THE AWARIF-U'L-MA'ARIF

by

SHAIKH SHAHAB-U'D-DIN 'UMAR B. MUHAMMAD SUHRAWARDI

TAJ COMPANY

THE AWARIF-UL-MA'ARIF

Written by : SHAHABUDDIN SUHRAWARDI

Translated by : LIEUT. COL. H.WILBERFORCE CLARKE

Revised Edition : 2021

Price : 300/-

Publisher

TAJ COMPANY

1397 Pahari Imli, Bazar Matia Mahal

Jama Masjid, Delhi-110 006

Ph: 9250010062 | 9711449086

Email: tajcompany1397@gmail.com

Printed at:

TAJ PRINTING SERVICE DELHI 110 006

PREFACE

The sources whence this note on Ṣūfism has been derived are:

(*i*) The introduction (pp. 1-29).

(*a*) *Disquisition on Ṣūfism* by Sir W. Jones.

(*b*) "Soofies" (*History of Persia*) by Malcolm.

(*c*) The *Gulshan-i-Rāz.*

(*d*) Other sources.

(*ii*) The definition of sixty-nine terms used in Ṣūfism (pp. 30-282).

The *Miṣbāḥ-u'l-Hidāyat* by Maḥmūd b. 'Alī al-Kāshānī, being a translation (in Persian) of the Arabic work, *'Awārif-u'l-Ma'ārif*[1] by Shaikh Shahāb-u'd-Dīn 'Umar b. Muḥammad Suhrawardī (*b.* 1145, *d.* 1234).

(*iii*) The Performances of Dervishes (pp. 283-298).

The Darvishes by Brown.

Neither the *Miṣbāḥ-u'l-Hidāyat* (in Persian), nor the *'Awārif-u'l-Ma'ārif* (in Arabic), has ever before been translated into English. What is here given to the reader comprises more than a half[2] of the *Miṣbāḥ-u'l-Hidāyat.*

Shaikh Shahāb-u'd-Dīn Muḥammad Suhrawardī, the son of Abū Najīb, was born at Suhraward, and he died at Baghdad.

1. Otherwise called the *'Awārif-u'l-Ḥaqā'iq.*

2. That is, out of 343 pages of the Persian text, 221 pages have been translated into English; and are herein given.

He was a pious *Shaikh*, assiduous in spiritual exercises and in the practice of devotion. He is author of the *'Awārif-u'l-Ma'ārif*, the *Ḥikmat-u'l-Arsār*, in Arabic, and many other works.

The matter (ten pages) taken from Brown's *Darvishes* has been arranged, corrected, collected and greatly condensed.

Those who wish further to pursue the subject of Ṣūfism will find useful the table of authorities on Ṣūfism, English and Persian (pp. vii-ix).

Unless Ṣūfism be understood, the *Dīvān-i-Ḥāfiẓ* cannot be understood.

In Vol. IV (pp. 196-211) of the works of Emerson (1882), wholly wrong is the view given of the work of Ḥāfiẓ; and mistranslated and misunderstood are the passages there given.

It is unnecessary to give instances; easily may the student verify this statement by referring either to my translation of Ḥāfiẓ, or to the original Persian. Let one instance suffice:

Emerson's Works, Vol. IV, p. 205	*Clarke's translation of the Dīvān-i-Ḥāfiẓ, Ode 371*
Oft have I said, I say it once more. I, a wanderer, do not stray from myself.	Times I have said; and again I say: That, heart-bereft, not of myself, have I gone this Path (of love).
I am a kind of parrot; the mirror is holden to me. What the Eternal says, I stammering say again.	Behind the (pure) mirror (of the holy traveller's heart), me, they have kept like the parrot. What the Teacher of eternity without beginning said: "Say"; I say.
Give me what you will: I eat thistles as roses, And, according to my food I grow and I give:	Whether, the thorn I be or whether the rose, there is a sward-adorner (God), By whose hand as (it) cherished me, I grew.

Scorn me not; but I know I have
the pearl,
And am only seeking one to receive
it.

O friends, me earth-bereft, astonied, censure not:
A great jewel, I have; and the master of vision (the jeweller, God) I seek.

Emerson (p. 201) says:

'We do not wish to make mystical divinity out of the Songs of Solomon, much less out of the erotic and bacchanalian songs of Ḥāfiẓ.

'Ḥāfiẓ himself is determined to defy all such hypocritical interpretation, and tears off his turban and throws it at the head of the meddling dervis, and throws his glass after the turban.

'Nothing is too high, nothing too low for his occasion. Love is a leveller, and Allah becomes a groom, and heaven a closet in his daring hymns to his mistress or to his cupbearer. This boundless charter is the right of genius.'

To this statement would agree no one who had, in the original Persian, read Ḥāfiẓ and had understood him.

Despite the fact that Emerson wholly fails to understand Ḥāfiẓ as the mystic poet, divine, immortal—strangely he admires him. For at p. 239, he says:

'You shall not read newspapers, nor politics, nor novels, nor Montaigne, nor the newest French book.

'You may read Plutarch, Plato, Plotinus, Hindu mythology and ethics. You may read Chaucer, Shakespeare, Ben Johnson, Milton; read Collins and Gray; read Ḥāfiẓ and the Trouveurs —fact-books which all geniuses prize as raw material and as antidote to verbiage and false poetry.'

At the head of the various sections, the figures refer to the Persian text of the *Miṣbāḥ-u'l-Hidāyat*:

Roman figures to chapters.

Arabic figures sections (of chapters).

To special notice, I wish to bring Maulavī Mīrzā Muḥammad Bisravī, who rendered me much help in this difficult work.

This translation was made in a tropical country, in leisure moments, amidst the pressure and the stress of professional duties most exacting; and under special circumstances of harass and worry that it is not permissible to describe.[3]

For these reasons, the reader's indulgence is solicited.

H. WILBERFORCE CLARKE

CALCUTTA
January 1891

3. See Clarke's Ṣūfistic translation of the Preface, *Divān-i-Ḥāfiẓ*, Preface, para 18 (p. xvi).

AUTHORITIES ON SŪFISM

Date	
1787	*Asiatic Miscellany*, vol. ii, pp. 50-53 ; 131-150.
1809	*Descriptive Catalogue* (pp. 34-45), *Oriental Library of Tippū Sulṭān*, by C. Stewart. This gives 115 excellent Persian works on Ṣūfism.
	De Bode's *Bukhārā*.
1818	*History of Muhammadanism* by C. Mills (p. 473).
1829	*History of Persia*, Malcolm—vol. i, pp. 322, 324, 400 ; vol. ii, pp. 382-426.
	Works of Sir W. Jones, vol. ii, pp. 131-150.
1856	*Journal, Asiatic Society, Bengal*, vol. xxv, pp. 133-150. 1857
	Note by Sprenger on the earliest work on Ṣūfism.
	Sind (chap. viii), Burton.
	Modern Egyptians (chap. iii), Lane.
	Die Morgenlandische mystik, by Tholuck.
1863	*Qānūn-i-Islām*, Herklot, pp. 187-200.
1868	*The Darvishes*, Brown.
1875	*Notes on Muhammadanism* (p. 227), C. E. Hughes.
1878	*Islām* (p. 201), Stobart.
1880	*Gulshan-i-Rāz*, translated by Whinfield.
1881	*Catalogue, Oriental Manuscripts* (pp. 35-45), British Museum (Quaritch).
?	*Paper on the Ṣūfis* by Captain Graham, Bombay.

Date	Author	Name of work
911	Shaikh Junaid Baghdādī	
1037	Shaikh Abū Sīnā (Avicenna) ...	*Maqāmāt-u'l-'Ārifīn*
1049	Abu'l-Qāsim Anṣārī	
1166	Shaikh 'Abd-u'l-Qādir Jīlānī	*Malfūzāt-i-Jalālī. Sharḥ-i-Ghauthīyah va Ghairah*
1230	Shaikh Farīd-u'd-Dīn 'Aṭṭār ...	*Asrār-Nāmah*
1234	Shaikh Shahāb-u'd-Dīn 'Umar b. Muḥammad Suhrawardī. ...	*'Awārif-u'l-Ma'ārif,*[1] *otherwise called 'Awārif-u'l-Ḥaqā'iq*
1239	Shaikh Muḥy-u'd-Dīn b. 'Arabī	
1273	Maulāna Jalāl-u'd-Dīn Rūmī ...	The *Mathnavī*
1292	Shaikh Sa'dī Shīrāzī ...	*Marghūb-u'l-Qulūb*
1317	Sa'd-u'd-Dīn Maḥmūd Shabistarī	*Gulshan-i-Rāz Haqq-u'l-Yaqīn Risālah i-Shāhid*
1382	Kamāl-u'd-Dīn Abu'l-Ghanīm 'Abd-u'r-Razzāq	*Iṣṭilāḥāt-i-Ṣūfiyā'* [2]
1389	Khwājah Shams-u'd-Dīn Ḥāfiẓ	The *Dīvān*
1492	Nūr-u'd-Dīn 'Abd-u'r-Raḥmān Jāmī	*Lawā'iḥ*
1591	Maulānā 'Urfī	*Qaṣā'id*
1610	Qāḍī Nūrullāh Shustarī ...	*Majālis-u'l-Mū'minīn*

1. See Preface, para 1.

2. Arabic text (p. 167), ed. Dr Aloys Sprenger, M D, 1845, entitled *Dictionary (in Arabic) of the Technical Terms of the Ṣūfīs.*

Date	Author	Name of Work
1659	Shāhzādah Dārā Shikūh Qādirī...	*Mushāhidah-i-Sulūk va Tarjumah-i-Wāsiṭī*
1669	Mīrzā Muḥammad 'Alī Tabrīzī Ṣā'ib	?
1670	Shaikh Muḥammad Muḥsin Fānī	The *Dabistān*
	Shaikh Farīd-u'd-Dīn Shakarganj	*Asrār-u'l-Auliyā'*

CONTENTS

INTRODUCTION

Sufism

Said Muḥammad: "In Islam is no monachism" (Qur'ān, v. 89).

Nevertheless, in 623 C.E.,[1] forty-five men of Mecca joined themselves to as many others of Medina; took an oath of fidelity to the doctrines of the Prophet Muḥammad; and formed a fraternity—to establish community of property, and to perform daily certain religious practices by way of penitence.

They took the name of *ṣūfī*, a word derived from:

(*a*) *ṣūf* = wool, woolly; a hair cloth used by penitents in the early days of Islam

(*b*) *ṣūfīy* = wise, pious

(*c*) *ṣūfī* = woollen

(*d*) *ṣafā'* = purity[2]

(*e*) *ṣafī* = pure

To the name of *ṣūfī* they added the title of *faqīr*, because they renounced the chattels of the world and its joys.

Said Muḥammad: "Al-faqru fakhrī" [Poverty is my glory].

During the life of Muḥammad, Abū Bakr (the first Khalīfah), and 'Alī (the fourth Khalīfah, *b.* 599, *d.* 661), established *Jamā'at* (assemblies) wherein vows were made and exercises practised.

1. The Hijrah dates from 15 July 622.

2. Some add *ṣafā'*, a station near the Ka'bah, Mecca. The man who wore the blue woollen garment was esteemed to be pure (*ṣafī*).

In 657 C.E., Uwais Qaranī (*d.* 657) established the first religious order of the greatest austerity.

In honour of Muḥammad, who, at the Battle of Uḥud, 625 C.E., had lost two of his teeth, he drew out his own teeth; and required his followers to do the same.

The term *ṣūfī* was first adopted by Abū Hāshim, a Syrian *Zāhid* (*d.* 780 C.E.); in his time was built the first *takyah* (convent). But some say that the seed of *ṣūfī'sm*:

was sown in the time of Ādam.
germed in the time of Nūḥ.
budded in the time of Ibrāhīm.
began to develop in the time of Mūsā.
reached maturity in the time of Christ.
produced pure wine in the time of Muḥammad.

Those who loved this wine have so drunk of it as to becomes selfless. They exclaim:

"Praise be mine! greater than I, is any?
"The truth (God), am I: there is no other God than I."

One of the earliest ṣūfīs was the woman Rābi'ah mentioned by Ibn Khallikān (*b.* 1211, *d.* 1282). At night, she used to go to the house-top, and to say "O God! hushed is the day's noise; with his beloved is the lover. But Thee I have for my lover; and alone with Thee, I joy."

In Volume I of his works, Sir W. Jones says:

"There is a species of Persian poetry that consists almost wholly of a mystical religious allegory, though on a transient view it seems to contain only the sentiments of a wild and voluptuous libertinism.

"Admitting the danger of a poetical style in which the limits between vice and enthusiasm are so minute as to be hardly distinguishable, we must beware of censuring it severely; for an ardent grateful piety is congenial to the undepraved nature of man, whose mind, sinking under the magnitude of the subject, and struggling to record its emotions, has recourse to metaphors, extending sometimes beyond the bounds of cool reason.

Ṣūfīs believe :

That the souls of men differ infinitely in degree but not at all in kind from the divine spirit whereof they are particles, and wherein they will ultimately be absorbed ; that the spirit of God pervades the universe, ever present to His work and ever in substance ; that He alone is perfect benevolence, perfect truth, perfect beauty ; that love for Him is true love (*'ishq-i-ḥaqīqī*), while love of other objects is illusory love (*'ishq-i-majāzī*) ; that all the beauties of nature are faint resemblances like images in a mirror of the divine charms ; that, from eternity without beginning to eternity without end, the supreme benevolence is occupied in bestowing happiness ; that men can only attain it by performing their part of the *primal covenant* between them and the Creator ; that nothing has a pure absolute existence but *mind* or *spirit* ; that material substances are no more than gay pictures presented continually to our minds by the sempiternal artist ; that we must beware of attachment to such phantoms and attach ourselves exclusively to God, who truly exists in us as we solely exist in Him ; that we retain, even in this forlorn state of separation, from our Beloved the idea of heavenly beauty and the remembrance of our primeval vows ; that sweet music, gentle breezes, fragrant flowers, perpetually renew the primary idea, refresh our fading memory, and melt us with tender affections ; that we must cherish those affections, and by abstracting our souls from vanity (that is, from all but God) approximate to this essence, in our final union with which will consist our supreme beatitude.

Sprenger[3] says :

The mysticism of the ṣūfīs is a hypertrophy of the religious feeling ; and a monomania in which man blasphemously attempts

3. See Preface to 'Abd-u'r-Razzāq's *Dictionary of Sufistic Terms*, 1845 ; the *Journal*, Asiatic Society, Bengal, Volume XXV, of 1856 (p. 145).

to fathom the depths of the essence of God.

The mystics give up worldly affairs; devote themselves to austerity; and are a nuisance to the world.

This disease attacks every nation after it has passed the meridian of its grandeur.

The mysticism of:

(*a*) the Neoplatonists marked the fall of Rome.

(*b*) the Ṣūfīs marked the *Khilāfat*.

(*c*) the later Fathers marked the darkness of the middle ages.

Because the noblest feelings of man are morbidly exalted by this disease, it has produced sublime poetry. Nothing can equal the beauty of the poems of Muḥy-u'd-Dīn, Ḥāfiẓ, Jalāl-u'd-Dīn Rūmī.

Ṣūfism is not due to the introduction of systems of philosophy from India, or from Greece. It is the result of the development of Islam; and is well worthy of the attention of the student.

Many consider Pantheism and Ṣūfism to be identical.

The *Shaikhs* and Ṣūfī-poets profess:

> The most ardent, although Platonic, attachment for individuals of their own sex, remarkable for beauty or for talent, declaring that they are adoring the Creator whilst admiring His beautiful handiwork (corporeal or intellectual); and boasting that their love is the more pure in being unmixed with carnal sensuality, such as it must be if bestowed on individuals of the other sex.

Maulānā Jalāl-u'd-Dīn Rūmī (*b.* 1207, *d.* 1273), says: Ṣūfīs profess eager desire but with no carnal affection; and circulate the cup but no material goblet. Since in their order, all things are spiritual —all is mystery within mystery.

Modern ṣūfīs believe in the Qur'ān; and in an

express covenant on the day of eternity without beginning (the day of Alast) between the assemblage of the souls (of men) and the supreme soul (of God), wherefrom they were detached.

In ṣūfism are four stages, which must be passed before man's corporeal veil can be removed; and his emancipated soul, mixed with the glorious essence, whence it has been separated but not divided:

(i) *Sharī'at.*[4] The *murīd* (disciple) observeth the *shar'* and the rites of Islam; ever beareth his *shaikh* in mind; in him effaceth himself through meditation; maketh him his shield against evil thoughts; and regardeth his spirit as his guardian spirit.

This is "effacement in the *shaikh*".

(ii) *Ṭarīqat.* The *murīd* attaineth power; entereth ṣūfism; and abandoneth the observance of religious form, exchanging outward for inward worship.

Without great piety, virtue, and fortitude (based on a knowledge of the dignity of the soul of man) he cannot attain this stage.

The *shaikh* passeth the *murīd* to the influence of the *Pīr* (long since deceased); and then, in all things, the *murīd* seeth the *Pīr*.

This is "effacement in the *Pīr*".

(iii) *Ma'rifat.*[5] The *murīd* hath attained to supernatural knowledge; and is, therein, equal to the angels.

By the *shaikh*, he is led to Muḥammad, whom, in all things, he seeth.

This is "effacement in the Prophet".

(iv) *Ḥaqīqat* (Truth). The *murīd* hath become joined to truth (God), whom, in all things, he seeth.

This is "effacement in God".

Many reach the second stage; few the fourth. Some make eleven stages:

4. Some call this *nāsūt*.

5. Some call this *'urf*.

Muwāfiqat. The *murīd* beareth enmity to the Friend's enemy—the world, *shaiṭān,* imperious lust; and love for the Friend (God).

Mā'il. The *murīd* inclineth to God; and, from the heart's page, effaceth "other than God".

Muwānisat. The *murīd* fleeth from all, and seeketh God.

Mawaddat. The *murīd* engageth in submission, in lamentation, in affection, and in agitation in the heart's chamber.

Hawā. The *murīd* keepeth the heart in austerity and in strife (against sin); and maketh it water (soft).

Khullat. The *murīd* maketh all the limbs full of recollection of God; and of aught else void.

Ulfat. The *murīd* maketh himself void of despicable qualities, and joined to laudable qualities.

Shaghf. The *murīd*, through ardency of desire, rendeth the heart's veil; and considereth the revealing of the mystery of love for God—infidelity, save under the mastery of *wajd* (ecstasy).

Taym. The *murīd* maketh himself the slave of love, and joineth himself to *tajrīd* (outward separation), and to *tafrīd* (inward solitude).

Walsh. The *murīd* keepeth the heart's mirror before God's glory; and becometh intoxicated with its wine.

'Ishq. The *murīd* keepeth so engaged the tongue in *dhikr* (creation of God), the heart in *fikr* (thought of God), and the soul in *mushāhadah* (viewing God's glory)—that he considereth himself non-existent.

Some consider *'ishq* to be: (*a*) effacing one's self in the essence of Absolute Unity (God); (*b*) the deposit of faith (Qur'ān, xxxiii. 72).

The following are terms used in ṣūfism:

ṣūfī	the *ṣūfī*
'ārif	the knower
sālik	the traveller (to God)
ṭālib	the seeker (of God)
'āshiq-i-ṣādiq	the sincere lover (of God)
ahl-i-taṣawwuf	one of mysticism

ahl-i-ḥāl	one of (mystic) state
ahl-i-ṭarīqat	one of the Path (to God)
ahl-i-mā'rifat	one of (divine) knowledge
ahl-i-ḥaqīqat	one of truth
ahl-i-ḥaqq	one of God
ahl-i-sharī'at	one of the *shar'*
taṣawwuf	ṣūfism
mutaṣawwif	sufistic
'abd, 'ābid	the servant (of God)
'abūdiyat	the service of God
ma'rifat	the knowledge of God
ṭarīqat	the path of God
jadhb	the attraction of God
jam' wiṣāl	the union (with God)
sukūnat	the dwelling (with God)
sāqī	the cup-bearer
maqām	degree
manzil	stage
ḥāl	the (mystic) state
wajd	rapture
shauq	desire
dhauq	delight
maḥabbat	affection
'ishq	love
ṣaḥābah	companions in the first generation after Muḥammad
tābi'īn	followers in the second generation after Muḥammad
zāhidān / *'ābidān*	devotees in the third generation after Muḥammad
ṣāḥib-i-dil	one possessed of heart, a *ṣūfī*
ṣāḥib i-ma'rifat	one possessed of (divine) knowledge
'ishq-ul-lāh	love for God
firāq	separation (from God)
dair / *takyah*	the convent
zāhid	the man of (dry) austerity
aṣḥāb-i-'ilm-i-zāhirī	the companions of outward knowledge

aṣḥāb-i-'ilm-i-bāṭinī	the companions of inward knowledge
ishtiyāq	ardour
mast	intoxicated
bī khud	void of self, selfless
Pīr	the founder of a religious order
shaikh	the chief of a convent
khalīfah / *naqīb*	the deputy *shaikh*
murshid	the spiritual guide, the *shaikh*
murīd	the disciple

The beginning of *taṣawwuf* (ṣūfism) is *īmān* (faith), which consists of "six columns" (principles):

(1) The existence of God
(2) The unity of God
(3) The angels
(4) The prophets
(5) The day of resurrection
(6) Good and evil, through God's predestination

The end of *taṣawwuf* lieth in pronouncing the six principles; and in conforming thereto with the heart.

The *īmān* of common folk (*'āmm*) is:

'Ilm (knowledge), which is only an imitation of "the six columns" learned from the *'ulamā'* or from the *imāms*. They know not why it is necessary to believe in these "six columns"; nor how thereby salvation can be obtained.

Many pursue the *'ilm-i-ṭarīqat* (knowledge of the Path) and wander into error, becoming:

ahl-i-jabrī	one disbelieving freedom of will
alh-i-qadrī	one believing in predestination
ahl-i-mujassamī	one believing only in the body
ahl-i-mushabbiyah	one believing in portraits of God
ahl-i-mu'tazalī	one sated (with God)

In all are seventy-three orders, whereof the true order is only one, the *firqat-i-najāt* (the party of salvation).

Manifest is their *īmān* (faith). Proceeding with only a lamp, they have reached the resplendent sun; at first only imitation, they have reached truth (God).

They find that the *ṭarīqat* (of the dervish) and the *sharī'ah* (of Islam) agree; and that whoever is imperfect in *sharī'ah* is also imperfect in *ḥaqīqat* (truth).

The Qur'ān (lxxviii. 18) says: "In the eternal life, my people will rise as monkeys, as hogs," etc., etc. These, in life, outwardly bore the form of man; but inwardly were brutes. From these evils, repentance before death will free one.

Give thyself to a *murshid* (spiritual guide) who, by his prayers, will show thee in dreams the evil parts of thy character till they shall pa s away. As the lover delights in his beloved, so doth the dervish in his *murshid*.

The dervishes say: "Neither fear we Hell, nor desire we Heaven." By this, they mean:

"O God, Thou bargainest with none; for purity of heart and love for Thee is our devotion. Be not Heaven nor Hell—we adore Thee.

"Put us into Heaven—'tis through Thy excellence; into Hell,—through Thy justice."

The ṣūfīs are divided into innumerable orders. The two original[6] orders are:

(1) Ḥulūliyah, *the inspired.* This order believes that God has entered into them; and that the divine spirit entereth all who are devout.

(2) Ittiḥādiyah, *the unionists.* This order believes that God is joined with every enlightened being; that He is as flame, and the soul as charcoal (ready to flame); and that the soul, by union with God, becometh God.

6. The original order is said to have been the Thabātiyah, the (ancient) Sabians.

From these two orders are derived the five following orders:

Wāṣilivah, the joined (to God)

'Ashāqiyah, the lovers (of God)

Talqīniyah, the instructed

Dhāqiyah, the penetrated

Wāḥidiyah, the solitary

For full information regarding the many orders of the ṣūfīs, I refer the reader to Malcolm's *History of Persia*, Vol. II, Art "Soofies".

The most celebrated of the ṣūfī teachers of Persia **have been** men as famed for knowledge as for **devotion**.

Of Ibrāhīm ibn Adham, they say:

"That holy man turned day into night;

"Night into day by his constant and undivided devotion to God."

Among the ṣūfīs, the most celebrated are the poets

The raptures of genius expatiating on an inexhaustible subject are deemed inspiration by those who believe that the soul can wander in the region of imagination, and unite with God.

In sweetest strains, Jalāl-u'd-Dīn Rūmī (*b*. 1207, *d*. 1273) teacheth that all nature abounds with divine love such as to cause the loveliest plant to seek the loftiest object of desire.

Nūr-u'd-Dīn 'Abd-u'r-Raḥmān Jāmī (*b*. 1414, *d*. 1492) breatheth ecstatic rapture in every line.

The *Gulistān* and the *Būstān-i-Sa'dī*[7] and the *Dīwān-i-Ḥāfiẓ* may be called the scriptures of the

7. Sa'dī, *b*. 1414, *d*. 1492.

Persian ṣūfīs.

Ṣūfī tenets are involved in mystery; for every gradation are mysteries never revealed.

Many of the most eminent ṣūfīs have been men of piety and of learning, whose self denial attracted a fame they sought not; others have cloaked themselves in humility to attain greatness, and fled from observation only to attract it.

To fame and power is no path however rugged, into which man will not enter.

Traces of ṣūfī doctrine exist in every country: in the theories of ancient Greece; in the modern philosophies of Europe; in the dream of the ignorant and of the learned; in the shade of ease and in the hardship of the desert.

In place of the usages of religion, ṣūfīs adopt the wild doctrines of their teacher; and embark on a sea of doubt under a *murshid* whom they deem superior to all other men and worthy of confidence that is only adoration.

Some deny evil, saying:

"Good is all that proceedeth from God."

They exclaim:

"The writer of our destiny is a fair Writer.
Never wrote He that which was bad."

All things in the world, they regard as the type and as the power of God. They see:

His beauty in the rose-cheek of lovely ones;
His power in the impious daring of Fir'aun (Pharaoh).

Sahl ibn 'Abdullah Tustarī saith:

"Revealed was the soul's secret when
Fir'aun declared himself to be god."

Jalāl-u'd-Dīn (*b.* 1207, *d.* 1273) maketh 'Alī (the first of ṣūfīs) say when he was wounded by an assassin:

Lord of the land am I; yet with my body no concern have I.

Me, thou hast not struck; only an instrument of God, thou art On God, who shall avenge himself?

Be not grieved: for to-morrow (the judgment day), thy mediator, shall I be.

Of 'Abd-u'l-Qādir Gilānī (*b.* 1078, *d.* 1166), Shaikh Muḥy-u'd-Dīn 'Arabī (*b.* 1166, *d.* 1239) says:

"I went to our house-top and saw all the pilgrims at 'Arafāt (near Mecca).

Descending, I told my mother that I must devote myself to God; and that I wished to proceed to Baghdad togain *ma'rifat*.

Weeping, my mother took eighty dīnārs; gave me half (my inheritance); made me swear never to tell a lie; and said: "Go, my son: to God, I give thee, not till the judgment day, shall we meet." At Hamadan, our *qāfilah* was plundered by sixty horsemen. One asking me what I had, I replied: "Forty dīnārs are sewed up in my garment." Disbelieving me, he laughed and left Another asked me and received the same reply. Whilst they were dividing the spoil, the Chief called me and said: "Boy, what property hast thou?" I replied: "I have already told two of your men that I have forty dīnārs sewn in a garment." He ordered the garment to be ripped, and found the money. He said: "How camest thou so openly to declare what has, so carefully, been hidden?" I replied: "Because I will not be false to my mother, to whom I have promised never to conceal the truth." Said the Chief: "Boy, art thou at thy age so sensible of duty to thy mother, and am I at my age insensible of my duty to God? Give me thy hand that, on it, I may swear repentance." He did so. His followers were struck with the scene, and said: "Leader in guilt, thou hast been; in virtue, to be same." They restored the spoil; and, on my hand, vowed repentance. At this time, I was sixteen years of age.

To those who sought him, Uwais Qaranī said: "Seekest thou God? If thou dost, to me why comest thou? If thou dost not, with me, what business hast thou?"

Qāḍī Nūr-u'l-Lāth Shustarī (*d.* 1610) says that ṣūfīs are of two classes:

(*a*) *Mu'takallim* (advocate, observer) if they desire human knowledge; the usages of religion; and pursue them in the ordinary way.

(*b*) Ṣūfīs, if they practise austerity, and look to the inward purity of the soul.

After His prophets, God esteemeth none more than the ṣūfī; because his desire is (through divine grace) to raise himself from this earthly house to the heavenly; and to exchange his lowly condition for the condition of the angel.

The accomplished are:

the *ḥukamā'*, men of wisdom.

the *'ulamā'*, men of knowledge.

These seek truth—the first by demonstration; the second by religion.

In this path to (God) are many dangers

For false teachers and deceived seekers vainly pursue the desert vapour; and wearied return, the dupe of their own imagination.

The *murshid-i-kāmil wa kamāl* (the perfect and

excellent *murshid*) is rare. When he exists, to discover him is impossible.

Perfection, who shall discover save he who is pefect?

The jewel's price, who shall tell, save the jeweller?

Hence, many miss the Path and fall into error. Deceived by appearances, they waste life in pursuit of defect, conceiving it to be perfection.

Neither austerity nor devotion can exclude *shaiṭān* who seeketh *zāhids* in the garb of religion. The only *ṭilism* whereby the good can be distinguished from the bad is *ma'rifat*.

Said Muḥammad:

> The irrational *zāhid*, God accepteth not;
> By pious fools, my back hath been broken.

From alarm at persecuting tyrants, ṣūfīs have often pretended to be of no particular faith.

Thus they confess not their religion; and to disclose the mystery thereof—is the deepest sin.

The *murshid* instructeth the *murīd* how to restore the inward man:

> by purifying the spirit
> by cleansing the heart
> by enlightening the head
> by anointing the soul

Then the *murshid* averreth:

that the *murīd's* desire shall be accomplished; that his despicable qualities shall be changed into laudable qualities; that he shall understand the revelation, the stages and the grades of exaltation——till he reacheth the ineffable joy of beholding God.

If the *murshid* be not perfect and excellent, the

murīd wasteth his time.

He will end by being an impostor, or by regarding all ṣūfīs alike and condemning them.

He will seek relief in infidelity, doubting all that he hath heard or read; and regarding as fable the accounts of holy men who have reached *haqīqat*.

The *murshid* is sometimes: (*a*) the dupe of his own imagination; (*b*) the wilful deluder of his own followers. He desireth to abolish the form of religion; alloweth no name to come between him and God, and yet desireth to come between all other men and God; destroyeth names reverenced by men in order to substitute his own name.

Without the *murshid*, no *murīd* can advance; his advance is in proportion to his faith[8] (in the *murshid*).

Ḥasan Ṣabbāḥ[9] Shaikh-u'l Jabal (*b*. 1071, *d*. 1124) and his descendants were of the order of *Bāṭiniyah*. They filled Persia with murders; and, by their mysterious power, made monarchs tremble.

God is ever renewing all the matter and the form of the universe. Not a leaf sprouteth, not a sparrow falleth, not a thought occurreth, without His impulsion.

Thus are Muslims brought face to face with evil in a way that Europeans cannot realise.

God is the only real agent, though He sometimes

8 The Murtaḍā Shāhī (an order of ṣūfīs) make in clay an image of the *murshid*.

This, the *murīd* keeps to prevent him from wandering; and to bring him into identity with the *murshid*.

9. The Historian of the Crusades calls him "the old man of the mountain".

From his name (al-Ḥasan) is derived our word "assassin".

See *Asiatic Researches*, Vol. XI, p. 42?; Malcolm's *History of Persia*, Vol. I, p. 395; Vol. II, p 416.

fashioneth some (Iblīs, Qābīl, Nimrūd, Fir'aun, Abū Jahl) to be His agents of wrath.

Equally with Mūsā was Fir'aun, an agent of God's will ; and he bewailed the impulsion that made him oppose Mūsā.

The *'Ārif* (the knower of *ma'rifat*) admitteth the ability to choose good. Not, like Iblīs, doth he cast his sins upon God ; but with Ādam, crieth : "O Lord, black our faces we have made."

The *'Ārif* saith :

God created all things, good and evil ; but evil is non-existence, a departure from the Only Absolute Existence. In relation to God, evil is naught.

If evil passion exist not, how can there be control ? If affliction exist not, how can there be patience ?

The jail is the criminal's *masjid* making him cry to God.

The ṣūfī disregardeth outward forms and rites. God judgeth not as man judgeth ; at the heart, He looketh.

Jalāl-u'd-Dīn Rūmī (vi. Prologue) saith : If with good and evil, a lover be befouled—these, regard not ; his aspiration, regard.

The ṣūfī practiseth voluntary poverty, mortification, obedience, renunciation of the world ; and the precepts of the gospel as to forsaking family, position, wealth, for religion sake.

All naught, he maketh save God : and giveth life to this non-existent universe by regarding it as permeated with God's presence.

Paradise, Hell, all the dogmas of religion are allegories,—the spirit whereof he alone knows.

He longeth for death ; for then he returneth to God whence he emanated, and in Him findeth annihilation.

On the unity of God, he meditateth to attain spiritual perfection; and unification with God.

This union, none can without *Faiḍu'llāh* (God's grace) reach; but to those who fervently ask Him, He refuseth not aid.

The Qur'ān and the Ḥadīth represent: (*a*) God as having created the world once for all, and as now removed to the highest heaven, leaving His creatures, by their own free will, according to the light given by prophets, to work out their salvation; (*b*) God as the being ever working in His creatures, the sun of all existence, the fulness of life, whereby all things move and exist—omnipresent, dwelling in, and communing with, each soul.

The ṣūfīs (men of heart; men looking behind the veil; inward men) developed the Greek mysticism popularised by

(*a*) Farābī	*d.* 954
(*b*) Abū 'Alī Sīnā	*d.* 1037
(*c*) Ghazālī	*d.* 1111
(*d*) Ibn Rushd	*d.* 1199

and made:

(*i*) God to be the One, the Necessary Being, the only Reality, the Truth, the Infinite, the First Cause (source of all action, good and evil).

(*ii*) The world of phenomena and of man—Not-being which like a mirror reflects being; and, by borrowing particles of being, rises to "contingent being" (which shares existence and non-existence).

In man, the spark of being is identical with the Infinite Being; but, while he is in "contingent being," he is weighed down and held apart from Being by "Not-being," whence evil proceedeth.

In this state, he requires laws and creeds to restrain him. Thus "Not-being" is when wanted something, and nothing when not wanted, and so do the ṣūfīs avoid the ill consequences of their theory.

The Muslim doctrine of *jabr* (compulsion) driveth some to fanatical deeds; some to cry *qismat*; some to regard the action and the existence of the universe as the manifestation of God's energy.

By divine illumination, man seeth the world, including man's self, to be an illusion, non-existent (and therefore evil).

He trieth to shake off this "Not-being," to efface himself, and to be united with the real Being, the Truth, that is, God.

The true course is to ignore self; to be passive that God may work. Then will God's light and grace enter the heart and draw man to Truth and unite him with the One.

The curl, the down, the mole, and the brow are the world now in *jamāl* (beauty), now in *jalāl* (terrible majesty).

The cheek and the curl are the types of mercy and of beauty; of vengeance and of majesty.

The mysteries of ecstatic vision cannot be interpreted by words, only by types; and license is in the mystic states of: (*a*) annihilation, effacement, (*b*) intoxication, (*c*) love's violence. Only those who know these states comprehend the meaning of these words.

The curl enchaineth hearts; beareth souls to and fro; plundereth the *kārvāns* of reason; and never resteth.

With its perfume, Ādam's clay became leavened. Thus, the material world.

The down is the vestibule of almightiness, a verdant growth in the spirit world, the well-spring of life, the hidden secret, the first plural emanation, that veileth the face of unity, the world of pure spirits that are nearest to God and the decoration of souls.

The mole is the point of unity, single yet embracing all phenomena. Fixed and stable is the point of unity; but the heart is disquieted by emotions, illumined by epiphanies and darkened by the veil of plurality in the *masjid*, now in the inward and now in the outward, now in the hell of lust, now in the heaven of *dhauq*.

It is the centre, whence is drawn the circle of two worlds; and whence is Ādam's heart and soul.

Unity (the mole) and the heart must be one Which is the original, which the reflection?

Sometimes is the heart:

sick, like His intoxicating eye.
fluttering, like His curl.
gleaming, like His face.
dark, like His mole.
a *masjid* of the inward and sometimes a *masjid* of the outward.
a hell of the inward and sometimes a heaven.

The cheek is the theatre of divine bounty, the divine essence in respect of the manifestations of its names and qualities; the manifestation of the seven (beauteous) names (of God); and is as the seven verses (of the Fātihah). Know His face and down,—verily thou knowest plurality and unity.

The eye betokeneth frowns and coquetry, now holding aloof from its slave, now granting union. From it proceed languishing intoxication, burning, plundering, and aching of heart; every corner thereof is a wine-shop.

Of His eye and lip, ask an embrace,—one saith nay; the other, yes.

The lip is the essence of being, the healing of the sick heart, the clothing of all souls. By His lip, souls are beside themselves, and compassion revealeth itself.

When, on His eye and on His lip, the world reflecteth, it giveth itself up to the worship of wine.

Beauty is Truth manifested and present; 'tis the beam of the light of spirits; 'tis the greatest of signs.[10]

Wine, the torch and beauty are epiphanies of Truth.

Wine is the rapture that maketh the ṣūfī beside himself at the manifestation of the emanation of the Beloved.

By it, this one becometh the philosopher, the traditionist, the righteous one, and the lover (of God).

By it, that one swalloweth at one draught the cup, the wine-house, the *sāqī*, and the wine-drinker; and yet open remaineth his mouth.

O ocean-heart! O mighty drinker! well done!

Drunken are:

reason.

the angels.

the soul.

the air.

10. The Qur'ān. liii 18.

the reeling heaven.
the revolving earth.

Better is the intoxicated than the self-righteous.

The wine of dying to self, drink; from thyself, thyself set free.

Wine is the transport and the light of the 'Ārif; the soul of that flashing light that in the consuming bush Mūsā beheld.

The "veil of darkness" betokeneth dwelling in iniquity. Who is veiled knoweth his wickedness.

The "veil of light" betokenth the practice of good deeds. Who is thus veiled knoweth not his wickedness, being clouded by his self-righteousness.

"Who are they that have lost their labour, and in life mistaken their aim?

"They who think that what they do is right" (Qur'ān, xvii. 103).

The tavern-haunter is one freed from self; one desolate in a desolate place (other than God, absent), headless, footless, neither the faithful nor the *kāfir*. One who, losing both head and foot, in every strain that he heareth from the minstrel, is seized with *wajd* from the hidden world.

Not of these words and sound, but of precious mystery, is every note of that mystic song.

The idol is the evidence of love and of unity. Idol-worshipping is making one; in it what is evil proceedeth from other than God.

The girdle is the emblem of obedience.

SHUYUKHIYAT (BEING A SHAIKH)

VI, 5

After the rank of being a prophet, no rank is higher than the being a deputy for a prophet, to call men, by the path of Muḥammad, to God.

The word *shaikh* signifieth being a *khalīfah*; hence its degree is excellent, in respect of the *shaikhs* of ṣūfīs, is in the *ḥadīth* stated.

The *shaikh's* purpose is to cleanse, from the rust of lust and of nature, the *murīd's* heart, so that in it, by attractions and inclinations, may be reflected the rays of the beauty of unity and the glory of eternity; so that, by beholding them, his eyes may be attracted; and so that, thus, divine love may rest in his sincere heart.

The rules of being a *shaikh* are fifteen.

(1) *The purifying of resolution and the searching for the cause.* First he should seek out of himself that the cause be not:

the desire of precedence;
the desire of being a *shaikh*;
the desire of being followed;

wherein are born the lusts of sons of Ādam; this he should do, though he may see his own lust at rest and the fires of nature extinguished.

When he seeth some of the seekers, with sincerity of desire, turn to him, and from him seek guidance, hastily he should not be their director, but should delay till, with penitence, true submission, and supplication to God, he discovereth the truth of the state and with certainty knoweth what God's purpose is to him in regard to their charge.

If he see that the charge of the crowd of the seekers is trial, he knoweth caution to be necessary, and is engaged in comprehending the hidden cause.

If he see that God's purpose is that he should instruct the seekers, he followeth God's order.

(2) *The knowledge of capacity.* The *shaikh* must regard the capacity of the *murīd.* If, in him, he see capacity for treading the path of those near to God, he inviteth him with skill, and by elucidating the states of him who is near to God.

If he see that he has not much capacity for the path of the pious, he inviteth him by admonishing, by inciting, by instructing, and by mentioning Paradise and Hell.

The *shaikh* urgeth the capable ones to deeds of the heart (*murāqibah,* observance of mystery, distinguishing thoughts), and to pure devotion.

Thus, if he see the *murīd's* welfare in abandoning the world's chattels, or in holding to them, he ordereth as may be suitable to his state.

Who acquireth not knowledge of the different kinds of capacity, and discrimination as to the forms of understanding, hath no true power over the *murīd.*

(3) *Being pure (having no lot or part) in respect of the* murīd's *property.* The *shaikh* must show no greed for the property, or for the service, of the *murīd.* With a gratification, he should not make vain his instructing and directing, which are the best of alms (for God).

When, by divine information or by true knowledge, he knoweth that, for the general good, he should take the property, he may do so.

If the *murīd* desire at once to give up his property, the *shaikh* may accept; because, in return for it, he can give to the *murīd* that state (for which he is fit) which is the cause of tranquillity of heart.

If he knoweth that the *murīd* will look with regret at his property, he will allow him to spend a portion.

Once, one of Junaid's *murīds* wished to give up all his property. Junaid refused saying:

"Keep what is sufficient and thereon subsist; the surplus, give. For, after the expending of all thy property, safe from the demands of thy desire, I shall not be."

(4) *Offering.* Delights of offering and of severing attachments are incumbent on the *shaikh* so that, by observing their effects, the sincerity and the conviction of the *murīd* may be greater; and the severing of attachments, easier; and the desire of celibacy, overpowering.

By offering, becometh sifted the *murīd's* suspicion as to the *shaikh's* state, and as to the truth of his sway.

According to necessity, he should distribute the excess among the poor.

(5) *Concordance of deed with word in invitation.* When the *shaikh* wisheth to invite the *murīd* to a practice, or to an abandonment, it is necessary that, in his own state, this (practice or abandonment) should be evident, so that, without suspicion, the *murīd* may accept.

Upon persons, the mere word has no great effect.

According to the *ḥadīth*, the *murīd* should choose *faqr* (poverty), which is the wealth of ṣūfism, and the condition of *ṭarīqat* (the path to God), although to him, poverty and riches are, as 'Umar hath said, one.

(6) *Compassion for the weak.* When, in the *murīd*, the *shaikh* seeth weakness of resolution, and knoweth that against lust and the abandoning of accustomed things, he hath no true resolution, he should display kindness.

To the limit of his power, he should abridge the austerities, so that the *murīd* may not shun him; and so that, in time, and by intercourse, he may gain kinship with *fuqarā'* (*faqīrs*).

Possibly, after resolution shall have been incited in him, he may gradually reach from the abyss of license (to disregard austerities) to the height of resolution.

Once one of the sons of favour (a rich man) joined the society of Aḥmad Qalānsī; and severed himself from the world.

In him, Aḥmad found a weakness, whereupon, when a few dirhams were gained, he used to purchase for him bread, round cake, roast meat, sweetmeat; and to say:

> "Out from the world's favour and from association therewith, this man has come; then fit it is to tread with him the path of compassion; and not to forbid him delights."

(7) *The purifying of speech.* Pure of the pollution of desire must be the *shaikh's* speech, so that its effect upon the *murīd* may be seen.

On the heart the effect of speech is like to seed: if the seed be bad, there is no fruit; iniquity of speech is in entering into, and associating with, desire.

Into speech desire falleth: (*a*) either for attracting the hearts of hearers, which is unfit for the state of *shaikhs*; (*b*) or from pride of himself on account of the beauty of his own speech, which (in the opinion of men of *ḥaqīqat*) is pure sin.

With the *murīd* the *shaikh* should winnow his speech from the pollution of desire, should plant it in the heart's soil, and entrust it to God to be preserved from the bird of forgetfulness and from the power of *shaiṭān*.

On account of the pride of self, sincerity appeareth not save by observing the lights of God's excellence and the effects of His boundless favours,—in the splendour of which lights the glance of lust becometh dimmed; and the darkness of pride, extinguished. Then in the buffeting of the waves of the ocean of perpetual bounty, he regardeth his own existence, much more his speech,—less than a drop.

(8) *Exalting the heart to God in the state of speech.* When the *shaikh* wisheth to speak to the *murīd*, he should turn his heart towards God, and from Him ask sense, that he may be the perfecter of time and the comprehender of the welfare of the hearer's state; that his tongue may be the speaker of God; and that his speech may be true in rendering benefit.

Thus they say: "In the hearing of his own speech he was equal to the other hearers."

Although sooner than the spectators on the shore, the diver in the sea collecteth pearl-shells and bringeth with himself the pearl, yet, as soon as he issueth from the sea and openeth the shell, he is only equal to the spectators on the shore.

(9) *Speaking ambiguously.* When in the *murīd*, the *shaikh* seeth something detestable, and wisheth to admonish him thereto, so that he may strive to remove it, he should not speak fluently and conspicuously.

Nay, ambiguously he should cast the matter before the assembly, that to its object, its tenor may lead.

Thus if, in the *murīd's* soul, he should see (*i*) a pride of his own deeds and states; (*ii*) a claim to nearness (to God) and to perfection; (*iii*) a crookedness and a turning from the path of firmness, he should relate to the assembly, in respect of it, a *ḥadīth* or a tale, of *shaikhs*; and briefly should hint at the abomination, so that those present may be profited.

In this way, counsel is nearest to courtesy and to *ḥikmat*.

(10) *Preserving the mysteries of the* murīd. The *shaikh* should preserve the mysteries of the *murīd*, and not reveal his manifestations and miracles. By speaking to him in private, he should render them contemptible, saying:

"Although circumstances like these are the favour of God, yet, expecting and looking for them, is the cause of the *murīd's* path being closed.

"In thanks for them, they should make return; from them, take off their glance; and, in observing the Benefactor (God) through observing His favour, be engaged.

"Otherwise in loss they remain."

(11) *Pardoning the* murīd's *blunder.* If, in the

murīd, the *shaikh* should see a defect in abandoning a service, or in neglecting a rule,—it, he should forgive him; and thereto by kindness, by courtesy, by indulgence, and by grace incite him.

(12) *Descending from (passing over) his own right.* Of the *murīd*, the *shaikh* should have no hope, although it is his right; and to his right, the keeping of the *murīd* is a most important rule. But the *shaikh's* expectation of it is not approved; and his descending from his right is best.

Wakī' says:

"Once, in Egypt, with an assembly of *fuqarā'*, I was in a *masjid*, where Abū Bakr Wirāq stood before a pillar and prayed.

"I said to myself, when the *shaikh* finisheth his prayer, I will salute him. When he had returned the *salām* of the prayer, he came and preceded me in salutation.

"I said: 'Best it would have been if I had first stood in respect.'

"The *shaikh* said: 'I have never been bound with the expectation that anyone should do me honouring.' "

(13) *The allowing of the* murīd's *rights.* In sickness and in health, the *shaikh* should not delay in allowing the rights of the companions.

(14) *The distributing of times in respect of* khilvat (*retirement*) *and of* jilvat (*rapid circular motions*). The *shaikh's* time should not be plunged in intercourse with the people. His power of *ḥāl*, his perfection, his *tamkīn*, and his presence (with others) should not be the excuse.

With perfection of *ḥāl*, and of *tamkīn*, Muḥammad was not, all day, in men's society. For asking the aid of God's bounty, of mercy, he chose *khilvat*; for diffusing the mercy on the people, he chose society.

For the *shaikh* is necessary a special *khilvat*, wherein he may be employed: (*a*) in portions of devotion; (*b*) in humbling himself and in supplicating God for his own sake and for others; (*c*) in asking aid so that his *khilvat* may be secure from being employed with people.

By the opposition of man's composition, displaying assiduity to God is difficult; and languor in deeds is expected, and at such times, it is proper that he should pass his time in society and thereby dispel that languor.

Again, through *shauq* and *dhauq*, he may incline to *khilvat* and to devotion; men may be benefited by his nature; and he may escape from languor.

(15) *The increasing of the works of supererogation* (nawāfil) The boiling of his *ḥāl* should not hinder him from repairing time with good deeds. For, with perfection of *ḥāl*, assiduous in respect to *nawāfil*, was Muḥammad:

in the *namāz-i-tahajjud*, prayer of midnight.
in the *namāz i-chāsht*, prayer between sunrise and noon.
in *namāz-i-zawāl*, prayer after noon.
in the *ruza-i-taṭawwū*, fasting during good deeds.
in other *nawāfil*.

At night so long used he to stand in prayer that his auspicious feet became swollen.

THE BEHAVIOUR OF THE MURĪD TO THE SHAIKH

VI, 4

For the *murīd*, in the society of the *shaikh*, the observance of manners (whereby love of hearts is attracted) is most important.

When he is possessed of manners, he taketh in love a place in the *shaikh's* heart; and is agreeable to God's sight. Because, with mercy, favour, and care, God ever looketh at the hearts of His own friends (the dervishes).

Then by dwelling in the *shaikh's* heart, the constant blessings of God's mercy, and of His endless bounty, comprehend his existence; and the *shaikh's* acceptance becometh his mark of the acceptance of God, of Muḥammad, and of all *shaikhs*.

Save by manners, one cannot gain the rights due to the *shaikh's* instruction.

The honouring of *'Ulamā'* and of *shaikhs* is a great right, the non-performance whereof is exceeding disobedience as is stated in the *ḥadīth*: "Whoever performeth not the *shaikh's* rights is defective in the performance of God's rights."

The *shaikh*, in the midst of the *murīds*, is as Muḥammad in the midst of his *aṣḥāb* (companions); for inviting the people to follow Muḥammad, he is in the Inn of the *Khalīfah*.

There are fifteen rules of conduct, which it is necessary the *murīd* should observe.

(1) *Perfect faith in the* shaikh *as regards his instructing, directing and purifying* murīds. If he regard another more perfect, love's bond becometh weakened; and the *shaikh's* words affect him little.

For the means whereby the *shaikh's* words and actions take effect is—love.

As his love is greater, so is his readiness for the *shaikh's* instruction greater.

(2) *Perfect resolve in respect to attendance upon the* shaikh. To himself, he should say: "Save by attendance on the *shaikh*, no door can be opened. Then at his threshold I will either surrender my life, or reach my object."

Its mark is that, by the *shaikh's* driving and rejecting, he turneth not away.

Abū 'Uthmān Ḥā'iri went to Nīshāpūr with the intention of visiting Abū Ḥafaẓ Ḥadād.

When he beheld the light of his holiness, he was attracted: and asked permission to stay. Abū Ḥafaẓ drove him away, saying: "Not in our assembly shouldest thou sit."

Abū 'Uthmān retreated till he was hidden from sight: then he resolved to dig a pit at the house-door; to sit therein and therefrom not to come forth till Abū Ḥafaẓ should consent to receive him.

When Abū Ḥafaẓ beheld such proof of sincerity of desire, he called him, welcomed him, made him of the number of his special companions; married him to his daughter; and appointed him *khalīfah*.

On the death of the *shaikh*, thirty years after, he, Abū 'Uthmān, sat as *shaikh*.

(3) *Being obedien to the* shaikh's *sway*. In respect

to his soul and his wealth, the *murīd* should admit the *shaikh's* sway: and be obedient to his orders. For, save this, his object is not reached, nor his sincerity known.

(4) *The abandoning of opposition.* Neither outwardly nor inwardly, should the *murīd* oppose the *shaikh's* authority. When, on the *shaikh's* part, something becometh difficult to him, and its truth is not revealed to him, he should remember the tale of Mūsā and Khiḍr.

Despite his power of prophecy, his knowledge and his great love, Mūsa refused obedience to Khiḍr's absolute commands, but when the mysteries and their *ḥikmat* were revealed, Mūsā returned to obedience.

(5) *The rejection of his own will.* The *murīd* should begin no matter of faith or of the world, wholly or partly, without reference to the *shaikh's* will.

Without the *shaikh's* permission, he should not: eat, drink, sleep, take, give, look. Without the *shaikh's* appointing, he should not begin : (*a*) fasting, (*b*) breaking the fast, (*c*) many of the *nawāfil* such as—attaching one's self to precepts, to *dhikr*, to meditation, and to *murāqibah*.

One night, Muḥammad passed by Abū Bakr's tent, and heard him reading with low voice the prayer of *tahajjud*.

Afterwards he passed by 'Umar's tent, and heard him reading with loud voice the prayer of the Qur'ān.

In the morning, he asked Abū Bakr : "With low voice why readest thou the *tahajjud*?" Abū Bakr replied : "Those who desire salvation, hear it." He asked 'Umar : "With loud voice why readest thou?"

'Umar replied: "To drive away Shaiṭān." Muḥammad said: "Read ye neither with low voice nor with loud voice. Nay, preserve ye the middle way."

This showeth that, with the existence of a *shaikh* (Muḥammad), to be one who doeth aught alone is not proper.

(6) *The observing of the* shaikh's *thoughts.* To no matter, which is abhorrent to the *shaikh's* heart, should the *murīd* proceed; nor having regard to the *shaikh's* excellence of character and of kindness, should he consider it a small matter.

(7) *Referring to the* shaikh's *knowledge in the explanation of dreams.* In the explanation of dreams, whether in sleepiness or in wakefulness, he should refer to the *shaikh*'s knowledge.

For, possibly, the source of that dream may be an evil desire, whereto his knowledge reacheth not, and wherefrom injury may arise. He should present it to the *shaikh* that with it the *shaikh* may become acquainted.

(8) *Purity of custom in respect to the* shaikh's *speech.* The *murīd* should recognise the *shaikh*'s tongue, as the link of God's speech, and should know for certain that he is the speaker of God not of lust. He should regard the *shaikh's* heart as a boisterous sea, filled with the pearl of *'ilm* (knowledge), and with the jewel of *ma'rifat*, which, at times, from the furious blowing of the winds of favour of the Eternal, casts some of those jewels on the shore of the tongue.

Thus, he should ever be expectant and present that he be not excluded from the advantages arising from the *shaikh's* speech.

Between the *shaikh's* speech and his own state, he should seek the suitable way, and with himself commune.

At God's door, with the tongue of readiness, he should seek rectitude of state; according to his readiness arriveth an address from the hidden.

With hypocrisy and the manifestation of his own *'ilm* and *ma'rifat*, he should not come, for thus he putteth far from himself his desire and becometh deaf to the *shaikh's* speech.

(9) *Lowering the voice* In the *shaikh's* society, the *murīd* should not raise his voice, for the doing so is the abandoning of good manners and the removing of the veil of dignity.

In the Qur'ān is reproved both the raising of the voice and the lowering of it beyond limit.

(10) *Forbidding* nafs *from ranging at large.* Neither by word nor by deed should the *murīd* tread the path of mirth with the *shaikh* By mirth, the veil of reverence becometh rent, and the way of grace, closed.

He should say: "O my Sayyid! O my Maulā!"

At first, the *ṣaḥābah* (companions) used irreverently to say to Muḥammad: "O Muḥammad! or O Aḥmad!"

For their reproof descended a divine address, and they afterwards said: "O sent one of God (the salutation and the safety of God be on thee)!"

In the *shaikh's* presence, he should not cast down his prayer-mat save at the time of prayer; should in *samā'* keep himself from moving and from *zaqa* (calling out), and should (so long as power of refraining and of containing himself shall be) keep himself from moving and from laughing.

(11) *Knowledge of times of speech.* When, on an important matter of faith or of the world, the *murīd* wisheth to speak to the *shaikh*,—he should first ascertain whether he hath leisure. Not hastily nor abruptly should he approach the *shaikh.*

Before speaking, he should display penitence, and, for grace of manner of speech, should (as the Qur'ān saith) seek aid from Muḥammad.

With much questioning, men importuned Muḥammad, and wearied him. Then descended a divine address whereby concord with hypocrites was severed.

(12) *Preserving the limit of his own respect.* In questioning the *shaikh,* he should guard his own respect, and, from his own state, should not discover every state (of the *shaikh's*) that may be closed to him. On a matter, that is neither his *maqām* nor his *ḥāl,* he should not speak.

Of the necessary matters of his own state, he should not ask much. The profitable word is that which they utter to the degree of the hearer's understanding; the profitable question, to the degree of the hearer's rank.

(13) *The concealing of the* shaikh's *mysteries.* Every state (of miracles, dreams, etc., etc.) which the *shaikh* keepeth concealed, and of which the *murīd* learneth—for its divulging, he should not seek permission.

Because in concealing it, the *shaikh* hath seen the profit of faith and of the world whereto his *'ilm* reacheth not, and in revealing it, great calamity may be caused.

(14) *The revealing of his own mysteries to the* shaikh. From the *shaikh* the *murīd* should not conceal his mysteries. Every miracle and gift that God may have bestowed on him, he should plainly present to the *shaikh's* judgment.

(15) *Speaking of the* shaikh *to the degree of the hearer's understanding*. That matter wherein is unintelligibility, and whereto the hearer's understanding reacheth not the *murīd* should not utter.

From such speech, no profit ariseth; and possibly the hearer's faith in the *shaikh* may become languid.

If the *murīd* observe this collection of rules of manner, his object (from the acquisition of the splendours of God's mercy and from the descending of His boundless blessings) becometh, by means of the *shaikh's* society, revealed openly and secretly.

THE CUSTOMS OF THE MEN OF THE KHĀNQĀH (CONVENT)

V, 5

The men of the *khānqāh* form two parties : (*i*) the travellers, (*ii*) the dwellers.

When ṣūfīs intend to alight at a *khānqāh* they try to reach it before the afternoon. If, for some reason, the afternoon cometh, they alight at the *masjid* or in some corner.

The next day, at sunrise, they proceed to the *khānqāh* and make: (*a*) two *rak'ats* (of prayer) as salutation to the spot; (*b*) *salām* (peace-wishing); (*c*) haste to embracing and to hand-shaking those present.

The *sunnat* is that to the dwellers they should offer some food or something as a present.

In speech, they make no presumption; so long as they ask not, they speak not.

For three days, for the business that they may have, beyond the visiting of the living and of the dead,—they go not from the *khānqāh* until the inward form, from the alteration caused by the accidents of travel, returneth, to its own ease, and they become ready for the interview with the *shaikhs*.

When from the *khānqāh* they wish to go out, they prefer their request to the men of the *khanqāh*.

When three days have passed, if they resolve to stay, they seek service whereby they may stay.

If their time be engaged in devotion, no service is necessary.

The dwellers of the *khānqāh* meet the travellers with: (*a*) *tarḥīb* (ye are welcome); (*b*) regard; (*c*) affection; (*d*) expansion of face (through joy).

The servant should offer light food, and be present fresh of face, sweet of speech.

If a traveller, unaccustomed to the customs of ṣūfīs, reach the *khānqāh,* they should not look at him with contempt, nor should they prevent him from entering. For many of the holy and pious are ignorant of the customs of this assembly (of ṣūfīs).

If through contempt injury reach them, their heart may possibly be vexed, and its effects may injure faith and the world.

Kindliness to man is the best of manners; ill-naturedness is the result of ill nature.

If to the convent reach someone who hath no fitness therefor, him, after offering victuals, with kindness and fair words, they remove.

The dwellers of the *khānqāh* form three parties: (*i*) *ahl-i-khidmat* (men of service); (*ii*) *ahl-i-ṣuḥbat* (men of society); (*iii*) *ahl-i-khilvat* (men of *khilvat*).

The *ahl-i-khidmat* are "the beginners," who, out of love, come to the *khānqāh.* They do them service, so that thereby they may become acceptable to the hearts of men of deeds and of stages, and may be regarded with the glance of mercy; may acquire fitness for kinship; and become a slipper out of the garment of alienation and of farness.

They gain capability of society and capacity for its advantages; and by the blessing of their society, words, deeds and manner become bound by the bond of dignity. After that, they become worthy of *khidmat.*

To the old men, the passing of their time in *khilvat* is best.

To the youths, the house-assembly sitting in *suhbat* is better than *khilvat*, so that, with the bond of *'ilm*, their lusts may (by the revealing of states, words, and deeds to those present) be bound.

Thus has Abū Ya'qūb Sūsī said.

The men of the *khānqāh* have—a portion, devotion and a service; and aid each other respecting important matters of faith and of the world.

Fitness for "service" is when a person hath, by outward resemblance, and inward and pure desire—acquired kinship with ṣūfis.

Who hath not kinship with one of these two ways,—him, it is not proper to do "service"; or with him to associate except in compassion.

Because sometimes, through the exigency of human nature, issue from them things that appear ugly in the sight of people of desire and of love.

If from the *khānqāh* is the allowance of their victuals; and the bequeather's condition is that they should expend the allowance on the purposes of the Lords of desire, and on the travellers of *ṭarīqat*, that allowance is not lawful to the habituated, nor to that crowd that, from deeds of body, have not reached the stages of the heart.

If the *khānqāh* have no bequest, and in it be present one possessed of vision, he, according to the exigency of the time and their capacity, instructeth *murīds.*

If he consider it good to abandon *kasb* (acquisition) and to remain in beggary, he putteth them on *tawakkul* (reliance on God), and on the abandoning of the means (of livelihood).

If the men of the *khānqāh* be a brotherhood, and no *shaikh* be present, they choose, as occasion demandeth, one of these three ways:

If they be of the crowd of the strong and of travellers, and resolute as to *tawakkul* (reliance on God), and as to patience, their sitting (in reliance) on the revealing (of God's aid) is worthy of their state.

Otherwise they should choose *kasb*, or beggary, which they consider the better.

The men of the *khānqāh* should, outwardly and inwardly, observe concord to each other, and should, at the time of eating, assemble at one table-cloth, so that outwardly they may not be separated; that the blessing of outward association may penetrate into the heart; that they may with each other pass life in love and purity; and may, in their heart, give no power to alloy and counterfeit (evil thoughts).

If from one to the heart of another, a foul deed should pass, they should instantly efface it, and with him not pass life in hypocrisy.

Every society, the foundation whereof is on hypocrisy and not on sincerity, giveth no result whatever.

When, outwardly to each other, they display reconciliation, and their heart is folded with hate,—hopeless is their good, and expected their destruction.

If an act of treachery appear, in it they should not persevere, but quickly for it make reparation by seeking pardon, and that pardon it is not right that the aggrieved one should withhold. For, in respect to this, promise (of blessing) hath arrived.

Outwardly and inwardly, they should strive to be in agreement with, and in equality to, each other; and to be in respect of all people free from impurity (of wrong).

Then to them may deferred Paradise be hastened, and the mere promise of others be their realisation.

In the heart of the ṣūfī or of the *faqīr*, how should there be the alloy and the counterfeit (of evil thought), the place of return whereof is the love of the world? By abandoning the world and turning from it are they special and chosen.

After seeking pardon, the pardon-seeker should present victuals, just as doeth he who cometh from journeying.

Because the sinner, who, for sin, shall have come out from the circle of being present and of being collected (of the *khānqāh*), and shall have entered on the journey of separation and of being hidden,—returneth not to this circle. To re-enter, it is first necessary that he should present victuals, which the ṣūfīs call *gharāmat* (fine).

When a person appeareth possessed of lust, with him they should strive to repel the darkness of lust by the luminosity of the heart.

The injurer and the injured both are in sin. Because if the injured one had heartily opposed the lust of the injurer, the darkness of lust would, through the luminosity of the heart, have departed.

The true ṣūfī is he who striveth in the purifying of his heart, and alloweth no pollution to abide in him.

As our allowance, may God grant us this state.

ON THE RULE OF THE SAFAR (THE JOURNEY)

VI, 9

Doubtless, in subduing refractory lusts and in softening hard hearts, *safar* profiteth much.

The being separated from one's native land, from friends and familiar things, and the exercising of patience in calamities cause lust and nature to rest from pursuing their way, and take up from hearts the effect of hardness.

In subduing lusts, the effect of *safar* is not less than the effect of *nawāfil*, fasting and praying.

On dead skins, by tanning, the effects of purity, of softness and of delicacy of texture appear; even so, by the tanning of *safar*, and by the departure of natural corruption and innate roughness, appear the purifying softness of devotion and change from obstinacy to faith.

Hence the master of *sharī'at* (Muḥammad) hath incited to *safar*, although to *safar* is not limited the acquisition of the objects of the seekers of *ḥaqīqat* and of *ṭarīqat*.

For there have been *shaikhs* who have, neither at the beginning nor at the end, made *safar*, but God's grace hath been their aid, and the noose of attraction hath drawn them from the lowest to the highest stage, and conveyed them to the stage of being a *shaikh*, the master of instruction.

Most *shaikhs* have made *safar*,—some in the beginning, for the sake of receiving profit; some at the end, for giving profit; and some both in the beginning and at the end, wherein they have regarded their own welfare of season and of *ḥāl*.

Ibrāhīm Khwāṣṣ used not to stay more than forty days in a city, because in this course, he regarded his welfare of *ḥāl* and of *tawakkul*.

With 'Īsā (Christ), the ṣufīs are associated, because, during the whole course of his life, he was in *safar*, and, for the safety of his faith, never stayed in a place.

Whoever maketh *safar* must observe twelve rules:

(1) *The advancing of proper resolution, and the establishing of honoured purposes—*

(*a*) *The acquiring of* 'ilm (*knowledge*).

(*b*) *The meeting of* shaikhs *and of brothers.* Because, on meeting men of *ṣalāḥ* and obtaining a glance from the Lords of prosperity, many advantages accrue to seekers of *ṭarīqat*.

He may be worthy of a happiness-giver's glance, and therefrom he may take up advantages of faith and of the world.

In respect of the special ones, not far is this sense.

In the glance of some serpents, God hath established a special quality whereby he, on whom they glance, becometh destroyed. Wonder is it if, in the glance of His own special ones, God should have placed a virtue whereby they give the seeker on whom they glance life and happiness according to his capacity!

In the *masjid* of Khīf at Minā, Shaikh Ḍiyā'-u'd-Dīn Abu'n-Najīb was making the *ṭawāf*; at all he glanced; and in inquiring as to, and reflecting upon, their state made excess.

They said: "What seekest thou?" He said: "Slaves of God there are whose glance giveth happiness; their glance, I seek."

(*c*) *The cutting asunder from familiar things and the swallowing the bitterness of separation from brothers and dear friends.* For patience, in separation from one's abode and friends, is worthy of many benefits.

(*d*) *The revealing of the hidden treasure of the soul's state; and the expelling its decorations and claims.* Because many reprehensible qualities (which, being rested in their purpose, are concealed in lusts)—become, revealed, in *safar*, through farness from accustomed things.

Thus if at the *khānqāh* (or at his abode), he see not (by reason of his rest with desire) a perturbation in his *nafs*, he thinketh that in him are existent patience and *riḍā'*.

When, in *safar*, calamities become continuous, and from his soul a passion or an abomination appeareth, he knoweth that he hath not these two qualities. Up he riseth in search of them, and the claim of possessing them vanisheth.

(*e*) *Solitude and abandoning the acceptance (of the people).* The breeze of the *ḥāl* of the master of *ḥāl* who dwelleth in a corner reacheth the soul of the true ones and of the seekers of that corner, and he becometh the *qiblah* of prosperity and the master of the people's acceptance.

This state is, for travellers of *ṭarīqat*, the source of trial; and, to those arrived at the stage, the mark of being chosen.

For travellers (who are afflicted with this calamity of trial) the journeying for solitude and for the abandoning of acceptance (of the people) is of the requisites (of *safar*).

Because the stage of acceptance (of the people) is the slipping place of travellers; here, do their feet slip; here, do they turn their face from God to the people—except the person whom the favour of the Eternal aideth and who avoideth that abode, and goeth elsewhere, so that preserved from this calamity he may remain.

(*f*) The reading of verses of singularity and unity of God from the books of the world and from souls; and reading the signs of *qudrat* (power) and of *ḥikmat* (God's mystery) and the wonders of created and destined things—so that thereby amplitude may appear to the power of thought, and proofs to the perfection of *qudrat* and of *ḥikmat* increase (in number).

(2) *Making safar with a friend.* In *safar* calamities (which everyone in solitude cannot bear) occur. Hence is necessary a friend who may aid.

Some of the strong, having power of endurance against afflictions, have in solitude made *safar*, yet to everyone it is not easy.

(3) *Of the party* (*who make together* safar) *making one* amīr *so that all shall obey him as in the* Ḥadīth. Greater is the capacity of power of that one who, in austerity, piety, liberality and in compassion, is greater.

It is related that Abū 'Abdullah Marūzī desired to make *safar*. His companionship, Abū 'Alī Rabāṭī asked. Abū 'Abdullah said: "Only on the condition that thou be *Amīr* or I." Abū 'Alī replied: "Be thou *Amīr.*"

Abū 'Abdullah took up his road-provisions, and on his head placed his load.

One night, in the desert, it rained. All night Abū 'Abdullah stood holding his blanket over Abū 'Alī to preserve him from the rain.

When Abū 'Alī said: "Do not," Abū 'Abdullah used to say: "I am *Amīr*; obedience on thy part is necessary."

Whoever in power hath his glance over many followers; and hath the desire for rule or for the acquisition of lust's desires,—his is no portion in ṣūfism.

(4) *The bidding farewell to brothers*. He should, as Muḥammad ordered, bid farewell to the brothers (of the *khānqāh*); and on the brothers, it is obligatory that they should pray for him.

For thus, when bidding farewell to travellers, did Muḥammad pray.

(5) *The bidding farewell to the stage (of sojourning)*. When the traveller taketh up his chattels, he should perform two *rak'ats* of prayer, and with them bid farewell.

In the *Ḥadīs* is a tale by Anas b. Mālik that Muhammad never alighted at a stage without performing, at the time of departure, two *rak'a's* of prayer, after which he used to pray: "O God, increase my piety; pardon my sins; turn me towards good-just as Thou wishest."

(6) When he wisheth to ride his steed, camel, litter or ship—he should say : "Praise be to God Who made subdued to us this steed. In the name of God. God is great. I depend upon God ; save with God, the great and powerful, is neither power nor command. Thoû art the rider of all backs ; and the aider of all matter."

(7) From the stage, he should start early in the morning on the fifth day (Thursday), because Ka'b Mālik relateth that, on that day, Muḥammad generally began his *safar* and despatched his troops.

(8) When he cometh near to the stage, he should say : "O God of the skies, of those that increase, of earth, of those that decrease : of *Shaiṭān*, of those that mislead ; of the wind, of those that blow ; of water, of those that flow ! O God, I pray for the good of this stage and of its people ; with Thee, I take shelter from the evil of this stage and of its people."

(9) *Salutation to the stage.* When he alighteth, he should, by way of salutation to the stage, offer two *rak'at* of prayer.

(10) *The arranging of the articles of* safar. With himself, he should keep the staff, the water-holder, and the girdle, because their association with him is the *sunnat.* Abū Sa'īd Khudrī relateth that Muḥammad, going from Medina to Mecca, thus ordered.

(11) When he reacheth a city whereat he wisheth to stop and from afar casteth on it his glance, he should make salutation to the living and to the dead, should read some of the Qur'ān ; should send the blessing thereof as a present to them, and should

utter this prayer : "O God ! in it bestow upon us good rest and fair allowance."

(12) Before entering the city, he should, if possible, bathe, because when Muḥammad wished to enter Mecca, he used first to bathe.

SAMĀ' (THE SONG, THE CIRCULAR DANCE OF DERVISHES)

V, 9

Of the number of most laudable ṣūfī mysteries, denied by outward *'ulamā'*, one is the assembly for : (*a*) the *samā'* (hearing) of the *ghinā'* (song) and *ilḥān* (lilt), (*b*) the summoning of the *qawwāl* (singer).

The reason of denial is that this custom is innovation, for in the time :

of Muḥammad,
of the *ṣaḥābah*,
of the *tābi'īn*,
of the *'ulamā'*,
of the ancient *shaikhs*,

this was not the custom.

Some of the modern *shaikhs* have established the custom ; and, since it is not opposed to the *sunnat*, held it laudable.

Samā' is the comprehender of three benefits :

(1) To the soul and the heart of the companions of austerity and the Lords of strife (against sin),—weariness, *qabḍ* and despair appear on account of many deeds. Then, for the repelling of this calamity, modern *shaikhs* have made a spiritual composition out of the *samā'* of sweet sounds, harmonious melodies and verses desire-exciting ; and made them eager for it at the time of need.

(2) Through the manifestation and the power of *nafs*, stoppings and veilings (of God's glory) occur

to the holy traveller. Thus, the increase of *ḥāl* closeth; and, through length of separation (from God), the violence of desire (for God) decreaseth.

Then, by hearing sweet lilts and *ghazals* (describing his *ḥāl*), that strange *ḥāl* (which moveth the claim of desire, and exciteth love's contest) appeareth to the hearer; the stoppings and the veilings arise and depart from before him; and the door of increase openeth.

(3) To men of the Path, whose state—from (slow) travelling to (swift) flight, from (laborious) travelling to (irresistible) attraction, from being a lover (of God) to being the beloved (of God)—shall not have ended, it is possible that, at the time of *samā'*, the soul's ear may open and gain the rapture of the address of eternity without beginning, and of the "first covenant"; that with one shaking the bird of the soul may shake from itself the dust of existence and the clamminess of impurities; and may—from the pollution of the heart, of lust and of the crowd of existences—become free.

Then, with swift flight, the soul cometh into propinquity to God; the holy traveller's slow travelling changeth to swift flight; his laborious journey, to irresistible attraction; and his being a lover, to his being the beloved (of God).

Then, in a moment, doth he travel, as without *samā'* he cannot travel in years.

The best of deeds (prayer) is for some the cause of prosperity; and for some of sorrow. Nevertheless, the abandoning of prayer is not lawful.

At this time in a way (which is the way of men

of the time and of ṣūfīs) *samā'* is the essence of disaster; for many are the assemblies the foundation whereof is on the claim of lust and of sensual delights —not on the principles of sincerity, and on the desire of increase of *ḥāl* whereon hath verily been the way of this *ṭarīq*.

The cause of being present at an assembly of *samā'* is: (*a*) the claim to victuals that in that assembly are expected; (*b*) the inclination to dancing, to sport and to pastime; (*c*) the delight of beholding things forbidden and abhorrent; (*d*) the attraction of worldly kinds; (*e*) the manifestation of *wajd* and *ḥāl*; (*f*) the keeping brisk the market of being a *shaikh*; and the making current the chattels of self-adorning.

All this is the essence of disaster, and abhorrent to men of faith.

Every assembly the foundation whereof is on one of these desires,—from it becometh difficult the search for increase of: *ḥāl*; inward purity; tranquillity of heart.

This complaint was laid in the time of Junaid, which was the time of revealing of *shaikhs* and of ṣūfīs.

At the end of his life Junaid held not the assembly of *samā'* of the singer.

They said: "Why holdest thou not *samā'*?" He said: "With whom may I hold *samā'*?' They said: "For thy own soul, hear." He said: "From whom may I hear?"

It is preper to make *samā'* with sympathising friands; and to hear one who sufereth pam (of love for God), and who, for the sake solely of the next world, speaketh.

Doubtless the sweet voice is one of divine favours.

Thus by the camel-driver's song, the camel easily beareth heavy loads and joyfully travelleth many stages in a day.

Waḥī saith: Once in the desert, I met an Arab tribe; one of them took me to his tent. Before the victuals appeared, I saw a black slave bound and several camels dead at the tent-door. The slave said: "Tonight thou art the guest; and the guest my Lord holdeth dear. Hope is mine that thou wilt intercede for my release from these bonds." When he had made ready the victuals, I said: "I will not eat till thou releasest this slave." He said: "This slave hath ruined my property and my camels; and cast me on the dust of poverty. My income used to be from the profit of these camels. But this slave hath a voice exceeding sweet; and he loaded the camels with heavy burdens; and to the melody of *Ḥudā* urged them so that in one day they traversed three days' space. When they reached the last stage, they cast their loads and fell dead. Him I will give to thee."

The next day I wished to hear the slave's voice; my host accordingly ordered him to begin for camel-driver's melody.

Near, there was a bound camel.

When he heard the slave's voice, he revolved his head and snapped his tether; and I became senseless and fell.

They asked Junaid: "Why doth a person, who is resting with gravity and who suddenly heareth a sweet voice—fall into agitation and tumult?" He said: "When, in the covenant of eternity without beginning and of *mīthāq*, God said to the atoms of the progeny of the sons of Ādam—Am I not your God?—the sweetness of that address remained in the ear of the soul. When they hear a sweet sound, the sweetness of the address cometh to mind; and they delight thereat, and fall into tumult.

Thus also say Dhu'n-Nūn Miṣrī and Samnūn Muḥib.

Bukā' (lamentation) is of two kinds: (*a*) the *bukā'* of joy, (*b*) the *bukā'* of *wajd*.

For *bukā'* is produced by fear, desire, joy or *wajd*.

The *bukā'* of joy is when, from exceeding joy, one weepeth—as when a son, or a beloved, long separated by seas, returneth.

The *bukā'* of *wajd* is when a ray of the splendour of *ḥaqq-u'l-yaqin* (the truth of certainty) flasheth, and the blow of *qidam* (eternity) cometh upon *ḥudūth* (calamities), the rest of the existence of the *wājid* (the enraptured one) riseth up and disappeareth in the dashing together of *qidam* and *ḥudūth*.

This state in manifested in the form of drops of tears.

Whatever hath dominion over humanity, *samā'* strengtheneth.

For those engaged in love for God, *samā'* is the aider to perfection; for those filled with lust, the cause of disaster.

Although *wajd* in *samā'* is the perfection of the *ḥāl* of "the first ones," it is the defect of "the last ones". Because *wajd* is the sign of resuming (after little losing) the state of witnessing. In *samā'*, the *wājid* is the loser; and the cause of the loss of the *ḥāl* of witnessing is the appearance of the qualities of *wujūd* (existence).

The qualities of *wujūd* are: (*a*) the darkness arising from lust, the veil of the vain; (*b*) the luminousness arising from the heart, the veil of the verified.

The source of *wajd* in *samā'* is: (*a*) either purely sweet melodies, the delight whereof is shared between the soul and the heart of the verified; and between the soul and the lust of the vain; (*b*) or pure melodies (whereby the soul alone is delighted) wherein the listening heart maketh *samā'* in respect to the verified, and the *nafs* in respect to the vain.

For freedom from the veil of existence, the *ḥāl* of witnessing is constant and the *samā'* of addresses (of God) perpetual—to "the last ones".

The *samā'* of melody cannot agitate, for agitation assault is a strange state.

The *ḥāl* of witnessing and the *samā'* of addresses (of God) appear not strange to the man of constant witnessing and of perpetual *samā'*, and therefore by them he is not agitated.

A companion of Sahl 'Abdullah saith: "Years in Sahl's society I was; and yet I never saw him changed by hearing—the *dhikr*, the Qur'ān, the other exercises, until at the close of his life, they read to him this Qur'ānic verse: "From you, sacrifice He will not take today."

Suddenly *ḥāl* turned to him; and he so trembled that he nearly fell.

I asked the cause; he said: "Me, weakness hath befallen." He became changed and agitated. Afterwards Ibn Sālim asked him of his state. He said: "It was from weakness." They said: "If that were from weakness, what is power?" He said: "Power is that when naught descendeth on a person but by the power of *ḥāl*, he suffereth it; and by it changeth not."

Once, Mumshād Dīnawarī passed a place where, in *samā'*, was a crowd of "the first ones". When they saw him, they left off. He said: "Upon your state ye continue intent. If all the musical instruments were gathered in my ear, they would engage naught of my purpose and relieve naught of my pain."

Whoever hath the state of perpetual witnessing, his state in *samā'* is even as it was before *samā'*.

The heart that is ever present with God, and rejecteth *samā'*,—understandeth from every sound that reacheth him, the address of God.

Then is his *samā'* not restricted to man's melodies even as Abū 'Uthmān Maghribī hath said. The voice within himself is *samā'*; of the external ear is no need, even as Ḥassr hath said:

Whose *samā'* is constant, ever present with the Hidden is he in heart; and ever void of lusts' tale is the ear of his heart.

He heareth sometimes the address of God; sometimes the praise of the atoms of existence; sometimes from the inward; and sometimes from the outward.

Once Shiblī heard one crying in the bāzār of Baghdad: "Ten *khiyār* (cucumbers) for a *dāng*." He cried out: "When ten *khayyār* (good men) are for a *dāng*, the state of the (worthless) wicked is what?"

Once a man of heart (a ṣūfī) heard a proclaimer shouting: "*Sa'tarbarī*." He fell senseless. When to sense he returned, they asked him the cause. He said: "From God, I heard—*asa tarbarī*."

Of the *Amīr u'l-Mū'minīn* ('Alī) it is said that once he heard the sound of a conch. To his companions, he said: "Know ye what this conch saith?" They said: "Nay." He said: "It saith, praise be to God! O God! O God! verily living is the Eternal Master."

'Abd-u'r-Raḥmān Salīmī says: "Once I went to Abū 'Uthmān Maghribī. There, with an ox, they were drawing water from a well. To me, Abū 'Uthmān said: 'Knowest thou what this ox saith?' I said: 'Nay.' He said: 'He saith—Allah! Allah!'"

Men of *samā'* are of three kinds:

(*a*) *The sons of truths.* These in *samā'* hear the address of God to themselves.

(*b*) *The men of needs.* These by means of the meanings of couplets that in *samā'* they hear heartily address themselves to God; and, in whatever they ascribe to God, are in sincerity of purpose.

(*c*) *The lonely fuqarā'.* These have severed all worldly ties and calamities. In goodness of hearts is their *samā'*; and nearest to safety (in God) they are.

THE RULES OF SAMĀ'

V, 10

The first rule of *samā'* is that, at an assembly of *samā'*, they should keep foremost sincerity of resolution and seek out its cause;

(*a*) If it be lustful desire, shun it.

(*b*) If the claim of sincerity, of desire and of search for the increase of *ḥāl* and for comprehending the blessing (of God)—be united, free from lust's impurities, the grace of such an assembly (despite the absence of a *shaikh*, or men of *samā'* of the brothers of concord, and of sincere seekers) is great gain.

If it be not free from the impurities of lust,—it is necessary, in its purification, to bring forward subtleties of vision and graces of practice.

If the cause be first the claim of sincerity and afterwards lustful desire, it is necessary to repair the injury done by lust: (*a*) by sincerity of penitence; (*b*) by seeking aid (of God) against the wickedness of lust; (*c*) by putting forward prayer.

If the cause be first lustful desire and afterwards good resolution for reparation,—they credit the former desire, not the succeeding resolution; and shun such an assembly.

If *samā'* comprehend: (*i*) prohibited things such as (*a*) the morsel of tyrants, (*b*) the being near to women, (*c*) the presence of beardless youths; (*ii*) abhorred objects such as: (*a*) the presence of one who as a *zāhid* hath no affinity for this crowd; who delighteth not in *samā'*; (*b*) the possessor of rank of the Lords of the world to whom it is necessary to be respectful; (*c*) the presence of one, who falsely revealeth *wajd*; and to those present, maketh time perturbed with false *tawājud*, it is necessary for true seekers to shun such an assembly.

At an assembly of *samā'*, he who is present should sit with respect and gravity; should keep restrained the parts of the body from excess of motion, especially in the presence of *shaikhs*; should not become agitated with a little of the splendours of *wajd*; should not affect intoxication with a little taste of the pure wine (of love for God); nor voluntarily express either the *shahqat* (murmuring noise) or the *za'q* (calling out).

If—let us flee to God for protection,—without the descending of *wajd* and of *ḥāl*, he manifesteth *wajd* and layeth claim to *ḥal*,—it is verily the essence of hypocrisy and of sin the foulest blameable act, and the most disgraceful of states.

In the time of Abu'l Qāsim Naṣrābādī (who was a companion of Shiblī, and renowned in knowledge of the *Ḥadīth*), the *shaikh* of Khurāsān delighted in *samā'*.

One day between him and Abū 'Amr b.. Najīd (who was a *murīd* of Abū 'Uthmān Ḥā'irī, and had seen Junaid) there chanced an assembly of concord.

Him, on account of his exceeding *samā'*, Abū 'Amr reproached.

Naṣrābādī said: "Thus it is, but an assembly, whereat one is a speaker in lawful song and the rest are silent—is better than an assembly whereat all are speakers in slander." Abū 'Amr replied: "O

Abu'l-Qāsim! alas, evil is motion in *samā'*; in it, is this and this."

The explanation of Amr's reply is this, that the error of *samā'* comprehendeth many errors:

(*a*) Falsely slandering the Lord of the world (God). Because the revealing of *wajd* in *samā'* referreth to the *mutawājid*, to whom God hath bestowed a special gift.

(*b*) Deceiving some of those present in *samā'* by the manifestation of false *ḥāl*. Deceit is treachery; treachery is the source of repulsion.

(*c*) Breaking the confidence of followers of the men of rectitude. Thus is cut off from them the aid of holy men (*ṣāliḥ*) which is the essence of sin.

The way of true *wājids* is this:

So long as they gain not fully the ardour of *samā'*, they move not in *samā'*; from them motion issueth only when they cannot restrain it,—even as the palsied one cannot restrain himself from the motion of palsy.

Tawājud is this:

When, not in the true way of *wajd* and of *ḥāl*, but in the way of indulging the heart and bathing lust, a person displayeth a weighed motion with weighed cadences,—so that *nafs* (lust) becometh rested from the labour of deeds; and the heart from the labour of deliberation.

Thus, the heart vainly seeketh aid in search of God.

Although in the *shar'*, dancing may be among the lawful pleasures, it is with the men of truths and the Lords of grandeur—vain.

Yet the vain thing which is aid to the search for God is the essence of devotion. This vain is verily a truth in the garb of the vain.

The *mutawājid's* resolution in *tawājud* is possibly

a portion of *wajd*, so that (by its blessing) he gaineth a portion (of good) from his *ḥāl*.

Though this be permissible to "the first ones," it is unsuitable for the *ḥāl* and the office of *shaikhs*. Because their *ḥāl* is all, outwardly and inwardly, pure truth, wherein is no entrance to sport and pastime.

From them, especially in the presence of *shaikhs*, should not voluntarily issue the *za'q* (calling out), but only at that time when the power of restraint is effaced. So the breather whose power of breathing cometh strait,—if he breathe not, his heart consumeth.

It is related that in Junaid's service, a youth used to display assiduity; and in *samā'* to make the *za'q*. One day Junaid forbade him saying: "If after this, thou restrain not thyself,—from us go far." After this, in *samā'* the youth restrained himself from *za'q*. So, from the root of every hair flowed the sweat of restraint, till one day he expressed a *za'q* and at the same time his life.

The condition of *za'q* is: "The being hidden from things felt."

In the best *ṭarīq*, when not done through the overwhelming power of *ḥāl* and through the loss of the power of repression, unlawful are: (*a*) motion in *samā'*; (*b*) the voluntary *za'q*; (*c*) the voluntary rending of one's garment. These are the pretensions to *ḥāl* without the truth of *ḥāl*, and the ruin of property.

In casting the *khirqah* to the singer, there should be advanced an intention void of hypocrisy just as he may (in support of *wajd* and of exciting desire) wish to give ease to the singer.

The *khirqah* (mantle) that passeth from the possessor of *samā'* to the singer is of two kinds: (*a*) *khirqah-i-ṣaḥīḥah* the unrent *khirqah*; (*b*) *khirqah-i-mumazzakah* the rent *khirqah*.

The rule of the unrent *khirqah* is as follows:

(*i*) If the *wājid's* purpose in casting off the *khirqah* and bestowing it be specially for the singer, in it, others have no concern.

(*ii*) If his purpose be not special, and a distinguished one, obedient to order, be present, he may give it to the singer, or to another. Over him, none hath authority, for his acts are from vision.

(*iii*) If those present at the *samā'* be all brothers, and there be no *shaikh*, they give the *khirqah* to the singer; because the exciter of *wajd* (which is the cause of casting off the *khirqah*) is his song.

Some say:

(*a*) The *khirqah* belongeth to the assembly; because the source of *wajd* is not only the singer's song but also the blessing of the assembly.

(*b*) If the singer be outside of the assembly, he is with all a sharer; otherwise he is portionless.

(*c*) If the singer be for hire, he is portionless; otherwise with the assembly he shareth.

(*d*) If some of the lovers (of God) present a gift, and with it, those present are satisfied,—everyone may go after his *khirqah* and the gift they give to the singer.

(*e*) If in casting off the *khirqah* someone shall have resolved not again to go after his *khirqah*—it, they give to the singer.

The rule of the rent *khirqah* is:

When the possessor of *samā'*, through the impetuosity of *ḥāl* and the capture of control, rendeth on his body the *khirqah*,—it, they divide among those present at *samā'* whether of the same, or of diverse, kind (of brotherhood).

In dealing kindly with those of diverse kind, it is necessary that the assembly should hold a favourable opinion of them and of their casting off the *khirqah*.

If, at the division, be present one who at the time of *samā'* was absent, to him they give a portion (of the *khirqah*).

If of the cast-off *khirqahs* some be unrent and some rent, they rend (if the *shaikh* consider it fit) the unrent *khirqahs* and part them among those present.

The rending of the *khirqah* and the parting of it among those present is a *ḥadīth* by Anas b. Mālik; but in it, they have made contrariety.

If by the *ḥadīth* in respect of the *samā'* of (singing), of moving, of rending garments, and of parting them among those present,—the truth should be verified, it would to the ṣūfī be the best document.

THE KHIRQAH (DERVISH MANTLE)

V, 2

A custom of the ṣūfīs is the putting on of the *khirqah*, which, at the beginning of their sway over the *murīds*, the *shaikhs* have considered laudable, but regarding which they have received no order from the *sunnat* except the *ḥadīth* of Umm Khālid.

It is related that once to Muḥammad they brought some raiment in the midst whereof was a small black blanket. Taking it up, he said to the assembly: "Who intendeth putting on this?" All were silent. He said: "I give it to Umm Khālid." They called Umm Khālid, and Muḥammad covered her with it. On that blanket were marks (stripes) yellow and red; at them Muḥammad looked and said: 'O Umm Khālid! this is admirable" (which is the *ḥadīth*).

In the arranging of the garment of the *khirqah*, which is the ṣūfī way, clinging to this *ḥadīth*,—is far.

Although from the *sunnat* is no clear command, since the *khirqah* is surety for benefits and not an obstacle to the *sunnat*, it is laudable.

The following of the excellences of the Path is lawful; the excellences are:

(*a*) The changing of custom and the turning from natural things and sensual delights.

For, as in eatables, potables and spouses lust hath delight —in garments also, it delighteth

The putting on of a garment, which hath become lust's custom, and in the particular form whereof it resteth—in it, doubtless, lust delighteth.

Then is the change of garment, the change of custom which is the essence of worship, as in the *Hadīth*.

(*b*) The repelling of the society of contemporaries in sin and of *shaiṭāns* of mankind, who (by resemblance in form) incline to the other (good) society.

When a change of garment and an alteration of form appeareth in the *murīd*, his equals and associates depart from him.

For the *khirqah* is the shadow of the *shaikh's* love and frighteneth *shaiṭān* from the shadow of men of love as is in the *Ḥadīth*.

For the *murīd*, society of the good is necessary, that from them he may take the colour of goodness.

Separation from the wicked is the condition of acceptance of the society of the good.

Even so the indigo-stained raiment taketh no colour till after the removing of the indigo.

(*c*) The revealing of the *shaikh's* sway in the *murīd's* heart—by reason of his sway outwardly, which is the mark of inward sway.

So long as the *murīd's* interior becometh not worthy of the *shaikh's* sway, and the *murīd* considereth him not perfect and one of consummate excellence—he becometh not outwardly obedient to the *shaikh*.

(*d*) The good news to the *murīd* is his acceptance by God. Because the putting on of the *khirqah* is the mark of the *shaikh's* acceptance, which is the mark of God's acceptance.

By putting on the *khirqah* by the *shaikh* possessed of love, the *murīd* knoweth that God hath accepted him; and his being united to the *shaikh* (by the bond of sincerity, of desire and of acceptance) becometh a mirror wherein he seeth the beauty of his end.

The being united with *shaikhs* is the result of the acquaintance of his soul with the *shaikh's* soul which is the mark of kinship, as in the *Ḥadīth*.

Even so the *murīd's* putting on of the *khirqah* (by the *shaikh* possessed of understanding) signifieth the *murīd's* desire for the *shaikh*, and the *shaikh's* love for the *murīd*.

The exalted states (*ḥāl*) are the result of these two meanings (*e* and *d*) being wedded.

The *khirqah* is of two kinds: (*a*) the *khirqah* of desire; (*b*) the *khirqah* of blessing.

The khirqah *of desire.* When the *shaikh* (with the penetration of the light of vision and with intelligence) looketh into the midst of the *murīd's* state, and beholdeth the sincerity of his desire for God, he indueth him with this *khirqah*, so that he may become his giver of glad tidings; and that the eye of his heart may become luminous by the blowing of the breeze of God's guidance, whereof the *khirqah* is the bearer.

So did Ya'qūb's eye, by the breeze of Yūsuf's shirt, see.

The khirqah *of blessing.* This *khirqah* is presented to him who with the *shaikhs* hath a good report.

That one who, through good opinion and resolve for blessing by the *khirqah* of *shaikhs*, desireth this *khirqah*, and is a seeker of the conditions of men of desire and of putting off the garment of his own desire for the *shaikh's* desire,—him, as regards two matters, they order: (*a*) attendance to the orders of the *sharī'at*; (*b*) the protection of the men of *ṭarīqat*, by whose protection he may gain kinship, and become worthy of the *khirqah* of desire, which is forbidden save to the man of desire and to the Lords of sincerity of resolution.

To these two, some add the *khirqah* of holiness: When the *shaikh* seeth in the *murīd* the effects of holiness and the marks of acquisition to the degree of excellence and instruction; and wisheth to appoint him his own *khalīfah*,—he clotheth him with the *khil'at* of holiness, and with the honour of his own favour, whereby may be effected the penetrating of his order and the obeying of the people.

THE CHOICE OF THE COLOURED *KHIRQAH*

V, 3

The choice of the coloured *khirqah* (for amending the defilements, and for evacuating man's heart of deeds and of contemplation) is (through solicitude for the care of the white garment and through being engaged in its cleansing) of the number of laudable deeds of *shaikhs*.

The *sunnat* is for the choosing of the white garment, and, in the opinion of ṣūfīs, this choosing is proved. But for those, whose times are immersed in devotion, the washing of the white garment occupieth too much time.

The coloured garment is best, because the excellence of *nawāfil* is greater than the excellence of garments.

Whenever the beginning of an excellence is the cause of abandoning the most excellent,—the abandoning of that excellence is excellence.

Blue colour is the choice of the ṣūfīs despite that black is better against defilements. The ṣūfī putteth on the garment with that colour suitable to his *ḥāl*.

Black is fit for him who is sunk in the darkness of lust, and whose times are surrounded with darkness.

Not thus is the *ḥāl* of the man of desire, because by the ray of the light of desire, the darkness of existence is trampled upon.

For them, the black garment is unfit, and since they have not wholly gained freedom from lust, the white garment is also unfit; for them is fit the blue garment, which is a mixture of light and darkness, of pureness and foulness.

In the flame of the candle are two portions—one pure light, the other pure darkness. Their place of union appeareth blue.

The white garment is fit for *shaikhs* that may have gained freedom from lust (*nafs*).

These aspects are only approximate.

The men of this Path are of three kinds:

(*a*) *Mubtadiyān* (the first ones) whose state is the abandoning of will to the *shaikh*; and with whom naught of garments, of goods and of other things is lawful save by the *shaikh's* desire.

(*b*) *Mutawassitān* (the middle ones), whose state is the abandoning of will to God, and who have no will as to special raiment; as occasion demandeth they submit.

(*c*) *Muntahiyān* (the end ones), who, by God's will, are absolute. What they choose is God's will.

When the true *murīd* entrusteth the rein of his will to the *shaikh*, perfect possessor of vision; and to him becometh submissive,—the *shaikh* withdraweth him from natural habits and sensual affections, and directeth him in all affairs of faith and of religion.

If he see that for a special garment the *murīd* thirsteth and desireth,—from it he bringeth him forth; and clotheth him with another garment.

If he see that his inclination is for splendid and soft raiment, he putteth on him the coarse grass *khirqah*; if he see that his inclination is for the coarse grass *khirqah* for the sake of hypocrisy and pretension, he clotheth him with soft silk raiment;

if he see that he desireth a special colour or form,—it, he forbiddeth.

Even so in all his circumstances.

The choice of the colour and of the form of the *murīd's* garment dependeth upon the *shaikh's* vision; and that dependeth on the good counsel of the time.

Some *shaikhs* have not ordered the *murīds'* change of raiment; their vision hath been intent upon concealing the *ḥāl*, and upon abandoning its manifestation.

Shaikhs are like to physicians; and of *murīds* many are the diseases, each one of a kind that *shaikhs* have known, and that they have applied the remedy to.

Their directions are on counsel and on rectitude, and the foundation of the path of salvation and prosperity.

KHILVAT (RETIREMENT)

V, 6

Keeping *khilvat* (retirement) in the way of the ṣūfīs is an innovation. In Muḥammad's time, the *sunnat* was naught save *ṣuḥbat* (society); and its excellence excelleth other excellences.

Thus, by *ṣuḥbat* they have described the *Ṣaḥābah* and by no other description; and outside the society of Muḥammad, their description is naught, because their souls were, by the grandeur of prophecy, described with rest, and by the light of integrity encompassed with purity; hearts were void of love for the world and solaced by the vision of the beauty of certainty, and filled with love for God, with affection, with purity and with fidelity.

When the sun of prophecy became hidden, the souls of the Companions came gradually into motion; opposition became manifest, and in time reached a place where *ṣuḥbat* (society) became overwhelmed, and *khilvat* (retirement), pleasant and beloved.

For the safety of faith, the seekers of God sought the *ṣauma'ah* (convent) and *khilvat*, as Junaid hath said.

Though in the time of the sending of the *sunnat* was no *khilvat*, yet before that time, Muḥammad, through exceeding love for God, and sincerity of desire—held esteemed *khilvat*; used to go to the caves of Ḥirā'; and there used to pass nights in *dhikr* and in devotion.

In the choice of *khilvat*, the tradition is firmly held by the ṣūfīs, but the appointing of forty days is from a tradition from Muḥammad and from God's word.

With Mūsā, God promised to speak, and appointed a place of meeting and a stated time. God said: "Keep fast thirty days and nights." Ten days more, He afterwards added. During that time Mūsā consumed neither food nor drink; he was engaged in worshipping God; and for talking with Him became prepared. Since, for propinquity to God and for talk with Him, Mūsā had need of *khilvat*,—so have others.

Even so in the case of Muḥammad:

his being cut off from *ṣuḥbat*;
his retiring (to talk) with God;
his separating himself from the people;
his reducing his daily food;
his constant *dhikr* in desire's path in the beginning of divine impressions;

are further proofs.

Thus for the seekers of God, acceptable is the obligation (of *khilvat*) and, indeed, *wājib* (necessary),

The source whence the *sharī'at* fixed the appointed time (forty days) is obscure, and knowledge of it difficult save by the Prophets, by the special ones, and by the holy ones.

In the *'Awārif-u'l-Ma'ārif* the *Shaikh-u'l-Islām* saith:

"When God wished to appoint Ādam to His own *khilāfat*, and to make him architect of this world after he had, by his existence, made Paradise prosperous,—He gave to him a composition of elements of earth, fit for this world, and for forty mornings made them ferment.

"Every morning signifieth the existence of a quality that becometh the cause of his attachment to this world, and every attachment became his veil against beholding the glory of *qidam* (eternity).

"Every veil is the cause of farness from the hidden world; every farness, the cause of nearness to the material world till that time when the veil becometh heaped up, and this world's fitness, complete in Ādam."

In the establishing of forty mornings with sincerity (which is the condition of *khilvat*) its *ḥikmat* (philosophy) is:

For every morning (of *khilvat*), a veil should lift and a nearness (to God) appear, so that in forty mornings, the forty-fold veil should lift, and refined human nature, from farness to the native land of nearness to God (the summation of beauty and of glory; the essence of *'ilm*, and of *ma'rifat*) return; and for it, the vision of the grandeur of eternity without beginning should be verified and painted; the sight of its resolution, from inclination to the world's impurity, be preserved; and the fountain of *ḥikmat* go running from its heart and on its tongue.

The mark of *khilvat* is: the preservation of the condition of that revelation of *ḥikmat*.

The revelation of *ḥikmat* is in the proof of the lifting of the veil and the doubtless manifestations.

Khilvat is like unto a smith's forge whereon, by the fire of austerity, lust becometh fused, pure of nature's pollution, delicate and gleaming like unto a mirror; and without (beyond, through) it, appeareth the form of the hidden; and is a collection of contrarieties of *nafs* (lust) and accustomed austerities:

Little eating.
Little talking.

Shunning the society of man.

Perseverance in *dhikr*.

Denying thoughts.

Constant *murāqibah* (fearful contemplation).

The meaning of *riyāḍat* (austerity) is the abandoning of desire and of the requisites of effort.

THE CONDITIONS OF KHILVAT

V, 7

In the opinion of the ṣūfīs, *khilvat* is not restricted to forty days. The being severed from the people and the being engaged with God is a desired matter, the duration whereof is for life.

The advantage of appointing forty days is that, on the completing of this period, the manifestation begins to appear.

If to a person who to life's end keepeth his time engaged in devotion to God, and in freedom from the people, that manifestation appeareth,—beyond it is no greater favour.

If this bounty of God be not his, it is necessary for him at certain periods to practise *khilvat*.

At least once a year, he should sit in *khilvat*, so that when, for forty days and nights, he shall have accustomed his *nafs*—to the preservation of times; to the observance of readings (of the Qur'ān) and of rules, he may be expectant that the order will not be extended to his former mixing with people; that, in God's protection, his *khilvat* may be; and that his *khilvat* may be the aider of the structure of the times of glory.

Only in the preservation of its conditions appeareth the advantage of *khilvat*.

Who resolveth upon *khilvat* must purify his intention from the pollution of desire for the objects of this world; and of prayers for (his welfare in) the next world.

According to intention is the reward of deeds. As intention is better than the deeds, more full is its reward.

No object is better than propinquity of God; whatever is exterior to Him is called the indigo of *ḥudūth* (calamity), and is directed by the disgrace of *fanā'* (effacement).

In the heart's purification, inclination to the polluted is the essence of pollution; propinquity thereto, especially impure.

Who hath desire for that exterior to God, great and glorious of both worlds, is polluted; from that pollution, purification is necessary for approach to the holy God, and for fitness of prayer to Him.

His intention should be restricted to propinquity to God by practising worship; and far from desire:

for rank, for hypocrisy, for the revelation of miracles, and for the explanation of the verses of power (the Qur'ān).

If to that crowd—whose desire from *khilvat* and austerity is the revelation of miracles and not propinquity to God,—something of that desired be revealed, it is the essence of deceit, and the cause of farness, of folly and of pride.

In the purifying of the interior, in the cleansing of the heart, in affecting *nafs*,—freedom from occupations, reduction of food, and continuity of *dhikr* have perfect effect.

When by *khilvat*, his interior becometh luminous and the outward form of some unattainable knowledge appeareth, and true thoughts appear to him and over his *nafs* gain sway,—the seeker of miracles thinketh that that is the lofty and far object of *khilvat*; and by the exalting of wicked *shaiṭān* becometh proud; and contemptuously glanceth at others—(let us flee to God for refuge).

Possibly out from his heart, he bindeth up the chattels of the *Sharī'at* and of prophecy; considereth not the abandoning of laws, of orders, and of the lawful and unlawful—so by the path of retrogression, he becometh cast out from the highway of the *Shar'* and from the path of Islam.

If, to one who is in intention pure, the manifestation of miracles falleth, it becometh the cause of the power of certainty and of the confirmation of resolve.

The condition of sincerity being observed, it is necessary that, out from the bond of debt, by cancelling tyranny; by making right (apologising for) calumny; by removing enmity, hate, malice,—he should come; and pure to all make his heart.

If, in his property, there be something whereto his heart clingeth,—it, from his property, he should expel.

If he be possessed of property in respect to family he performeth (so that outwardly and inwardly he may be free and pure) complete washing; exerciseth care as to the cleansing of raiment and of the prayer-mat; and chooseth for his *khilvat* a place where, from occupations, he may be free.

When he reacheth the door of *khilvat*, he saith:

"O God! by the right ingress, let me enter; by the right egress, let me pass out. By Thy grace, me make a conquering king."

When to the prayer-mat he wisheth to go, he first advanceth the right leg and saith:

"In the name of God; by the grace of God; praise be to God, and peace and blessing be on the Prophet of God!"

"O God! my sins pardon; open me the door of mercy."

Then, with the desire of the presence of God, he performeth two *rak'ats* of prayer with *khushū'* and with *khuḍū'* (humility of the heart and of the limbs).

In the first *rak'at*, after the Fātiḥah, he saith:

"O God of ours! on Thee is our reliance; in Thee, be our refuge; in Thee, our shelter."

Then, with sincerity and humility, he asketh pardon for all his sins. To God, he displayeth in his heart penitence for turning to that exterior to Him.

Before the *Qiblah* he sitteth, and, as long as he can, is in *tashahhud*.[1]

With himself he reflecteth that God is present, also the Prophet of God, so that he may be bound with the bond of reverence, and is ever wishing within that he may, outwardly and inwardly, offer himself in devotion and in praise, and in the raiment of concordance with divine decrees.

Thus, may he become the meeting-place of divine breathings, ready for the descending of boundless bounty.

In *khilvat*, after the purifying of resolution, penitence and continuity of employment with God, he must observe seven conditions:

(*i*) *Constant ablution*. When he seeth in himself lassitude, he should renew ablution, so that in his

1. "I profess that there is no God but God; I acknowledge Muḥammad to be the Apostle of God."

interior the light of outward purity may be brightened, and be the aider of the heart's luminosities.

(*ii*) *Constant fasting* Ever should he be in fast, so that the blessing of the *Sunnah* may comprehend his times.

(*iii*) *Little eating.* At breakfast the quantity of food should be not more than a riṭl. If he restrict as to bread and salt, 'tis well.

If to relish (that is in the place of food) he stretcheth his hand, to its extent, he should reduce the bread. If he begin with a riṭl, he should in the last tenth (of the period of forty days) reduce to half a riṭl. If he be strong and begin with half a riṭl he should reduce to quarter of a riṭl.

The companions of *khilvat* are of three kinds: the strong ones, the middle ones, the weak ones.

The weak break their fast every night; the middle every two nights; and the strong every three nights.

He may devour all on the first, or on the last, night; or some on the first night and some on the last night.

The last division is the best, so that he may have power (*a*) for devotion, (*b*) for standing up for the midnight prayers.

In reducing the clayey parts—the source of pollution, of darkness, of coarseness—scantiness of food is wholly effective.

(*iv*) *Little sleep.* So long as he is able he should not sleep. If sleep be overpowering, he should repel it by renewing ablution, or by reading the Qur'ān. If it cannot be repelled and involuntarily sleep seizeth him, he should (when he returneth from sleep) renew ablution and be engaged in prayer.

Every sleep that is of necessity is the essence of devotion when thereby is attainable the repelling of lassitude of the senses and of *nafs* (which are the cause of weariness of the soul of devotion and of the delight of worship).

By sleep, the purity of the senses and the expansion of the interior (which are the cause of *wajd* of the soul) return to him. Then are his times immersed in devotion.

In putting lust to death and in keeping the heart alive,—ever keeping awake is profitable by loosening the humours of the body, by weakening the points of forgetfulness, of sins, of ignorance and of carelessness.

(*v*) *Little talking*. He should ever guard his tongue from talking with people.

The sage practiseth silence though no calamity he expecteth.

Whether the speech be beautiful or ugly, it is not void of calamity. For so long as to perfect purification it shall not have reached, *nafs* hath in the revealing of beautiful speech a delight, wherefrom is expected the revealing of the qualities of pride and the thickening of the veil. Doubtless, ugly speech is followed by punishment.

Save by silence, not attainable is the path of safety.

In the tale of Maryam and of 'Īsā, God maketh Maryam's silence the forerunner of 'Īsā's speech. Even so the 'Īsā of the heart cometh into speech when the Maryam of *nafs* is silent of talk.

(*vi*) *The negation of thoughts*. By *dhikr* and by

the occupation of the heart in contemplation of the divine aspect, he should repel the crowd of thoughts.

Excellent though the penetration of some thoughts is, discrimination of thoughts occurreth not to beginners. Then, the being engaged in thought is for him the way of the *ḥadīth-u'n-nafs*, and to him is formidable.

The meaning of *ḥadīth-u'n-nafs* is this. The *nafs* of man, by its connection with the *rūḥ* (soul) of speech, is innate in the qualities of speech; and is ever expectant of the opportunity of converse with the heart which is its beloved.

Whenever *nafs* seeth the heart inclined to itself, and findeth its ears void of other sayings, immediately with the heart, it cometh into speech; and to it, by way of remembrance, confirmeth past matters of things spoken, heard, seen, tasted, touched; or giveth future news of hope; and keepeth engaged the ear of the heart with hearing its own speech rather than with hearing the speech of the soul and of God,—so that the heart may ever be before it, and averse to aught save *nafs*.

When the possessor of *khilvat* persevereth in the heart as to negation of thoughts, and as to the confirmation of *tauḥīd*,—the source of *ḥadīth-u'n-nafs* becometh effaced; *nafs*, silent; the ear of the heart, void of its saying, ready for the hearing of divine words.

(*vii*) *The perpetuality of deeds*. Outwardly and inwardly, he should keep himself arrayed in the garb of devotion. Every moment in a work which at that time is most important and best, he should be engaged. Thus who is "a first one" should limit himself to divine precepts, and to the *sunnah* of prayer, and at other times to *dhikr*.

Out of all the *adhkār* (*dhikrs*) the *shaikhs* have chosen: *Lā ilāha illallāh* (no god but God), because its form is formed of negation and of affirmation, so that at the time of the flowing of this speech on his tongue, the *dhākir* is present (alive to God) and preserveth conformity between the heart and the tongue.

As to negation, he regardeth the existence of *ḥādith* wholly with the glance of *fanā'*; as to affirmation, the existence of *qadīm* with the eye of *baqā'*.

By repeating this creed (*Lā ilāha*, etc , etc.) the form of *Tauḥīd* reposeth in his heart; its root is established in his heart, its branches are extended to the soul.

At this time, *dhikr* becometh the necessary quality of the heart; its aid is continuous. To it, at times of lassitude, the *dhikr* of the tongue of languor findeth no path; after that, it reacheth a place where *dhikr* becometh enjewelled in the heart.

The *dhākir* in *dhikr*; the *dhikr* in the heart; the heart in *madhkūr* (the origin of *dhikr*, God) become effaced.

At this stage if the form of the phrase of *Tauḥīd* (which is the meaning of *dhikr*) become effaced from the outward face of the heart, to the inward face of the heart its truth is joined. The meaning of this is *ḥāl*.

Dhikr, *dhākir* and *madhkūr* are one.

But for the "middle one" assiduity in the reciting of the Qur'ān after the performance of divine precepts is best.

Verily that speciality (that to "the first one" from assiduity in *dhikr* appeareth) becometh acquired from reading the Qur'ān with other specialities as the glory of the qualities (of God), the various spiritual truths, the subtleties of understanding and the truths of knowledge,—by readings of various Qur'ānic verses.

To "the last one," to whom the light of *dhikr* may have become his innate quality,—excellent is the reading (of the Qur'ān), and perfect, the act of prayer (*ṣalāt*).

Because this form of prayer is a devotion completely comprehending, wherein are comprehended:

dhikr.
tilāwat reading.
khushū' humility (of the limbs).
khuḍū' humility (of the heart).

As long as *nafs* is in obedience,—in it is concordance with the heart.

The aid of the soul of propinquity, the proclaiming, the delight of society, and the need of forms of prayer become joined to the prayer-mat.

In it, perseverance is best.

If, on account of it, an abhorrence should appear in *nafs*, the descending from praying to reading is best, for reading in comparison with praying is easy.

If reading end in weariness, the descending from it to *dhikr* is best.

For perseverance in respect to *dhikr* merely, and the repeating of light phrase is easier to *nafs* than the preservation of words weighty and of varied signification.

If languor fall upon the *dhikr* of the tongue,—best is assiduity in *dhikr* of the heart—which they call *murāqabah* (fearful contemplation), that is, considering the manifestations of God—in respect to his own state.

If as to *murāqabah* languor chance, he may rest awhile his limbs and senses, and in sleep give ease.

Thus from *nafs*, fatigue may depart; and, again with pleasure, he may advance to deeds.

Verily it is unfit that, with detestation and compulsion, he should engage *nafs* in a work (whereby it may be vexed and the power whereof it hardly hath).

The possessor of *khilvat* should devote all his time to these readings, so that the path of hidden events may be disclosed.

THE DREAMS OF THE MEN OF KHILVAT

V, 8

In the midst of *dhikr*, it sometimes happens to men of *khilvat* that, from things felt (this world) they become concealed (in unconsciousness), and that to them become revealed, as to the sleeper truths of hidden matters. It the ṣūfīs call *wāqi'ah* (dream). Sometimes this (revelation of truths) appeareth in the state of being present (in consciousness) without being absent (in unconsciousness).

Often the *wāqi'ah* is like to *nawm*; of *wāqi'ah* and *manāmāt* some are true and some false.

In most *waqā'i'* and *manāmāt*, *nafs* is partner with the *rūḥ* (soul), and in some absolute (alone). Truth is the quality of *rūḥ*, and falsehood of *nafs*.

Mukāshafah is never false; it signifieth oneness of soul by contemplating mysteries in the state of freedom from the gloomy thoughts of the body.

Wāqi'ah and *mānām* are divided into three parts.

(1) *Free revelation* (kashf). Thus, with the eye of the free soul, by the imagination, a person, in sleep (*khwāb*) or in *wāqi'ah* (dream), contemplateth the state of things which is yet in the hidden.

After that, even as he may have seen, it happeneth in the material world. But to the beholder it hath, on account of its concealment from outward sense, the order of the hidden.

If in *khwāb* (sleep), a person seeth that a certain spot containeth hidden treasure, and on searching findeth it,—it is *kashf-i-mujarrad* (pure revelation).

If this meaning fall to the understanding: (*a*) by way of manifestation, it is "the vision of the soul"; (*b*) by invisible messengers, it is "the ear of the soul".

Once in Baghdad was a dervish, who took the path of reliance on God, and closed the path of question. One day great need befell him, and he wished to beg. Becoming penitent, he said: "Much time in reliance on God I have passed; that reliance shall I now reject?" That night, in *khwāb*, he beheld a vision. An invisible messenger said: "In a certain place is deposited a blue rent *khirqah* wherein are folded gold filings. Take it, and expend upon thy need." When out from sleep he came, he found it to be even so. This *khwāb*, they call true *ruyā'* (a dream) which is a part of prophecy. For, in the beginning of prophecy, every *khwāb* (dream) that Muḥammad beheld came true. In this kind (of dream) is no falsehood, for, to the wise, after proof given by the traditions of the Prophets, the sense in this revelation is a proof.

After separation from the body, the soul knoweth even of the small things heard and seen of this world.

The soul's knowledge is not restricted to small matters in respect to the outward and the inward senses. Nay, from the use of the outward senses, gain occurreth. By it, in the free state from the body, it discovereth the form of things felt. From using the vision, in it becometh painted the eye; from using the hearing, the ear.

(2) *Imaginary revelations from kinds of* naum *and* wāqi'ah. In *khwāb* or in *wāqi'ah* the soul beholdeth some of the things hidden; and in it, through connection with the soul, *nafs* displayeth partnership.

On the soul, by the power of imagination, *nafs* putteth the garment of a form fit for things felt, and thus beholdeth it.

In *wāqi'ah* the *murīd*-warrior seeth that he is in contest with the lion, and wild beasts; with serpents and scorpions; and with *kuffār.*

The true *shaikh* knoweth that *nafs* is with him in strife, and its meaning he seeth to be: (*a*) in the form of wild beasts, violence; (*b*) in the form of serpents and scorpions, enmity; (*c*) in the form of *kuffār*, disobedience and separation (from God's mercy).

If he see that he travelleth deserts and wastes, passeth over rivers and seas, ascendeth in the air, or passeth over the fire—the *shaikh* knoweth that he travelleth the stages of lust, and beholdeth him in the form of the elements (the four natures).

If he see that from the qualities of a

clayey,
watery,
airy,
fiery,

nature, something passeth, the imaginary power giveth it glory to the dreamer's eye in the fancy-garment of travelling

over wastes,
over seas,
in the air,

over fire.

The natures are:

Clayey

parsimony
slothfulness
ignorance
iniquity
darkness
foulness

Watery

haste to society
union with wicked lusts
acceptance of change and of effect of society
forgetfulness
inclination to sleep

Airy

inclination to lust
great grief
haste to change from state to state

Fiery

anger
pride
desire for rank
exaltation

The last stage of the stages of *nafs*, over which he passeth, is this.

If it be revealed to him, he seeth:

(*a*) the soul's truth in the form of the sun;
(*b*) the heart's truth in the form of the moon;
(*c*) the heart's qualities in the form of the constellation.

Every truth that is revealed to him, he seeth in

a suitable fancy-garment. Hence, this is called *kashf-i-mukhayyal* (fancied revelation).

In this is possibility of falsehood but not of pure falsehood, for it is not void of the soul's understanding.

If, in the state of the soul's understanding, sensual thoughts join not with the soulish[1] understanding, and the imaginary power clothe not the soul with the fancy-garment,—that *wāqi'ah*, or *khwāb*, is all true.

If some of the sensual thoughts join with the soulish understanding, and the imaginary power clothe all with the fancy-garment,—some are true, some false.

The dream interpreter freeth the soulish truths of understanding from the impurity of sensual thoughts, and interpreteth.

(3) *Pure fancy, when sensual thoughts have superiority over the heart, whereby the* rūḥ (*soul*) *is veiled from considering the hidden world.* In the state of *naum* and *wāqi'ah*, those thoughts become more powerful. Each one the imaginary power clotheth with the fancy-garment; the form of those thoughts is seen by the eyes of the imaginary power; and its deceit becometh clear.

Thus, that one who ever hath the thought of finding treasure, and who in *khwāb* seeth that he hath found it; or the austere one, who claimeth the people's acceptance of him, and seeth in *wāqi'ah* that he is their adored,—the *shaikh* knoweth that this manifestation is only the result of lust's desire, which on its beholder hath become depicted.

If he calleth it vain desire; or

1. *Rūḥāni*, soulish.

(*a*) in *khwāb, azghāth-i-aḥlām*, confused uninterpretable dream.

(*b*) in *wāqi'ah*, false dream.

In these, the truth never appeareth, because *nafs* possessed of doubt is void of partnership with *rūḥ* (soul), the composer of those thoughts. From *nafs*, truth is far.

The conditions of true *wāqi'ah* (dream) are:

(*i*) the being immersed in *dhikr*, and being hidden from things felt.

(*ii*) the existence of sincerity and freedom of desire from the observance of others.

Possibly, free fancy, in respect to the sincere man, becometh "fancied revelation"; and, by reason of being immersed in *dhikr* and in God's presence, the *rūḥ* (soul) of revelation becometh transmitted into the form of the fancy of *nafs*.

Then becometh true *wāqi'ah*, and capable of interpretation.

In all states, *wāqi'ah* with *naum* is similitude,—except when free fancy (*khayāl i-mujarrad*) in *khwāb* is not proved. In *wāqi'ah*, free fancy may be proved.

It is evident that in *wāqi'ah* and *manām*, truth occurreth and also falsehood. In other manifestations, truth is impossible, because there is naught save "free revelation (*kashf-i-mujarrad*)".

Free revelation is:

(*a*) in *mukāshafah* in the state of wakefulness.

(*b*) in *khwāb* or in *wāqi'ah*, in the state of being hidden from things felt.

In *mukāshafah*, the soul's understanding is attached to what is:

(a) either in the hidden world;
(b) or in the material world.

In the first case, its appearance in the material world

(a) is impossible such as:
Paradise,
Hell,
God's throne and seat,
the preserved tablet,
the pen of creation.

(b) is possible in the natural form as—possible events, necessary of acquirement, the form whereof shall not, in the hidden world, have yet been manifested.

(c) is possible in an accidental form as:
angels,
souls free from the body.

To Muḥammad, Jibrā'īl used to appear in the human form, sometimes as a divine inspiration and sometimes as a desert-dweller, as in the *ḥadīth* of 'Umar: Once a desert-dweller with white raiment and very black hair saluted Muḥammad, and sat close to him, knee to knee. Of Islam, of faith and of bounty he asked Muḥammad and heard his reply. When he disappeared, Muḥammad said to the Companions: "Know ye who this asker is?" They said: "God knoweth and His Prophet." He said: "It was Jibrā'īl who came from God to teach you the dogmas of faith." In this form, 'Umar and the other Companions beheld him.

Then it became known that the form was not the result of imaginary power, otherwise everyone, according to contrariety of state, would have seen it in a different form as the semblance of free soul—

(*a*) in separation from the body;

(*b*) in attachment to the body.

The semblance of angels and of free souls in the human form is an accidental form. The manifestation of their natural (spiritual) state is, save in the hidden world, impossible.

In every way that they desire, they make semblance of the human form, as is stated in the *ḥadīth* and in the verified speech of holy *shaikhs*.

In the second case, we have the following instances:

(*a*) Muḥammad's beholding the *masjid* of Jerusalem, when he returned from the *Mi'rāj*[2] (ascent to the highest heaven).

The infidels denied this tale and said: "If truly thou speakest, say how many columns there are in that remote *masjid* (of Jerusalem)?"

In *ḥāl*, it became revealed; from his gaze the world uprose; he counted its columns; and gave the information.

(*b*) They asked Muḥammad to give some news of a *qāfilah* near unto Shām.

The veil being lifted, Muḥammad saw that the *qāfilah* has reached to a distance of one stage from Mecca. He said: "Early in the morning, the *qāfilah* will arrive." Even so it did.

(*c*) Once at Medina, 'Umar Khaṭṭāb was on the *mimbar* reading the *khuṭbah* after he had sent Sāriyah

2. See the Qur'ān, P.D., xvii, i, 95; Clarke's translation of the *Sikandar Nāmah-i-Niẓāmi*, canto 4.

with an army to Nihāẓar. Suddenly, in the midst of the *khuṭbah,* he went into *mukāshafah* and saw that, against him, the enemy had made an ambush. He cried out: "O Sāriyah! (go) to the mouhtain." Sāriya heard; went to the mountain; and gained the victory.

The *Shaikh-u'l-Islām*—Shaikh Shahāb-u'd-Dīn 'Umar b. Muhammad Sahrawardī—telleth many a tale like unto these.

The true *murīd* is he whose *khilvat* is not weakened by the desire for semblances of these revelations and miracles, and whose spirit is not restricted to their acquisition.

For to the *rāhibīn* (Christian monks) who are not on the highway of the *Sharī'at* and of the *Sunnah* of Islam, this kind of revelation is not withheld.

This *kashf* (revelation) is naught save deceit, for, in its *wajd*, the *rāhibīn* are daily prouder and farther from the path of salvation.

If in the path of the true and the sincere, this *kashf* fall, it is a miracle, for it is the cause of strengthening of certainty, and of increase of devotion.

ON 'ILM (KNOWLEDGE)

II, 1

'Ilm is a light from the candle of prophecy in the heart of the faithful slave whereby he gaineth the path

(*a*) to God.

(*b*) to the work of God.

(*c*) to the order of God.

'Ilm is the special description of man; from it is excluded the understanding of his sense, and *'aql* (reason).

'Aql is a natural light, whereby becometh distingoished good from evil.

The *'aql* that distinguisheth between the good and evil:

(*a*) of this world is an *'aql* that belongeth to the *kāfir* as well as to the faithful.

(*b*) of the next world is an *'aql* that belongeth only to the faithful.

'Ilm is special to the faithful; *'ilm* and *'aql* are necessary for each other.

The eye of *'aql* (of the next world) is luminous with the light of guidance, and anointed with the *kuḥl* of the *Sharī'at.* In its essence, it is one, but it has two forms:

(*a*) *One in respect of the Creator.* Its meaning is the *'aql* of guidance, special to the faithful.

(*b*) *One in respect of the created.* Its meaning is the *'aql* of livelihood.

For people of faith and for seekers of God and of the next world, "the *'aql* of livelihood" is obedient to "the *'aql* of guidance".

Whenever these two *'aqls* agree, they credit "the *'aql* of livelihood," and according to exigency act: whenever they disagree, they discredit it, and to it pay no attention.

Thus, to the seekers of God, the man of this world ascribe weak *'aql*. He knoweth not that outside their *'aql* is another *'aql*.

'Ilm is of three kinds:

(*i*) *'ilm-i-tauḥīd*, knowledge of the unity of God.

(*ii*) *'ilm-i-ma'rifat*, knowledge of the work of God:

in respect of annihilation.
in respect of creation.
in respect of propinquity (to God).
in respect of distance (from God).
in respect of making alive.
in respect of putting to death.
in respect of dispersing.
in respect of assembling.
in respect of reward.
in respect of punishment.
in respect of other things.

(*iii*) *'ilm* of the orders of the *'Sharī'at* of orders and of prohibitions.

Each one of these three paths hath a separate traveller. The traveller of:

(*a*) the first path is the "sage of God." In his *'ilm* are, without opposition, included the other two *'ilms*.

(*b*) the second path is the "sage of the next world". In his *'ilm* is, without opposition, included the *'ilm* of the *Sharī'at*.

(*c*) the third path is the "sage of this world". Of the other two *'ilms*, no knowledge is his. If he had possessed it, he would have brought it into use. For the decline of good deeds is the result of defect of faith. If he had had his heart with God, and belief in the next world, he would not have passed below the doing of good deeds.

The sages of God have, with reason and conviction, faith in the unity of God; in the next world; and in the work of God.

Obedient to the orders of Islam are: the first ones (near to God), the ṣūfīs.

The sages of the next world, despite their belief in the next world, have a share (as much as is needed) of the knowledge of Islam, and employ it. They are: (*a*) the *abrār* (the pious); (*b*) the companions of the right hand.

The sages of this world have no share at all except the outward knowledge of Islam, which they have gained by being taught. What they have learned, they use not. Through defect of faith, they are not secure from passing into deeds, prohibited and detested. They are: (*a*) the companions of the left hand; (*b*) the wicked ones of men; (*c*) the sages of sin, upon whom have descended threat upon threat of God's wrath.

In the account of the *Mi'rāj* (the night-ascent to the highest heaven), it is said of Muḥammad:

"I passed by a crowd, whose lips they had cut with fiery scissors. I asked saying: 'Who are ye?' They cried: 'We are those who ordered for goodness, and prohibited from badness; and yet to badness we ourselves proceeded'" (*Hadīth*).

Better than the sage of God and of the next world is none; worse than the sage of this world, none (*Ḥadīth*).

Than *'ilm*, when they seek it for God's sake, naught is more profitable; when for the world's sake, naught greater loss.

'Ilm is like to victuals that essentially have, as regards the healthy, whose temperament is firm and quarters of the body free from humours, the power of nutrition; and that are, as regards the sick, whose temperament is declining and quarters of the body filled with humours, the source of disease.

In its own *nafs*, *'ilm* is a useful food, the cause of the expanding of *nafs* and of the heart, on the condition,—that the follower is not infirm of desire, and of temperament; nor in love for the world; nor a turner from God.

When the temperament of the heart turneth in love to the world, and the parts of existence become filled with low humours, *'ilm* becometh the cause of increase of desire, of pride, of haughtiness, of hate and of the rest.

For the destruction of this great deceit, there is naught:

(*a*) save when that *'ilm*, which is the guide of salvation, becometh the cause of destruction.

(*b*) save when that sage by whom the captives of the leader of desire gain freedom, becometh foot-bound in the snare of desire.

In *nafs* profitable *'ilm*
increaseth piety.

increaseth humility.
inflameth the fire of love and desire.
increaseth non-existence.

It is the aid of life; its severance from the heart is putting to death. Thus have spoken *Fatḥ-i-Mūṣilī* and *Amīr-u'l-Mū'minīn*, 'Alī.

In *nafs*, noxious *'ilm* increaseth:

pride.
haughtiness.
presumption.
desire for the world.

Profit from *'ilm* appeareth to that one who displayeth the service of resolution, not the following of license as Abū Yazīd Bisṭāmī hath said.

In the midst of men the existence of the sage of God is God's best favour, his being hidden, the absence of God's favour, and the source of the darkness of *kufr* and of error.

ON MA'RIFAT (DEEP KNOWLEDGE)

III, 1

Ma'rifat signifieth the recognising of the abridged *'ulūm* (knowledge) in detail:

'Ilm-i-Naḥv is the knowing how each agent (of word or of meaning) acteth.

Ma'rifat-i-Naḥv is the recognising of every agent in detail, at the time of reading, without either delay or consideration and its use in its place.

Ta'rīf-i-Naḥv is the recognising of the agent by thought. To be careless of this (despite the *'ilm-i-naḥv*) is a blunder.

The *ma'rifat* of God is dependent upon and bound up with the *ma'rifat* of the *nafs*. *Ma'rifat* of God signifieth:

> The recognising of the nature and the qualities of God in the form of detailed circumstances, of accidents, of calamities; after that it shall (in the way of abridgment) have become known that He is the True Existence and the Absolute Agent.

The possessor of the *'ilm-i-tauḥīd* seeth in the form (of details, of dreams, and of state):

of loss the causer of loss who is God.
of profit the causer of profit who is God.
of prohibition the causer of prohibition who is God.
of gift the causer of gift who is God.
of contraction the causer of contraction who is God.
of expansion the causer of expansion who is God.

And recogniseth them without delay; him, they call *'ārif*.

If at first he be careless of *ma'rifat,* and soon present (alive to it) becometh, and in the form of different powers, recogniseth the Absolute Agent,—him, they call *Muta'arrif.*

If he be wholly careless, and (despite his *'ilm*) recogniseth not God in form, in means, in links, and to means assigneth the effects of deeds—him, they call—

sāhī, negligent, or *ghāfil,* careless.

lāhī, playful.

mushrik, secret believer in partnership with God.

For instance, if he explaineth *tauḥīd* (the unity of God) and in its sea immerseth himself—and another, in the way of denial, refuseth him, saying: "Not the essence of *ḥāl* is this speech; 'tis the result of thought and of consideration," he grieveth and becometh enangered.

He knoweth not that his grieving is a proof of the truth of the denier's speech, otherwise he would have recognised the Absolute Agent in the form of this denial, and against the denier would not have gathered anger.

In *ma'rifat* of *nafs,* every unapproved quality (which is known by abridged *'ilm*) at the time when at the very beginning in *nafs,* it appeareth, he recogniseth and as to it exerciseth caution,—him, they call *'ārif*: otherwise *muta'arrif* or *ghāfil.*

If in detail the abridged *'ilm* he knoweth not,—him, they call *ghāfil* (careless). To him, this *'ilm* is a source of loss.

If by *'ilm,* he knoweth that pride is a blameable quality in *nafs,* and when in *nafs* this appeareth, he fleeth into the screen of humbling himself—so that, recognising this quality in himself, his *nafs* may not again be with outward pride.

This, they call the *ma'rifat* of *nafs*.

The portion of

(*a*) the *'ārif* is *riḍā'* (agreement) with God's decrees.

(*b*) the *muta'arrif*, patience in respect of God.

(*c*) the *ghāfil*, detestation and perturbation.

The *ma'rifat* of God hath degrees :

(*i*) every effect that he gaineth, he knoweth to be from the Absolute Agent (God).

(*ii*) every effect that appeareth from the Absolute Agent, he knoweth to be result of a certain quality of His.

(*iii*) in the glory of every quality, he recogniseth God's purpose.

(*iv*) the quality of the *'ilm* of God, he recogniseth in his own *ma'rifat*; and expelleth himself from the circle of *'ilm*, of *ma'rifat*, and of existence.

The greater the degrees of propinquity (to God), the more apparent the effects of God's grandeur.

By ignorance,[1] *'ilm* is generally acquired; the *ma'rifat* of subtlety becometh greater; astonishment on astonishment increaseth; and from the *'ārif* ariseth the cry—"Increase in me astonishment at Thee."

This is all the *'ilm* of *ma'rifat*, not *ma'rifat*, because *ma'rifat* is a matter of rapture the explanation whereof is defective, but its preface is *'ilm*.

Then without *'ilm*, *ma'rifat* is impossible; *'ilm*

1. Till one knoweth one's ignorance, *'ilm* (knowledge) cannot be acquired.

without *ma'rifat*, disaster.

'Ilm and *ma'rifat* have some forms:

(*i*) *'ilm-i-ma'rifat.*

(*ii*) *ma'rifat-i-'ilm.*

(*iii*) *'ilm-i-ma'rifat-i-ma'rifat.*

The last form is the perfection of form.

ON ḤĀL (MYSTIC STATE) AND MAQĀM (STAGE)

IV, 1

In the opinion of ṣūfīs, *ḥāl* signifieth a hidden event that, from the upper world, sometimes descendeth upon the heart of the holy traveller and goeth and cometh, until the divine attraction draweth him from the lowest to the loftiest stage.

Maqām signifieth a degree of the Path that cometh in the way of the holy traveller's foot; becometh the place of his staying; and declineth not.

Ḥāl (which relateth to the zenith) cometh not in the traveller's sway; in its sway is the traveller.

Maqām (which relateth to the *nādir*) is the place of the traveller's sway.

The ṣūfīs have said: "The *ḥāl* is a gift (*mauhab*); the *maqām* an acquisition (*kasb*)."

Void of the entrance of *ḥāl* is no *maqām*; separate from union with *maqām* is no *ḥāl*.

As to *ḥāl* and *maqām*, the source of contention of holy *shaikhs* is that some call this *ḥāl*, and some, *maqām*. For all *maqāms* are at the beginning *ḥāl*, and at the end *maqām*, as:

taubah = penitence
muḥāsibah = calling one's self to account
murāqabah = fearful contemplation

Each one is at the beginning a *ḥāl* in change and in decline; and when by propinquity to *kasb* (acquisition), it becometh *maqām*, all the *ḥāl* are lightened by *makāsib* (acquisitions) and all the *maqām* by *mawāhib* (gifts).

In *ḥāl*, the gifts are outward, the acquisitions inward: in *maqām*, the acquisitions are outward, the gifts inward.

The *shaikhs* of Khurāsān have said: "Ḥāl is the heritage of deeds." Hence the word of 'Alī ibn Abī Ṭālib: "The path of union with *ḥāl* (which through superiority relateth to the heavens) ask not of me"

The *maqāms* are:

taubah, penitence,
zuhd, austerity,
ṣabr, patience,

and others.

These are the means of the descent of *ḥāl*.

Some *shaikhs* urge that:

(*a*) ḥāl is that which findeth neither resting nor confining. Like lightning it appeareth, and effaced becometh. If it be left, it becometh the *ḥadīth-u'n-nafs*.

(*b*) so long as it is not left, it is not *ḥāl*. Because resting demandeth permanency; that which like lightning flasheth and expireth is not truly *ḥāl*.

This is the religious order of Shaikh Shahāb-u'd-Dīn Sahrawardī.

It is said that if *ḥāl* be left, it is not the source of *ḥadīth-u'n-nafs*. Its source is a weak *ḥāl*, which at the time of glittering strong *nafs* seizeth; to *nafs*, strong *ḥāl* never becometh accustomed.

Every event that like lightning glittereth, and in *ḥāl* expireth,—they call in ṣūfī idiom:

lā'iḥ = evident
lāmiḥ = glittering

ṭāli' = arising
ṭāriq = exploding
bādih = apparent

Its manifestation is followed by concealment. Thus hath said Abū 'Uthmān Ḥā'irī.

This hinteth at perpetual *riḍā'* (contentment), and doubtless *riḍā'* is of all *ḥāls* then perpetual *ḥāl* is unnecessary for *ḥadīth-u'n-nafs*.

Is the amending of a *maqām* (which is his foot-place), before ascending to a higher stage, possible or not?

Junaid hath said: "Possible it is before the first *ḥāl* is finished for a slave to advance to a higher *ḥāl*. Thence he gaineth information of the first *ḥāl* and amendeth it.

'Abdullah Anṣārī hath said: "Impossible is the amending of any *maqām* till from a higher *maqām* the holy traveller looketh into the lower *maqām*, of it gaineth information and it amendeth."

Shaikh Shahāb-u'd-Dīn Sahrawardī hath said:

"Impossible is advance to a higher *maqām* before amending the *maqām* (which is his foot-place). But before advancing, there descendeth from the higher *maqām* a *ḥāl* whereby his *maqām* becometh true. Hence his advance from *maqām* to *maqām* is by God's sway and of His gift—not of his own acquisition.

"So long as from the low to the lofty, advance approacheth not; from the lofty to the low, no *ḥāl* descendeth."

In the *Ḥadīth* is the imputing of the slave's approach to God; and of God's approach to the slave.

ON TAUḤĪD (UNITY OF GOD), AND DHĀT (EXISTENCE OF GOD)

I, 2

The *'Ulamā'* of ṣūfism who, through being detached from affairs, have gained union with the wine of *'ilm*; the step of whose souls and hearts hath become firm; the eye of whose vision by the light of beauty of eternity without beginning hath become anointed,—know, see and find by the path of *'ilm-i-yaqīn*, established proof, of *kashf* (revelation), of seeing, of *dhauq* (delight), and of *wajd* (ecstasy).

Witness do they bear that no person nor thing is worthy of being worshipped save the one God, the God of unity, the Eternal, pure (void) of parent, of offspring, of aid; pure (void) of resemblance, of equal, of *wazīr* and of counsellor.

Neither in opposition to His order is an opposition, nor in the government of His realm, an enemy.

Ever is described His ancient existence by unity, and known by singularity.

Expelled from His holiness and purity are the qualities of accidents, of form, similitude, union, separation, association, descent, issue, entrance, change, decline, alteration, and translation.

From the understanding of the reading of men's thoughts, the perfection of His beauty and the beauty of His perfection (unconnected with the beauty of His singularity)—free; from the trouble of the clothing of *dhikrs*, the grandeur of His eternity—free.

In description of Him, narrow is the power of the warriors of the plain of eloquence; in praise of Him, lame is the foot of the chiefs of the plain of *ma'rifat.*

Than the offering of the senses, than the discussion of conjecture, loftier is the column of understanding Him; of the passing of imaginings and the happening of understandings, void is the honour-plain of His *ma'rifat.*

In the beginning of His *ma'rifat* is no guide save astonishment and perturbation to the pure ones of Lordship, who are at the limit of reason; in the splendour of the light of His grandeur is no path save blindness and ignorance to the vision of the possessors of Sight.

If thou say : He hath created His abode,—where ? The answer is : (In the place of)—He. If thou say : (Visible) to the eye, brought He time,—when ? The answer is : (At the time of)—He. If thou say : Resemblance and sufficiency made He—how ? The answer is :—(By means of)—He.

No limit hath He. Within this limit are comprehended eternity without beginning and eternity without end; folded in the fold of His plain are existence and dwelling (the universe); in beginning, all His beginnings—the end; in His ending, all endings, the beginning; in His outwardness, the outward manifestation of things, the inward; in His inwardness, the inward parts of worlds, the outward; in His eternity without beginning, the collection of eternities without beginning only an accident (*ḥādith*); in His eternity without end, all eternities without end, only an event *muḥdath*).

From whatever is contained in reason, in understanding, in the senses, in conjecture,—exempted and free is the nature of the Lord.

For these all were *muḥdathāt* (accidents) save understanding *muḥdath* (accident), *muḥdath* can do naught.

The argument of His existence is His existence; the proof of His witnessing is His witnessing.

Naught save the beauty of eternity without beginning is the bearer of the beauty of eternity without beginning. In this stage the limit of understanding is weakness.

To the substance of the understanding of *Wāḥid* (unity of God), save *Wāḥid*—no *muwaḥḥid* (professor of unity) can reach.

Where his understanding is ended, there is the limit of *his* understanding not of *Wāḥid* (God).

Who considereth *Wāḥid* comprehended in his knowledge is verily deceived and presumptuous.

Tauḥīd is the negation of separation, and the affirmation at the limit of collection.

In the beginning of the *tauḥīd* of *ḥāl* (mention whereof will presently be made), this description is necessary.

But, possibly, at its end, one in separation may be immersed in collection, and in collection, the spectator (with the eye of collection) of separation—as each collection, or separation, is not a forbidder of the other. In this is the perfection of *tauḥīd*.

Tauḥīd hath degrees :

(*i*) *tauḥīd-i-īmānī*, the *tauḥīd* of faith.

(*ii*) *tauḥīd-i-'ilmī*, the *tauhīd* of knowledge.
(*iii*) *tauḥīd-i-ḥālī*, the *tauhīd* of *ḥāl*.
(*iv*) *tauḥīd-i-ilāhī*, the *tauhīd* of Godship.

(*i*) *Tauhīd-i-īmānī* is:

When (according to the urgency of the order of Qur'ānic verse and of the *Ḥadīth* the slave verifieth to his heart, and confesseth with the tongue, as to the singularity of the description of Godship and to the unity of rights of the adored Lord.

This *tauḥīd* is the *mukhbir* (news-bringer) and the belief of sincerity is the *khabar* (news). Profit from outward *'ilm* and holding thereto is freedom from open partnership; turning in the thread (entering the circle) of Islam giveth profit.

Through necessity, with Muslims, ṣūfīs believe in the *tauḥīd*; but, in other degrees, are separate.

Tauḥīd is:

An *'ilm* of benefit from the heart of *'ilm* which they call the *'ilm-i-yaqīn* (the knowledge of certainty).

This *'ilm-i-yaqīn* is such that, in the beginning of the path of ṣūfism, the slave knoweth, from the desire of *yaqīn* (certainty), that the true existence and absolute Penetrator is none save the Lord of the world.

In His *dhāt* (nature) and qualities, effaced and naught he (by *'ilm*) regardeth his own *dhāt* and qualities.

The splendour of every nature, he recogniseth from the light of Absolute Existence, and every ray, from the light of the quality of the Absolute (God).

When he gaineth:

an *'ilm*
a *qudrat*
a desire
a hearing
a seeing

he knoweth them to be the effects of:

an *'ilm* of God
a *qudrat* of God
a desire of God
a hearing of God
a seeing of God

Thus for all qualities and deeds.

This degree is of the first degrees of *tauḥīd* of the man of speciality and of ṣūfism; its preface is joined to the column of *tauḥīd-i-'āmm*; and the semblance of this degree, those short of sight call *tauḥīd-i-'ilmī*, but verily it is the *tauḥīd-i-rasmī*, mutilated of the rank of credit.

This *tauḥīd-i-rasmī* is such as a person, with desire of intelligence and of understanding, might, through reading and hearing, conjecture as a meaning of *tauḥīd*. In his mind, a *rasm* (impression) of the form of *'ilm-i-tauḥīd* becometh painted; thence, in the midst of argument,—since, in him is no effect from the *ḥāl-i-tauḥīd*—he uttereth brainless words.

(*ii*) *Tauḥīd-i-'ilmī*, although it is a low degree of the *tauḥīd-i-ḥālī*, wherefrom fellow-traveller with it is a temperament: "Its temperament is one of *tasnīm*, a fountain wherefrom those near to God drink," is the description of the wine of this *tauḥīd*.

Hence, its possessor is often in *dhauq* and joy, because, by the effects of the temperament of *ḥāl*, some of the darkness of his impressions becometh lifted. As in some changes, he worketh according to the demand of his own *'ilm*, and bindeth up, in the midst, the existence of causes which are the links of the deeds of God, but, in many a *ḥāl*, by reason of the residue of the darkness of existence, he becometh veiled from the demand of his own *'ilm*.

In this *tauḥīd*, some of the hidden *shirk* (the giving companions to God) departeth.

(*iii*) *Tauhīd-i-ḥālī* is when the *ḥāl* of *tauḥīd* becometh the necessary description of the nature of the *muwaḥḥid* (professor of unity).

Save a little residue in the superiority of the rising of the light of *tauḥīd*, all the darknesses of impressions of His existence vanish, and, in the light of his *ḥāl*, veiled and included (like to the being rolled together the light of the constellations and the light of the sun) becometh the light of *'ilm-i-tauḥīd*.

In the stage of existence, in viewing the beauty of the existence of *Wāḥid* (unity), the *muwaḥḥid* becometh so immersed in *jam'* (union) that, in the vision of his witnessing, naught cometh save the nature of the qualities of *Wāḥid*—so much so that he regardeth *tauḥīd* the quality of *Wāḥid*, not his own quality. This (act of) regarding (of his) he regardeth His quality.

In this way, his existence falleth like a drop in the power of the dashing waves of the ocean of *tauḥīd*, and in *jam'* (union) becometh immersed.

The source of: (*a*) *tauḥīd-i-ḥālī* is the light of manifestation; (*b*) *tauḥīd i-'ilmī* is the light of *murāqabah* (fearful contemplation).

By *tauḥīd-i-ḥālī* (like to the light of the sun in whose superiority of manifestation, most parts of darkness rise up and disappear from earth's surface) become repulsed many of the impressions of humanity.

By *tauḥīd-i-ḥālī* most of the hidden *shirk* (giving companions to God) ariseth (to disappear), and from the truth of pure *tauḥīd* (wherein all at once the effects and the impressions of existence vanish) to the special *muwaḥḥids* in the *ḥāl* of life sometimes the flash like unto flashing lightning becometh bright, and immediately is extinguished.

The residue of other circumstances aideth; in this state, the residue of hidden *shirk* becometh wholly repulsed; outside this digree of *tauḥīd* is possible no other degree.

By *tauḥīd-i-'ilmī* (like to the light of the moon in whose manifestation, parts of darkness become repulsed and some are left), become uplifted (to disappear) some of the impressions of humanity.

The cause of existence of some of the residue of impressions in *tauḥīd-i-ḥālī* is this:

On the *muwaḥḥid's* part not possible is the issuing of the arranging of deeds and the purifying of words; for this reason in the *ḥāl* of his life, the right of *tauḥīd* (as is necessary) becometh not discharged.

(*iv*) *Tauḥīd-i-ilāhī* is that whereby in the eternity without beginning of eternities without beginning by His own *nafs*, not by the *tauḥīd* of another—God is ever described with singularity and qualified with praise.

Now, in praise of eternity without beginning He is *wāḥid* and one; and thus, to the eternity without end of the eternities without end, is.

So that today it became known that in His own existence, the existence of the beauty of things vanish.

For the veiled ones is the promise of beholding this *ḥāl* (of God) till tomorrow (the Judgment Day).

But for the Lords of vision and for the companions of beholding (who have obtained freedom from the restricted place of time and of abode), this promise is cash indeed (immediate).

The honour of His singularity and the wrath of His unity gave not power in His existence, to other existence.

The right of *tauḥīd* is this: this is the *tauḥīd* that is free from the reproach of defect.

By reason of defect of existence, the *tauḥīd* of angels and of man is defective.

Thus, Shaikh Abū 'Abdullah Anṣārī hath said.

THE AFFAIRS OF THE NEXT WORLD

I, 10

The preface to pure *'ilm* is true faith.

So long as increase of faith descendeth not into the stages of the hearts of will, the *qāfilah* of *'ilm-u'l-yaqīn* (the knowledge of certainty) taketh not down its chattels of staying in the heart; the treading of the path by verification and by seeking the traces of the Prophets is impossible save by the foot of faith and of submission and by the guide of love and of reverence; and the effort in desire of advance, without preserving one's self from sin by the rope of God and by the *sunnat* of prophecy, is error and disaster.

If, with the foot of defective reason and understanding, a person wisheth to advance from the abyss of ignorance to the summit of *'ilm*, although he may put forward great effort, he seeth himself in the end, at the first place, momently descending into degrees of loss.

For when the path with lofty degrees becometh closed, and yet the motive of desire is left,—*nafs* turneth to decline and rolleth about in the seventh Hell to the lowest of the low.

As to the hidden world and the circumstances of the next world (as by the Qur'ān-i-Majīd, and by the *Ḥadīth* of prophecy have arrived), it is incumbent on everyone to have faith:

in the torment of the grave, in the questioning of *munkir* and *nākir*, in the assembling and dispersing, in the account and the balance, in the bridge and *ṣirāt*, in Paradise and Hell, in the issuing of nations (through the intercession of the Prophet) from fire and, not with weak reason and fine understanding, to begin for one's self upon its interpretation, and not to wander about the sufficiency and the wherefore.

Because in respect to *'ilm-i-īmānī* (the knowledge of faith), the limit is not the degree of human understanding. In it, even the Prophets have not exercised power.

What from revelation they have seen, in it with certainty they have had faith, the faith which (from the Prophets) to the hearts of nations (according to their purity) hath reached.

Reason hath a limit beyond which when it passeth, into error it falleth.

The limit of the five senses is:

When things felt by them are apparent and existing as:

things seen.
things heard.
things smelt.
things tasted.
things touched.

When out of these something issueth and the understander is in his senses, true is the understanding of it.

When he perceiveth something not existing (as things comprehended by the distraught),—not true is the understanding of it.

The limit of *khiyāl* (fancy) is:

When, after effacement, it regardeth things comprehended of the outward senses, when it passeth its limit and trieth to comprehend things not perceived,—the fancy is error.

A person heareth the name of one whom he hath never seen; he evoketh a form purely imaginary. When the hidden becometh present, the imaginary form may, or may not, be concordant with his (real) form.

The limit of *vahm* (imagination) is: when out of a form of things perceived he gaineth in part a sense of things not perceived; as a sheep from seeing the wolf comprehendeth the sense of enmity not perceived.

When he transgresseth and imagineth things sensible and spiritual, he falleth into error.

Thus he cannot imagine *rūḥ* (the soul) merely from the form of the body as to:

its entering.
its issuing.
its union.
its separation.
its nearness.
its farness.

He cannot find the limit of the world of bodies.

When beyond it he beginneth imagining, he falleth into error.

The limit of *'aql* (reason) is the understanding of the world of *ḥikmat*; no path into the world of *qudrat* is its.

The world of *ḥikmat* signifies:

the existence of cause. For to a cause, the absolute Wise One hath bound every existing thing in the world of dominion and of witnessing (the world material); and by means of that cause hath caused to pass the *sunnat* (the creation of that existence)—not in this sense that, without that cause, existence is impossible in God's power For the arrangement of the world of *ḥikmat*, God hath joined existence to cause. Guardian over the world of *ḥikmat*, they have made reason; to it not true (is) a power in the world of *qudrat* (the creating of something without the means of a cause).

Whenever out of the world of *qudrat*, he heareth something, he saith it is not reasonable; or ordereth as to its alteration.

He knoweth not that—not inexcused is what is unreasonable.

Not reasonable is the existence of the child. Without the seed of the father, the acceptance of it by the mother, its settlement in the womb, and the passing of the appointed time in the world of *ḥikmat* —it existeth not.

But, in the world of *qudrat*, it is possible and doth occur. As the existence, of Ādam, of Ḥavvā, of 'Īsā.

When to the world of *qudrat*, reason findeth no path, and desireth sway in it,—it falleth into error.

To explanation, he hasteth saying, the meaning is such and such.

Verily the imputation of ignorance he accepteth not, and knoweth not whence is the source of error. If in his own limit (the world of *ḥikmat*) he had stood, into this error he would not have fallen; evident it would have been that from the garment of *ḥikmat* one cannot find the world of *qudrat* save by faith.

Possibly if words like these reach the ear of hypocrites, they will in the way of jest laugh at the speaker's reason, and name it delirium.

No knowledge have the helpless ones. At them, the man of vision and the Lords of explanation look with pity, and, at the lowness of their reason and at the poverty of their understanding, laugh. Like a captive, they are in the world of *ḥikmat* veiled from the world of *qudrat*.

Like this is the confining of the embryo in the narrow place of the womb.

If, by chance, to it a person were to say:

"Outside the narrow place of the womb is another world, a great space, a great breadth, a sky, a land, a sun, a moon, and other things"

never would the imagining and the reasoning of it appear true save by faith.

Even so the dwellers of the narrow world of *ḥikmat* cannot save by faith gain the circumstances of the world of *qudrat* until man's soul from the narrow place of the womb of the world of *ḥikmat* cometh to the space of the world of *ghaib* and of *qudrat*; or by the death of nature and of will which they call "the second birth,"[1] even as 'Īsā hath written.

Before faith, whatever they have accepted, only by the eye, they see; so long as the veil of humanity is not uplifted, only the eye revolveth.

Today save by the power of inward taste (which meaneth faith), one cannot find the *dhauq* (delight) of the limit of (this given by) the Prophets.

There is a crowd in whom that power is not created, and whose directing is impossible, and a crowd in whom this power is created.

But, by the power of sickness of desire, they have been ruined, and in their palate, the food of truths, like the *'ilm* of faith, appeareth bitter.

On all men of faith, it is incumbent to aid God:

by raising the faith of Muṣṭafā (Muḥammad); by destroying the vain; by repelling the deceit of men of error; and by prohibiting the power of *shaiṭāns*, man-in-form.

1. John, iii, 3

The *Sharī'at* of Muḥammad and his creed is the straight path and trodden highway; the seal (last) of the sent ones (Prophets), trusted one of the Lord of both worlds with so many thousands of troops of nations (holy ones, pure ones, martyred ones) hath gone on that highway and swept it of thorn, of rubbish, of doubt and of suspicion; hath established knowledge of it and of its stages; hath left behind a trace of every pace; hath established an alighting place at every stage; hath for the repelling of the robbers of the path sent the guide of resolution as fellow-traveller.

If a strange surveyor claimeth that the path is not straight, and inviteth the people to another path,—his word should not be regarded; and for its repelling, the aid of the true faith is of the number of ordinances and of requisites.

The men of deceit and of error are a crowd who outwardly wear the robe of Islam, and towards Islam inwardly keep concealed *kufr* and hate; outwardly mix with the men of Islam; show themselves to the people as verified *'ulamā'* and confirmed *ḥukamā'*; instruct in the eternity of this world and in the denial of the resurrection; regard the *'ulamā'* and the *shaikhs* of Islam as the enemy; and (because by the light of their *'ilm*, their own hiding and dark places become discovered) render contemptuous their form.

The God-like *'ulamā'* are the stars of the sky of *Sharī'at*; it, they ever keep preserved from the sway of *shaiṭāns* of men. Their luminous breath like to the penetrating meteor pelteth those (the *shaiṭāns* of men) concealing and carrying off the mysteries of the

Sharī'at; keepeth them on every side perturbed and restless; and repelleth from the people their deceitful wickedness.

Wherever these men of deceit gain sway, they make the people shun the *'ulamā'*; begin in the souls of those ready, satanic sway and (by iniquity of faith, and by the cutting off of the link of Islam from the order of man) the ruining of their faith; turn the pure simple heart from the purity of nature; conceal themselves behind the shield of Islam; make sure the arrow of treachery and of loss at the butt of faith and of religion; and secretly, with courteous glance, call man to destruction.

They are the enemies of faith, the brothers of *shaiṭān*; ignorant of rules, the causer of injuries.

Before the Lord of both worlds, no devotion hath such a lofty degree as the repelling of this crowd and the uplifting of the foundations of their deceit and hypocrisy.

The men of submission (to repel these men of deceit and error) are: (*a*) men of *qudrat* (power); (*b*) men of *'ilm* (knowledge).

The men of *qudrat* act, by way of slaughter and of rapine; of chastisement and punishment; of denial and of banishment.

The men of *'ilm* act, by manifesting deceit, hypocrisy and heresy.

Who, on one of these two ways, hath power is by it ordered; by accepting it, rewarded; and by abandoning it, requited.

ʻILM-I-QIYĀM (KNOWLEDGE OF GOD'S STANDING AS THE SLAVE'S OBSERVER)

II, 5

In the opinion of the ṣūfīs, *ʻilm-i-qiyām* signifieth: a special *ʻilm*, wherein, in all movings and restings, outward and inward, the slave seeth God standing over him and observing him. This sense is from the Qur'ān. Hence, the slave keepeth himself adorned, outwardly and inwardly, with the garment of rules agreeing with the orders of God and separated from the garment of opposition (to Him).

This is a precious *ʻilm* which, in ṣūfistic idiom, they call *ʻilm-i-murāqabah.*

Who maketh it his inward habit becometh delighted with all exalted *maqāms* and precious *ḥāls*; the reverence and the fear of God become his teacher in all affairs as Muḥammad hath said.

Sahl ʻAbdullah Tustarī mostly ordered his *murīds* by this *ʻilm* of precept, and said:[1]

"Void of four things, be ye not:

(*i*) *ʻilm-i-qiyām*, that ye may,— in every *ḥāl*, witnesser and observer of you,—see God.

(*ii*) the service of devotion, that ye may ever keep yourselves established in conformity with devotion to Him.

(*iii*) constantly ask God for the aid of His grace in respect of the above two things.

(*iv*) persevere in these three things till death; for, in

1. To the end, is ʻAbdullah's discourse.

these four things are the good of this, and the next, world, and happiness inwardly and outwardly."

'Ilm-i-qiyām is the *dhikr* of the heart at the time of motion of limbs and resolution of the heart in respect to: (*a*) *qiyām*, on himself, (*b*) *shuhūd-i-ḥaqq* on himself, so that in conformity with that ordered, the motion and the resolution may be. This they call:

(*a*) *dhikr-i-fariḍah*, the *dhikr* of God's ordinance.
(*b*) *dhikr-i-zabān*, the *dhikr* of the tongue.
(*c*) *dhikr-i-faḍīlat*, the *dhikr* of excellence.

Thus, they say: Yesterday is dead; tomorrow is not born; today is in the agonies of death.

Who is engaged in the *dhikr* of the past and of the future is in destruction.

The safety and the salvation of the people is in their being engaged in the ordinance of the time (*'ilm i-qiyām*), with the practice of the pleasurable deed. Because, in this *ḥāl*, theirs can be:

breathing.
doing anything.
rest.
favour.

Than other *'ilms*, this *'ilm* is more dear, more strange, more profitable.

Yours the service of that in surety whereof are included perpetual country and constant favour.

Who perpetually seeketh this fortune without preface maketh severance of connections; without shunning the society of strangers, patience as to the opposition of *nafs* appeareth not.

ʻILM-I-ḤAL (KNOWLEDGE OF THE MYSTIC STATE)

II, 6.

Of the special ṣūfistic *ʻilms*, one is *ʻilm-i-ḥāl* which consisteth:

in regarding the heart and considering the mystery of that state (which is between the slave and the Lord) by equalling the increase and the loss; by levelling powerfulness and feebleness by the touchstone of proof, so that by observing truths and by preserving rule he may establish *ḥāl*.

For, there is a rule for every *ḥāl* in respect to its own *nafs*, according to: (*a*) the time, (*b*) the *maqām*.

Thus from the *ḥāl* of *riḍā'*, in respect to its *nafs*, is a rule,—the rest of *nafs*.

As to the calamities arising from God's order, according to the time when calamity:

(*a*) increaseth is a rule,—the performance of thanks so long as the increase of the *ḥāl* of *riḍā'* and the folding of *nafs* in the folds of despair are not confirmed until the quality of independence and of pride becometh not evident.

(*b*) ceaseth is a rule—asking God for help so that He may open the door of advance and of increase; may preserve *nafs* from motion; and (for desire of increase) may into the slave's heart bring a desire *shauq*, exciting, and a *shauq*, affliction-mixing.

For the increase of the *ḥāl* of *riḍā'* is another order and rule in the stage:

(*a*) of concordance (with the orders of God),—*riḍā'* and joy.

(*b*) of opposition—denial and grief.

In each of these two stages, contrary to the rule of increase, is a rule for the decrease of the *ḥāl* of *riḍā'*.

Who regardeth the form of his own state between him and the Lord, according to its rule, according to every time and stage, is preserved; and, to the maturity of perfection and to the stage of men (devoted to God), reacheth.

Who is careless of it is not secure of the robbers of the Path. This is an employment wherein if his life be expended, not discharged is its due.

The holy travellers of this Path are separate according to difference of power of capacity and of weakness thereof.

Some, in their *nafs*, know this difference of circumstances (joy and sorrow) and thereby discriminate between their increase and decrease.

Momently, in respect of a former moment they discover the difference of their *ḥāl*.

Some discover this change at times; some in hours; some in days.

Sahl 'Abdullah Tustarī hath said: "Safety, the slave gaineth not, save when he is learned in his *ḥāl* and forgetteth it not; and, by it, is obedient to God." They asked saying: "What is the *'ilm-i-ḥāl?*" He said: "Whose state with God is the abandoning of will and the negation of desire, ever regardeth this *ḥāl* according to exigency; and ever abandoneth design; whenever in himself, he findeth inclination to a plan, he denieth it; what knoweth he but that it is the repeller of his *ḥāl*."

Sahl hath by the abandoning of will made the speciality of the *'ilm-i-ḥāl*, because loftier than it is no *ḥāl*.

'ILM-I-YAQĪN (KNOWLEDGE OF CERTAINTY)

II, 9

'Ilm-i-yaqīn (the knowledge of certainty) signifieth: the revelation of the light of *ḥaqīqat* in the state of concealment of humanity by the evidence of *wajd* (ecstasy) and of *dhauq* (delight), not by the guidance of *'aql* (reason) and *ḥadīth* (report).

They call this light: (*a*) beyond the veil,—the light of faith, (*b*) through the veil,—the light of *yaqīn*.

Verily, not more than one light—the light of faith—is there when it becometh the heart's agent.

Without the veil of humanity, it is the light of *yaqīn*. As long as a residue of existence is, ever the cloud of the qualities of humanity go rising from the soul of humanity, and covereth the sun of *ḥaqīqat* (truth).

Sometimes, it becometh scattered; and by way of *wajd*, the heart from the flashing of the light gaineth *dhauq*, as the cold-stricken one, on whom suddenly shineth the sun's light from its splendour and warmth gaineth *dhauq* (delight).

Regard the sun as the *ḥaqīqat-i-ḥaqā'iq* (the truth of truths); its light, like the flashing of *ḥaqīqat*, shining from outside the veil of the light of safety, manifested through the veil of the light of *yaqin*; and the cold-stricken one, like that one veiled with the qualities of humanity in the light of faith.

Then is the light of faith ever firm; the light of *yaqīn*, sometimes flashing and bright, as in the *ḥadīth*.

Yaqīn hath three degrees. Thus, as to the sun's existence, a person is void of doubt:

(*i*) by seeking guidance from beholding the sun's splendour and understanding its heat. This is *'ilm-u'l-yaqīn.*

(*ii*) by beholding the sun's body. This is *'ain-u'l-yaqīn.*

(*iii*) by the dispersing of the eye's light in the sun's light. This is *ḥaqq-u'l-yaqīn.*

Then—

(*a*) in *'ilm-u'l-yaqīn,* it is known, verified and evident.

(*b*) in *'ain-u'l-yaqīn,* it is manifest and witnessed.

(*c*) in *ḥaqq-u'l-yaqīn,* a double way ariseth in consequence of:

the witnesser.
the witnessed.
the looker on.
the looked on.

Thus, the seer becometh the eye; the eye, the seer.

In the *ḥāl* of the residue of the composition, this sense (like lightning that cometh into flash and immediately expireth), appeareth not more than a moment to the perfect and to those joined with God.

If an hour it be left, the thread of composition looseneth, and the way of existence ariseth (and departeth).

Of *yaqīn*:

(*a*) the root is *'ilm-u'l-yaqīn.*

(*b*) the branches are *'ain-u'l-yaqīn* and *ḥaqq-u'l-yaqīn.*

Faith hath many degrees, whereof one is *yaqīn.*

Yaqīn giveth the heart freedom from the perturbation of doubt: it, the *Shar'* hath called faith as in the *ḥadīth*.

What by way of adducing reasonable proof becometh known is far from *'iml-i-yaqīn*, because:

(*a*) that (the adducing of reasonable proof) is the *'ilm* of adducing proof.

(*b*) this (*yaqīn*) is the *'ilm* of *ḥāl*.

Not all at once, save by the rising of the sun of *haqīqat*, becometh the darkness of doubt removed.

NAFS (ESSENCE)

III, 2

Nafs hath two meanings:

(*a*) *nafs-i-shay* (the *nafs* of a thing) which is the *dhāt* (essence) and the *ḥaqīqat* (truth) of a thing. Thus they say: "By its own *nafs*, a certain thing is standing."

(*b*) *nafs-i-nāṭiqah-i-insānī* (the human rational *nafs*) which is the abstract of the graces of the body, which they call—the human natural soul, and a luminosity (which is bestowed on it from the lofty human soul) by which luminosity the body becometh the place of revelation of iniquity and of piety, as the Qur'ān hath said.

The *ma'rifat* of *nafs* is in all qualities difficult, for *nafs* hath the nature of the chameleon.

Momently appeareth a different colour; hourly cometh forth another form. It is the Hārūt of the Babel of existence; momently, another vanishing picture on water *nafs* expresseth, and beginneth another sorcery.

Hints as to the *ma'rifat* of *nafs* are (found) in the links and conditions of the *ma'rifat* of God.

The recognising of *nafs* in all its qualities, and the reaching to a knowledge of it, is not the power of any created thing. Even so difficult is the reaching to the substance of the *ma'rifat* of God, and even so, to the *ma'rifat* of *nafs*, as 'Alī hath said.

The names of *nafs* are:

Nafs-i ammārah, imperious *nafs* (concupiscence).

Nafs-i-lawwāmah, reproaching *nafs*.

Nafs-i-muṭma'innah, restful *nafs*.

They call *nafs*:

(*a*) *Nafs-i-ammārah*. At the beginning, as long as under its sway, is existence.

(*b*) *Nafs-i-lawwāmah*. In the middle when obedient to the heart's sway it becometh, while is left yet some residue of the *nafs* of obstinacy whereon it ever reproacheth itself.

(*c*) *Nafs-i-muṭma'innah*. At the end, when extirpated from it, become the veins of contention and of abhorrence; when from contention with the heart it gaineth rest, and becometh obedient to order; when to *riḍā'* becometh changed its abhorrence.

In the beginning, when *nafs* is yet firm in the dwelling of nature, it ever wisheth to draw to its own low dwelling the *rūḥ* (soul) and the heart from the lofty region, and ever giveth to itself in their sight the splendour of a new decoration. As a broker, *shaiṭān* adorneth the worthless majesty of *nafs*; and restless for it maketh souls and hearts, so that he may make low the exalted soul, and polluted the purified heart.

Thus have said Sahl 'Abdullah, Abū Yazīd, and Junaid.

The crowd who consider rational *nafs* and heart to be one do so because at the end they find *nafs* described with the description of rest and contentment (the specialities of the heart).

The suspicion is that between the heart and rational *nafs* is no difference.

Nafs-i-muṭma'innah is indeed another *nafs*. They know not that it is verily *nafs-i-muṭma'innah* which is stripped of the garment of vagrancy, and clad in the honour-robe of rest and of *riḍā'*, and which hath taken the heart's colour.

Whenever *nafs-i-ammārah* taketh the heart's colour, the heart also taketh the soul's colour (and pursueth good deeds).

ON SOME OF THE QUALITIES OF NAFS

III, 3

The source of the blameable qualities in man is *nafs*; the source of the laudable qualities is *rūḥ* (the soul).

The blameable qualities of *nafs* are ten.

(1) Hawā' (*desire*). *Nafs* desireth to advance as to its desires; to place in its bosom the desires of nature; to bind on its waist the girdle of its consent with desire and to hold God in partnership, as saith the Kalām-i-Majīd.

This quality departeth not save by austerity and by love for God.

(2) Nifāq (*hypocrisy*). In many outward states, *nafs* is not concordant with its interior; not one before it, is man's being absent or his being present.

In man's presence, *nafs* praiseth and displayeth sincerity; in his absence,—just the contrary.

This quality departeth not save by the existence of sincerity.

(3) Riyā' (*hypocrisy*). Ever in its bond is *nafs* that, in man's sight, it may keep itself adorned with laudable qualities (though in God's sight through hypocrisy they are blameable).

abundance of property and boasting thereof.

pride.

violence.

independence.

Whatever is reprehensible before the people, *nafs* shunneth and concealeth,—though in God's sight it be laudable:

faqr (poverty) submission humility	laudable in God's sight; reprehensible in the people's.

This departeth not save by knowledge of the paltry worth of the people as Junaid and Abū Bakr Warāq have said.

Nafs is a hypocrite like unto fire that revealeth the good quality (light), and concealeth the bad quality (consuming).

Although *nafs* revealeth the beautiful and concealeth the ugly,—it is not concealed save to those of defective vision.

It is like unto an old woman detestable of appearance, who adorneth herself with sumptuous apparel of varied colour and with henna. Only to boys doth that decoration appear to be good; to the wise, abhorrence increaseth.

(4) *The claim to Godship, and obstinacy against God. Nafs* ever desireth that people should praise it; should obey its orders; should love it above all; should of it be fearful and display the bond of dependence upon its mercy.

Thus against these orders, God cautioneth His own slaves.

These qualities depart not save by the glory of the qualities of God.

(5) *Pride and self-beholding. Nafs* ever looketh at its own beauteous qualities; regardeth with contentment the form of its own *ḥāl*. The paltry benefaction

that from it occurreth to another, it exalteth; for years forgetteth it not; and regardeth him as being immersed in obligation.

If to *nafs*, great benefaction cometh, it regardeth it as paltry and almost forgetteth it.

This is of the number of deadly sins as Muḥammad hath said, and as is entered in the *Ḥadīth*.

This departeth not save through self-contempt.

(6) *Avarice and parsimony*. Whatever chattels of goods and of desire it gathereth, it letteth not go save through pride, or through fear of poverty (in the future).

When this quality is strong in *nafs*, from it springeth envy, for envy is the breeding of miserliness for the property of others.

If it see another with special favour, it seeketh his decline; when it gathereth power, hate appeareth.

Him, who with itself gaineth equality in affluence; whom it seeth distinguished for an excellence, whom it regardeth as the cause of a favour being refused,—his destruction, *nafs* ever desireth

This departeth not save under the power of the light of *yaqīn*.

(7) *Greediness and asking for more*. *Nafs* is ever in prolonged delights, and restricteth not itself. Never becometh full the stomach of its need.

It is like the moth that with the candle's light contenteth not itself; by understanding the injury of its heat it becometh not warned; and casteth itself on the body of the fire so that it becometh consumed.

As *nafs* suffereth calamity, so its greed for delight becometh greater.

This departeth not save by *wara'* (austerity) and by *takvā* (piety).

(8) *Levity and light-headedness. Nafs* resteth on nothing. When thoughts of lust and of desire arrive, it putteth not in the first place steadiness or delay; it immediately desireth to enact it; therefore in their (proper) place evident become not rest and motion. For its desire, it displayeth celerity.

The sages have likened it to the spherical globe which they place in a court, plain and smooth. It is ever in motion.

This departeth not save by patience.

(9) *Haste to fatigue.* To *nafs*, fatigue of things quickly appeareth; and to it showeth the false idea that its being up plucked from the present state and its being employed in a following state—will be its rest.

It knoweth not that the guidance of ideas like to these will never convey it to its idea. Mostly, the form of occurrence is contrary to its purpose.

If it gain success, then everything that was pleasing becometh abhorrent to it.

From this calamity it is impossible to escape save by the establishing of the ordered thanks (to God).

(10) *Negligence.* As towards desires is haste, so towards devotion and good deeds is slothfulness. This disease departeth not save by great austerity and rigorous effort, which fighteth nature by coldness and dryness; and maketh it acceptable of order and gentle and smooth like tanned skins.

To each of these qualities, of *nafs*, physicians of

nafs (Prophets and holy men, their followers) have applied a remedy.

These ten qualities are the mother of qualities, wherefrom many other qualities are derived.

The roots and the branches of lustful qualities are all sprung from the root of the creation of *nafs*. That is the four natures:

heat
cold
wetness
dryness

MA'RIFAT-I-RŪḤ (DEEP KNOWLEDGE OF THE SOUL)

III, 5

The *ma'rifat* of the soul and the majesty of its understanding is lofty and inaccessible. Not attainable is its acquisition with the noose of reason. It is a *sīmurgh* that hath its nest on the Qāf (Caucasus) of majesty ; and as the prey of understanding entereth not the dwelling of writing.

It is a jewel that hath risen from the abyss of the ocean of grandeur ; not possible is the writing of its qualities by the scale of conjecture.

The Lords of revelation and the Masters of hearts (who are prefects of the mysteries of the hidden, and who have become free from the following of desire and from the servitude of *nafs*) have grudged explanation save by hint.

The most honoured existence, and the nearest evidence to God,—is the great soul[1] which to Himself God hath joined.

Great Ādam, the first *khalīfah*, the interpreter of God, the key of existence, the reed of invention and the paradise of souls,—all signify the qualities of *rūḥ* (the soul); and the first prey that fell into the net of existence was the soul.

The will of the ancient one assigned it to His own *khilāfat* in the world of creation; entrusted to it the keys of the treasuries of mysteries; dismissed it

1. See the Qur'ān, P.D.; xvii. 87.

for sway in the world; opened to it a great river from the sea of life—so that ever from it it might seek aid of the bounty of life; might add to the parts of the universe; might convey the form of divine words from the establishment-place of collection (the Holy Existence) to the place of separation, (the world) might give, with the essence of abridgment, dignity in the essence of division. To it, God gave two glances of divine blessing:

(*a*) One for beholding the majesty of *qudrat*.

(*b*) The other beholding the beauty of *ḥikmat*.

The first glance signifieth natural reason; its result is love for God.

The second glance signifieth reason, common and low; its result is wholly *nafs*.

Every bounty, the aid whereof the soul of increase seeketh from the essence of collection (God), —worthy of it, universal *nafs* becometh.

By reason of active deed, of passive deed and of power, of weakness, the attribute of male[2] and of female[3] appeareth; in the soul of increase and universal *nafs*,—the custom of love-making became confirmed by the link of temperament; by means of marriage, the races of worlds became existing; and by the hand of the midwife of Fate appeared in the apparent world.

Then all created beings are the outcome of *nafs* and of *rūḥ* (the soul).

Nafs is the result of *rūḥ*; *rūḥ*, of order. Because by His own self, without any cause (whereto the order

2. The male qualities are: the active deed and power.

3. The female qualities are: the passive deed and weakness.

is the hint) God created the soul; and by the means of *rūḥ* (whereof creation is the hint), the crowd of created beings.

Since it is necessary that every *khalīfah* should be the comprehender of varied qualities, He clothed the God-like grace and the endless bounty of the soul, in the *khilāfat* of creation, with the honour-robe of all names, and with the qualities of His own beauty and grandeur; and made it honoured in the chief seat of creation.

When the circle of causing to create reached accomplishment, in the mirror of the existence of dusty Ādam, the soul became reflected; and in it, all the names and God-like qualities illuminated.

Spread abroad in lofty places became the rumour of Ādam's *khilāfat*; and on the mandate of his *khilāfat* came this royal seal; on the standard of his blessing became revealed this Qur'ānic verse: "To Ādam, all names He made known" (ii. 31).

In the grasp of his sway, they placed the gate of subduing and the eye of decreeing.

For his adoration, they ordered the angels, for that tranquillity (collectedness) was not the angels'.

Some of the angels are in the stage: (*a*) of *jamāl* (beauty) only; they are the angels of kindness and of mercy, (*b*) of *jalāl* (grandeur) only; they are the angels of wrath, of mercy and of vengeance.

By all names, Ādam knew God but the angels only by that name, which was their stage.

The existence in the material world:

(*a*) of Ādam became the stage of the form of *rūḥ* in the hidden world.

(*b*) of Ḥavvā (Eve) the stage of the form of *nafs* in the hidden world.

Ḥavvā's birth from Ādam is like unto the birth of *nafs* from *rūḥ* (the soul); and the effects of the marriage of *nafs* and *rūḥ*, and the attraction of male and of female, became assigned to Ādam and Ḥavvā.

Like to their issuing from *rūḥ* and *nafs* came into existence the atoms of progeny (which were a deposit in Ādam's backbone) by the union of Ādam and Ḥavvā.

The existence of Ādam and Ḥavvā became the exemplar of the existence of *rūḥ* and *nafs*.

In every person of mankind, another exemplar becometh—by the union of *rūḥ* (in part) and of *nafs* (in part) transcribed from the exemplar of Ādam and Ḥavvā.

Became produced the birth:

(*a*) of the heart from the two (soul and *nafs*).

(*b*) of the form of the male of the sons of Ādam from the form of the universal soul.

(*c*) of the form of the female from the form of universal *nafs*.

In the form of the female, no Prophet hath been sent. Because by reason of sway in the souls of men and by its effects in creation, prophecy hath the attribute of the male; and the means of revealing the mystery of prophecy is the soul suitable to the form (of man).

JAM' (COLLECTED) AND TAFRAQAH (DISPERSED)

IV, 2

In the idiom of the ṣūfīs:

jam' signifies:	*tafraqah* signifies:
(*a*) the repelling of structures (creation).	the accepting of structures (creation).
(*b*) the dropping of additions (worldly advantages).	the confirming of devotion and of Godship.
(*c*) the withdrawing *shuhūd-i-ḥaqq* from creation.	the separating of God from creation.

Jam' without *tafraqah* is impiousness; *tafraqah* without *jam'* is uselessness; *jam'* with *tafraqah* is the very truth, for it hath the order of *jam'* joined to souls, and of *tafraqah* to forms.

As long as the soul and the body are linked, the union of *jam'* and *tafraqah* is of the requisites of existence.

The true *'Ārif* is ever joined:

(*a*) to *rūḥ* (which is the dwelling of *mushāhadah* in the essence of *jam'*.

(*b*) to the body (which is the instrument of strife) in the *maqām of tafraqah*.

Thus have Junaid and Wāsiṭī written.

This state, the ṣūfīs call *jam'-u'l-jam'*.

In devotion, who looketh:

(*a*) at his own acquisition is in *tafraqah*.

(*b*) at God's grace, is in *jam'*.

(*c*) at neither himself nor at his own deeds, is in *jam'-u'l-jam'* (wholly effaced).

Thus Abū 'Alī Daqqāq and Junaid have said.

Jam' signifies:

the veiling and the concealment of the people in the superiority of *ẓuhūr va shuhūd-i-ḥaqq* (revelation and manifestation of God).

Tafraqah signifies:

the veiling and the concealment of God in the *shuhūd-i-wujūd-i-khalq* (manifestation of the existence of creation).

TAJALLĪ (EPIPHANY) AND ISTITĀR (BEING HID)

IV, 3

Tajallī signifieth the manifestation of the sun of the *ḥaqīqat* of God out from the clouds of humanity.

Istitār signifieth the cloud of the light of *ḥaqīqat* in the revelation of the qualities of humanity.

Tajallī is of three kinds.

(1) Tajallī-i-dhāt. Its mark (if of the holy traveller's existence something hath remained) is the *fanā'* (effacement) of *dhāt*, and the annihilation of qualities in the glories of their lights. They call it "falling into a swoon," as was the state of Mūsā, whom (by beholding *tajallī*) they took out of himself and effaced.

When from God he sought the appearance of *dhāt*[1] he had not yet after *fanā'* reached *baqā'*; in conformity with the guidance "let me see," at the time of the *tajallī* of the light of *dhāt* on the Ṭūr of the *nafs* of his existence,—the residue (which is the seeker of manifestation) of the qualities of his existence became effaced.

If from the residue of his existence, *fanā'* be wholly separated; and after the *fanā'* of existence, its truth be joined to absolute *baqā'* (God),—he seeth, by the light of the eternal, the *dhāt* of the eternal.

This is an honour-robe that they specially gave to Muḥammad, and is a draught that they caused him to taste.

1. This is the *dhāt* of God.

From desire for this cup, they cause to drop a draught into the jaw of the soul of the special ones of his followers.

This sense demandeth the exaltation of the *walī* (saint) above the *nabī* (prophet).

For the *walī* gaineth this rank not of himself,—nay by the perfection of his following the prophet.

(2) Tajallī-i-ṣifāt. If the Ancient Existence display *tajallī*:

(*a*) with *jalāl*, he is (on account of His glory, *qudrat*, and force) in *khushū'* and *khuḍū'* (humility of heart and of limbs).

(*b*) with *jamāl*, he is (on account of His mercy, grace and blessing) joyous and loving.

The *dhāt* of the Eternal changeth not, but according to exigency of will, contrariety of capacity, are evident sometimes outwardly *jalāl* (grandeur) and inwardly *jamāl* (beauty), and sometimes the contrary thereto.

(3) Tajallī-i-af'āl. This signifies the averting of one's glance from the deeds of other people; from them, the severing of additions of good and of evil, of profit, and of loss; the moderating of their praise and blame; of their acceptance and rejection (of one).

For the bare manifestation of divine deeds dismisseth to themselves the people from the addition of deeds.

To the holy traveller in the stages of travelling come in order: (*i*) *tajallī-i-af'āl*; (*ii*) *tajallī-i-ṣifāt*; (*iii*) *tajallī-i-dhāt*.

Deeds are the effects of qualities, and enfolded in *dhāt* are qualities.

For the people, deeds are nearer than qualities,

and qualities, nearer than *dhāt.*

They call:

(*a*) the *shuhūd-i-tajallī-i-af'āt* (the manifestation of the glory of deeds), the *muḥāḍarah* (the being present).

(*b*) the *shuhūd-i-tajallī-i-ṣifāt* (the manifestation of the glory of qualities), the *mukāshafah* (the manifestation).

(*c*) the *shuhūd-i-tajallī-i-dhāt* (the manifestation of the glory of *dhāt*), the *mushāhadah* (the beholding).

They call:

muḥādarah, the *ḥāl* of hearts.

mukāshafah, the *ḥāl* of mysteries.

mushāhadah, the *ḥāl* of souls.

Cometh truly *mushāhadah* from a person who is standing in the existence of the witnessed (God), not in his own. For the power of the glory of the light of eternity (God) is not of accidents (*ḥādith*).

So long as in the witnessed, the *shāhid* (witnesser) in not effaced, and in it becometh not left, His *mushāhadah* one cannot make.

After beholding the effects of the flame of separation, and the violence of desire on Majnūn's state, a party of the tribe of Majnūn interceded with the tribe of Lailā, they said: "What would it be if, a moment, Majnūn's eye become illumined and anointed with the sight of Lailā's beauty?" The tribe of Lailā said: "To this extent is no harm. But Majnūn himself hath not the power of beholding Lailā." At last, they brought Majnūn, and uplifted a corner of Lailā's tent. Immediately his glance fell on the fold of Lailā's skirt,—senseless he fell.

In short, the glory of God is the cause of the people being veiled; His being veiled is the cause of manifestation (of glory) of the people.

When God becometh glorified:

(*a*) in His own deeds,—in them, the deeds of the people become veiled.

(*b*) in His *dhāt*,—in it, the *dhāt*, the qualities, and deeds of the people become veiled.

For the welfare of the world of *ḥikmat* and for enlarging the effects of mercy on His own special ones,—the Absolute Wise one (God) leaveth the residue of the qualities of lusts (which are the source of being veiled), so that, for them and for others, there may be mercy.

For them (the special ones),

that by the occupations of lusts, they may remain persevering; and by permanency may acquire nearness (to God).

For others (the people in general),

that annihilated in the essence of *fanā'* and immersed in the sea of *jama'* they may not become, and that to others their existence may become a source of profit.

Some of the *'Ulamā'* (who are ṣūfīs) have said:

The *istighfār* of Muḥammad is the demand for this veil in order that he may not be immersed in the sea of *shuhūd*; and that, by him through the link of humanity, men may be benefited.

WAJD (RAPTURE) AND WUJUD (EXISTENCE)

IV, 4

Wajd (*wajdān*) signifieth:

(*a*) an event that from God arriveth, and turneth the heart from its own form to—great grief, or to great joy.

(*b*) a state wherein all the (mortal) qualities of the *wājid* become cut off, and his nature becometh painted with joy.

The *wājid* (possessor of *wajd*) signifieth:

one who hath not yet come forth from the veil of sensual qualities, and is, by his own existence, veiled from God's existence.

Sometimes in the veil of his existence appeareth an opening whence a ray from the light of God's existence shineth and helpeth him. After that the veil becometh folded, and *maujūd* (existence), lost.

Wajd is intermediate between the preceding disappearing and the following disappearing (of *maujūd*).

Wujūd signifieth:

(*a*) that in the superiority of the light of the *shuhūd* of *maujūd* (the existence of God), *wujūd* and *wājid* become lost and naught.

(*b*) the quality of *muḥdath* (accident).

(*c*) the existence of the quality of *qadīm* (the Ancient One, God).

As Dhu'n-Nūn hath said: "When, out from his own existence, the possessor of *wajd* is not effaced, —he is *wājid*, and standing in him, is *wajd*."

When, out from his own existence, the possessor of *wujūd* is wholly effaced, and in the existence of *maujūd* is left standing—he is the *dhāt* of *maujūd* (the existence of the existence of God), not the *dhāt* of *wājid* (or the *dhāt* of the slave).

Wājid signifieth one who is the disappearer of his existence.

Thus hath Shiblī said.

Who, by the appearance of his own *wajd*, becometh veiled from the seeing of the *wajd* of the *maujūd* (the existence of God),—in him joy cometh.

Who, by seeing the *wajd of maujūd* (the existence of God), becometh deprived of the appearance of his own *wajd*,—from him descendeth the possibility of joy.

Thus hath Junaid said.

Wajd is the preface to *wujūd*.

In victory over the fortress of human *wujūd* (existence) every *wajd* is like to a *manjanīq* (catapult) established by the attraction of the divine world, so that, when the fortress of *wujūd* (existence) is subdued—it becometh the *wajd* of *wujūd*.

The end of *wajd* is the beginning of *wujūd*. That is, the *wujūd* of *wajd* is the cause of the *wājid's* being deprived of existence, which is the condition of the *wujūd* of *maujūd* (the existence of the existence of God).

Thus have said: (*a*) Abu'l-Ḥusain Nūrī; (*b*) Shiblī.

The taking away of the addition of *wajd* to self is the essence of accepting *tauḥīd*; and its addition to self is the essence of denying (*tauḥīd*).

Thus hath Bāyazīd said.

As *wajd* is the preface to *wujūd*, so *tawājud* (*wajd*-making) is the preface to *wajd*.

Tawājud signifies the asking for and the attracting of *wajd*, by way of:

(*a*) *tadhakkur* (repeating);
(*b*) *tafakkur* (reflecting);
(*c*) sincere resemblance to the man of *wajd* (in motion and in rest).

Although apparently *tawajud* is preparation, preparation is the opposite to sincerity, yet since the resolution of the *mutawājid*, in this form of *tawājud*, is wholly inclination for acceptance of the aid of divine bounty, and (is) true offering for snuffing up divine odours,—it is not contrary to sincerity.

Thus the *Sharī'at* hath permitted and ordered.

The description of the man:

(*a*) of the beginning is *tawājud*.
(*b*) of the path is *wajd*.
(*c*) of the acquisition is *wujūd*.

ON WAQT (PERIOD) AND NAFAS (MOMENT)

IV, 6

To *waqt* ṣūfīs assign three meanings. *Waqt* may mean a quality such as *qabḍ* (contraction), *basṭ* (expansion), sorrow or joy,—that prevaileth over the slave.

From exceeding superiority of *ḥāl*, the possessor of this *Waqt* cannot understand another *ḥāl*.

So the possessor of the *ḥāl* of *qabḍ*, with the superiority of the *ḥāl*, is so impressed and filled that he findeth an impression neither from the passed *basṭ*, nor from the coming *basṭ*. All his time, he seeth the *waqt-i-ḥāl*; over the *ḥāl* of others, according to his own *ḥāl*, is his own sway which thus becometh the source of error.

Every *ḥāl* concordant with his own *ḥāl*, he decreeth as to its truth, otherwise, as to its falsity.

In this explanation, the sense of *waqt* is general, —both for the holy traveller and for him who is not.

Waqt may mean a *ḥāl* that, by assault, appeareth from the *ghaibat* (the hidden); taketh by the superiority of its sway the holy traveller from his own *ḥāl*; and maketh him submissive to its own order.

Special to the holy traveller is this *waqt* and is a hint to the saying: "Son of his time is the ṣūfī."

When they say "by the decree of *waqt*," they mean that, by God's will, out of his own will, he is seized and veiled.

In respect of the order of "other than God,"—who showeth contentment, cometh into strife (with God); and by its influence, is subdued.

Hence they have said: "Waqt is the slaying sword."

The sword hath two qualities,—one soft and smooth, the other the keen, cutting edge. Who displayeth to it softness and rubbeth it with gentleness—findeth from it softness; who displayeth to it roughness suffereth the wound of its violence.

Even so *waqt* hath two qualities—gentleness and wrathfulness.

Agreement and concordance with it who maketh, enjoyeth its grace; repulsion and opposition to it who maketh, becometh overpowered by its violence.

By the passing of God's purpose, *waqt* is over all purposes and states the prevailer; and, according to its own decree, fashioneth them—like the sword, the severer.

Waqt may mean the present time, which is middle, between the past and the future.

They say: "Master of *waqt* is such a one." That is, being engaged in the performance of recitations of the present time, solicitude for a thing (which at that time may be important and best) keepeth him engaged from mention of the past, and from thinking of the future. Thus, his time he loseth not.

In this *waqt*, decline is not passed save in connection with holy travellers, to whom, by reason of the *talwīn* of *ḥāl*, this *wāqt* is sometimes existent and sometimes lost; and who, into the volume of credit, bring not the account of their own life save at the time when *waqt* is existent.

For those joined to God and for the companions of *tamkīn*, this *waqt* is constant; and to it the path of decline is closed.

Thus hath Shiblī said.

The possessor of this *waqt* is issuer from beneath the sway of *ḥāl*.

In the second sense, *waqt* is not powerful in him. Nay, he is powerful in *waqt* in the sense that he keepeth all *waqt* engaged in important affairs.

Some ṣūfīs call the possessor of *waqt* the father of *waqt*, not the son of *waqt*.

Nafas signifieth the succession of *ḥāl* of *mushahadah* (manifestation), whereto is joined the life of hearts of men of love, which is like unto the succession of breaths, whereto is conditioned the permanency of the life of bodies.

If for a moment from the path of the heart, the succession of fresh breath be cut off,—from the volume of natural heat, it becometh inflamed; if for a moment, from the essence of the desirous heart, the succession of *shuhūd*,—from the violence of its thirst and rage, it consumeth with desire.

The difference between *waqt* (in the second sense) and *nafas* is this:

Waqt is a *ḥāl* in the place of languor and of stoppage; and an event in the pursuit, and in the observing, of *mushahadah* (manifestation) and of *ghaibat* (concealment).

Nafas is a *ḥāl* ever free from languor and stoppage. Hence they have said: *Waqt* for the beginner, for the finisher, *nafas*.

SHUHUD (BEING PRESENT) AND GHAIBAT (BEING ABSENT)

IV, 7

Shuhūd signifieth:

being present. With whatever the heart is present, *shāhid* (witness) of it, it is, and that thing is *mashhūd* (witnessed) by it (the heart).

If the heart be present with God, it is *shāhid* (witness) of God: if the heart be present with the people, it is *shāhid* of the people.

The way of ṣūfīs is to call the *mashhūd* (witnessed) *shāhid* (witnesser), because with whatever the heart is present, that thing also is present with the heart.

For the sake of the unity of God and the plurality of the people, they mean: (*a*) by *shāhid* (singular) God; (*b*) by *shawāhid* (plural) the people; (*c*) by *shuhūd* (singular) being present with God; for ever is their heart *shāhid* (witness) of, and *ḥāḍir* (present) with, God.

Men of *shuhūd* are two parties: (*a*) the companions of *muraqabah* (fearful contemplation); (*b*) the lords of *mushāhadah* (manifestation).

Ghaibat is a description opposed to *shuhūd*:

(*i*) the blameable *ghaibat*, opposed to *shuhūd-i-ḥaqq*.

(*ii*) the laudable *ghaibat*, opposed to *shuhūd-i-khalq* which (through the superiority of the *shuhūd-i-ḥaqq*) is of two kinds:

(*a*) the *ghaibat* of beginners; the *ghaibat* of things left.

(*b*) the *ghaibat* of the middle ones; the *ghaibat* of his own existence; this is the limit of *ghaibat* and the beginning of *fanā'* (effacement).

The stage of "the last ones" is outside the *ḥāl* of *ghaibat*. For *ghaibat* is the *ḥāl* of that one who hath not freed himself from the narrow place of existence, nor reached the amplitude of Absolute Existence (God); nor gained the limit as to *ghaibat* (the being hidden) and as to *shahādat* (the being present).

Men of blameable *ghaibat* are hidden from the *shuhūd-i-ḥaqq* by the *shāhid* of the people: men of laudable *ghaibat* are hidden from the *shuhūd-i-khalq* by the *shāhid* of God.

To the man of perfection, they conceal neither the *shuhūd* of God from the people, nor the *shuhūd* of the people from God.

The observing of rules and the following of *shuhūd* and of laudable *ghaibat* is for holy travellers and for men of *talwīn*.

For those joined to God and for the established ones at rest is no *ḥāl* save constant *shuhūd-i-ḥaqq*. For them is no *ghaibat*, laudable or blameable.

At the beginning of the superiority of *ḥāl*, and at the time of manifestation of the good news of the morning of revelation, Shiblī went before Junaid, and present was Junaid's lawful spouse.

She wished to go behind the screen. Junaid said: "Shiblī is *ghā'ib* (hidden); be thou in thy place." Even as Junaid was speaking to her, Shiblī wept.

To his wife, Junaid said: "Now thou shouldest be concealed, for to sense Shiblī hath come."

The state of beginners is *ghaibat* from the people in *shuhūd* of the beloved; from out of it, "the last ones" have passed.

The tale of Zulaikhā (Potiphar's wife), who, in love for Yūsuf, had the degree of *tamkīn*, and in *shuhūd* of him became not *ghā'ib* from the senses as her companions and reprovers (yet beginners in love for Yūsuf and in the *shuhūd* of his beauty), who, by the force of the *ḥāl* of *shuhūd* for him, were *ghā'ib* from the senses; and were unaware of the cutting of their own hands (through the passion of love for him).

TAJRĪD (OUTWARD SEPARATION) AND TAFRĪD (INWARD SOLITUDE)

IV, 8

Tajrīd signifieth outwardly abandoning the desires of this world, and inwardly rejecting the compensation of the next world and of this world.

The true *mujarrad* is one who as to *tajarrud* (*tajrīd*) from the world is not the seeker of compensation, nay, the cause of *tajarrud* is propinquity to God.

Who outwardly abandoneth request of the world, and for it expecteth compensation, in this fleeting world, or in the next world,—freed from the world verily hath not become, and is in the place of exchanging and trafficking.

In all his devotions, by worship only his gaze is on the performance of his rights to God, not on compensation nor on other desire.

Tafrīd signifieth the rejecting the increase of deeds of himself, and the concealing their appearance by regarding on himself God's favour and bounty.

Tajrīd is the abandoning of the expectation of compensations.

Because when he knoweth the grace of *tajrīd* and of devotion (to be) God's favour—not his own deed nor his own acquisition,—for it, he expecteth not compensation. Nay, immersed in God's favour, he seeth his own existence.

Tajrīd in form is not necessary to *tajrīd*; for

possibly, in abandoning, he may be expectant of a compensation. So *tafrīd* is not necessary to *tajrīd*, for possibly, in abandoning hope of compensation, he seeth himself in the acquisition of entrance (to God).

MAḤV (OBLITERATION) AND ITHBĀT (CONFIRMATION)

IV, 9

In the opinion of the ṣūfīs, *maḥv* signifieth the obliterating of the slave's existence.

Ithbāt signifieth the confirming (after *maḥv*) of the slave's existence.

Related to the will of the Eternal are *maḥv* and *ithbāt*.

Maḥv hath three degrees:

(1) the lowest degree—the *maḥv* of blameable qualities and of dark deeds.

(2) the middle degree—the *maḥv* of blameable and of the laudable qualities.

(3) the highest degree—the *maḥv* of *dhāt*.

In opposition to every *mahv* is an *ithbāt*.

Near to each other is the meaning of:

fanā' (effacement).
baqā' (permanency).
maḥv (obliteration).
ithbāt (confirmation).

The difference between *maḥv* and *fanā'*, between *baqā'* and *ithbāt*, one cannot comprehend save by the aid of the kind Friend, and of gracious faith.

After the *fanā'* of *dhāt*, (*a*) *baqā'* appeareth not; (*b*) *ithbāt* is not necessary.

Thus the *ithbāt* of agreeable qualities and of beautiful deeds is not necessary after the *maḥv* of misdeeds of natures and of the sins of deeds of the companions of purifying and of the Lords of glorying.

The *fanā'* of deeds and of qualities becometh not wholly acquired save after the *fanā' of dhāt*, but their *maḥv* is not restricted to the *maḥv* of *dhāt*.

Maḥv and *ithbāt* are generally (derived) from *fanā'* and *baqā'*, because they practise not *fanā'* and *baqā'*, save in the *maḥv* of humanity and in the *ithbāt* of Godship.

In the sense of *maḥv*, they use:

- *saḥk* (grinding), the effacing the essence of qualities.
- *maḥq* (abolishing), the effacing the essence of *dhāt*.
- *ṭams* (effacing), the effacing the effects of qualities and of *dhāt*.

TALWĪN (CHANGE) AND TAMKĪN (REST)

IV, 10

Tamkīn signifieth perpetuity of manifestation of *ḥaqīqat* by reason of the tranquillity of the heart in the place of nearness (to God).

Talwīn signifieth the subjugating of the heart between manifestation and veiling by observing times, and by the pursuit of the *ghaibat* of *nafs*, and its manifestation.

Possessor of *talwīn*, they call not him who shall not have passed beyond the qualities of *nafs*, nor reached to the world of the qualities of the heart, for *talwīn* is through the succession of varied states.

Possessor of *ḥāl*, they call not him who is bound in the qualities of *nafs*.

Then *talwīn* is possible for the Lords of hearts, who may not have traversed the world of qualities (of God), nor reached to (knowledge of) *dhāt*, because they are innumerable qualities.

Talwīn is possible where numbering is possible.

The Lords of revelation of *dhāt* have passed the limit of *talwīn* and reached to the stage of *tamkīn*, because in *dhāt* by reason of His unity change appeareth not.

Escape from *talwīn* is for that one whose heart ascendeth from the stage of the heart to the stage of the soul; cometh forth from beneath the sway of the numbering of qualities; and becometh a dweller in the open space of propinquity to *dhāt* (God's existence).

When, from the stage of the heart to the stage of the soul, the heart arriveth,—from the stage of *nafs* to the stage of the heart, *nafs* emigrateth.

Talwīn (which before was the heart's) becometh in this stage the accident of *nafs* through:

qabḍ (contraction).
basṭ (expansion).
sorrow and joy.
fear and hope.

Nafs becometh the *khalīfah* of the heart of the possessor of *talwīn*.

By reason of the light of manifestation and the certainty of the existence of this *talwīn* not being veiled,—this *talwīn* is verily not the reviled *tamkīn*.

So long as the custom of humanity is left, impossible is it that out of nature change should be wholly obliterated, but change excludeth not the possessor of *tamkīn* from the stage of resting.

THE AURĀD (PRAYER-EXERCISES) AND THE KALIMĀH-I-SHĀHĀDAT (THE CREED)

VII, 2

On his tongue, the slave should urge the two *shahādats* (witnessings) saying: "I declare no god but God; I declare Muḥammad, His slave and prophet." For the verifying of his own heart, he should witness to this confession.

The confession of *shahādat* is special, because, in respect to his own *nafs*, every confession is *shahādat*; the *shahādat* is not confession.

As every confessor is taken as to the confessed, so the confessor (of faith) is taken as to his own faith and questioned to the limits of the *Shar'* as to his service.

The *shahādat* of confession is not the place of suspicion. Although confession is of the crowd of (mere) words, yet it is a most honoured column of deeds.

Because the meaning of: (*a*) *'amal* (deed) is the use of the limbs upon the orders of the *Sharī'at*, (*b*) *iqrār* (confession) is the use of the tongue in the creed of faith whereto most men are subjected.

The tongue is the interpreter and the witness of the heart, whose mystery it relateth, and to whose faith it witnesseth.

The other limbs are interpreters and witnesses of the heart, whose mystery they relate, of whose *ḥāl* they give evidence.

This *shahādat*, they perform by the tongue of deed (not by the tongue of the mouth).

Thus the tongue hath inwardly a word, outwardly a deed; all the columns have inwardly a word and outwardly a deed.

The limb that men use in the requisites of the *Shar'*, it, with the tongue of *ḥāl*, witnesseth to the existence of faith in their heart.

Iqrār and *'amal*, each, is a witness to the existence of faith, not a part thereof. Faith is verification by the heart; confession, by the tongue; action, by the limbs. This signifieth not that the essence of faith is confession, or deed; for faith alone is the verification of the heart. Confession and deed both are the marks, though it is possible that the witnessing of these two may be false: as in the case of hypocrites, in whom are strong confession and deed, while faith languid is.

But because the base of rules is on outward things, the order in respect to the faith of one (for whom witnessing is made) is dependent upon the *shahādat* of these two witnesses, and to it opposition declineth.

After the witnessing (*shahādat*) of witnesses the order in respect to one (against whom witnessing is made) is incumbent upon the *qāḍī*, although the witnessing be suspicious.

Once Bilāl cast down in battle one of the infidels who presented the *shahādat*. To it Bilāl paid no consideration and separated his head from his body. When he related this to Muḥammad, he was reproved.

He replied: "O Prophet, his confession was from fear, not from faith." Muḥammad saith: "How splitedest thou his heart? How knowest thou that in his heart was no faith?"

ZUHD (AUSTERITY)

IX, 3

Zuhd signifieth:

(*a*) the heart's turning away from the pleasure of the world's goods, and shunning its desires.

(*b*) the third stage of *taubah* (penitence) and of *wara'* (piety).

The holy traveller on the path to God at first forbiddeth his own *nafs* with the elephant-goad of sincere penitence from falling into difficulties as to sins; to it maketh straight the power of delights, and maketh, with the polisher of piety, his heart pure of the rust of greed, so that therein may appear the verity of this, and of the next, world.

Therein, he seeth this world ugly and transitory, and therefrom turneth; the next world, beautiful, and thereto inclineth.

The abandoning and the being alone is:

(*a*) for "the last ones," not the necessity of the truth of *zuhd*.

(*b*) for "the first ones," of the requisites of *zuhd*.

In praise of *zuhd*, for the distinguishing of pretenders from the sincere, most of the words of *shaikhs* comprehend the necessity for abandoning property and delights.

There are three *zuhds*:

(*i*) the *zuhd* of the common in the first rank.

(*ii*) the *zuhd* of the special in the second rank is *zuhd* in *zuhd*. It signifieth change of delight from the acquisition of *zuhd* which is the prop—of delight; of the will of the slave; and of his *nafs* being filled with delights of the next world. By the *fanā'* (effacement) of his own desire in the will of God, this sense cometh true.

(*iii*) the *zuhd* of the special of the spencial ones in the third rank, which is *zuhd*, with God. It is peculiar to the Prophets and to other holy men; and is in the world after the *fanā'* of his own will by God's will.

Zuhd is the result of *ḥikmat* and of the birth of knowledge.

In the application of *zuhd*, pleasure in the world is the result of ignorance, and the birth of the heart's blindness as in the *Ḥadīth*.

For the shunning of the fleeting world and for delight in the lasting world,—the *zāhid* hath laid on a sure foundation (God's will) the foundation of his own work.

Thus have Luqmān and Shiblī said, and so is it in the *Ḥadīth*.

Benefit by *ḥaqīqat* is not the denial of the stage of *zuhd*, of its excellence, and of exaltation of the rules of effort; but—through the humbling of *zuhd* in the glance of *zāhids*,—the purpose of *ḥaqīqat* is the repelling of pride.

FAQR (POVERTY)

IX, 4

At the stage of *faqr* (which meaneth taking possession of no chattels) the holy traveller of the path of *ḥaqiqat* arriveth not, till he hath passed through the stage of *zuhd* (austerity).

For one who hath desire for the world although he hath no property, the name of *faqr* is illusory.

Faqr hath a name, a custom and a truth.

Its name is taking possession of no chattels despite desire; its custom is taking possession of no chattels, despite *zuhd*; its truth is the impossibility of taking chattels.

Since the man of *ḥaqīqat* seeth by its means all things in the sway of the master of lands (God), he regardeth not lawful the consigning of property to others.

The *faqr* :

(*a*) of men of *ḥaqiqat* is a natural quality which,—despite having, or not having, chattels—becometh not changed. If in their power be the whole world, free from taking it they regard themselves.

(*b*) of spectators who have found only an impression of the truth of *faqr*; in whose hearts its meaning hath not become enjewelled—is an accidental quality. By the accession of chattels they become changed, and of them regard themselves possessed.

For the sake of being numbered for excellence of *faqr*, and for desire of the good of the next world, they shun wealth more than the man of wealth shunneth *faqr*.

On the excellence of *faqr* over wealth, and of wealth over *faqr*, the man of meaning hath urged speech.

Faqr

(*a*) is with "the first and the middle ones" more excellent than wealth;

(*b*) is with "the end ones" equal to wealth;

because wealth cannot deny them the sense of *faqr* and its truth, as 'Abdullah b. Jallād hath said. Although to him *faqr* and wealth are one, the quality of gift leaveth not in him the impression of the form of wealth, as Nūrī hath said.

Who is independent of God, how may he grasp aught? Save in God, the quality of the *faqr* is naught.

There are several crowds of *fuqarā'*:

(*a*) Those who regard as no property the world and its chattels. If it be in their power, they give it away, for it, in this and in the next world, they have no desire.

(*b*) Those who regard not their own deeds and devotion, although from them they issue—them their own property they know not, and in return for it expect no reward.

(*c*) Those who with these two qualities regard not as their own *ḥāl* and *maqām*. All they regard the favour of God.

(*d*) Those who regard not as their own *dhāt* and existence, nor even their own self. Their,—*dhāt* is none, nor quality, nor *ḥāl*, nor *maqām*, nor deed. No trace have they in the two worlds.

Need is the quality of the needy one, and in his nature standeth. Here is neither confirmed nature nor quality. This is the meaning of *faqr*, which some of the ṣūfīs have not.

The possessor of this *faqr* in both worlds, none recogniseth save God, because the Lord of the world is jealous. So concealed from the glance of strangers keepeth He His special ones that concealed from their own sight they are.

This *faqr* is the stage of the ṣūfīs and of "the last ones,"—not of holy travellers.

Because after passing the stages, in every stage (for the joined one), the pace is (according to his state) sometimes beyond the foot of the traveller.

Like *taubah* (penitence), which is the first stage of the stages of holy travellers, it is his foot-place which (after traversing all the stages and the *maqāms*) becometh attained.

TAJARRUD (CELIBACY) AND TA'AHHUL (MARRIAGE)

VI, 8

The tales of the Prophet in respect of *tajarrud* and of *ta'ahhul* are contradictory.

The source of this opposition is the contrariety of states and of lusts of some who are captive to exceeding passion.

Marriage is necessary:

(*a*) for those, from whom are expected,—weakness of piety, poorness of patience (as to abandoning desire); the falling into contrarieties (of state); and the committing of adultery.

(*b*) for those whom *nafs* hath turned away from following desires; hath obtained rest from excess of desire; hath, from contention with the heart, become torn up, and to the heart's suggestion become obedient.

Tajarrud and *tafarrud* are excellent for those who are in the flower of desire; whose *nafs*, in the seat of desire, is vain; and who are in the midst of travelling.

To a dervish they said: "Why desirest thou not a wife?" He said: "A wife is fit for man; the stage of man I have not reached. Wherefore should I desire a wife?"

Thus to another they spake. He replied: "Of the divorcing of *nafs*, my need is greater than of marriage. When I divorce *nafs*, it will be lawful to desire a wife."

To Bashar Ḥārith they said: "Of thee, men say so and so." He said: "What say they?" They said: "They say that thou hast abandoned the *sunnat* of marriage." He said: "Tell them that since I am engaged in enjoined observances, in the *sunnat* I engage not."

For the travellers of *ḥaqīqat*, it is known that, at the beginning of journeying, there is no help of severing attachments, of avoiding delay, of holding to resolution, and of shunning the license of nature.

Marriage is the cause of binding the heart to the chattels of livelihood, of descending from the height of resolution to the abyss of license; and of inclining towards the world, after austerity and faithfulness of desire (for God).

Freedom from wives and offspring aideth to tranquillity of heart, to purity of time, to the delight of ease, to freedom for devotion, and to loftiness.

As long as in respect to celibacy, and to strife against *nafs*, he hath power, it is necessary for the celibate traveller to esteem as booty—license of time, tranquillity of heart, so that he become not dull through solicitude for the wife.

Submission to the heart's orders becometh easy to him who beareth the celibate life till *nafs* becometh worthy of kindness; its vein of contention torn up, and to it stubbornness, forbidden.

Then to him God giveth a pure wife who shall be his aider in faith and in the chattels of livelihood in a way that shall be the tranquillity of the heart, and his preservation from the calamities of *nafs*.

Shaikh 'Abd-u'l-Qādir Jabalī said:

"A long while I had thought of marriage, but to it for fear of time's distress I advanced not; between impulsion and repulsion, I hesitated; at last when I had displayed perfect patience,—God gave me four concordant wives, each of whom voluntarily bestowed on me her property."

In the preferring of marriage to celibacy, the firm *'ulamā'* have the *'ilm-i-sā'at* (the knowledge of expansion), whereby they know:

(*a*) when, in respect of the observance of limits of "rights," they may satisfy *nafs*;

(*b*) when in respect of taking "delight," they may give it the power of expansion.

Ḥuqūq (' rights")[1] signify the requisites of *nafs*, whereby are preserved the prop of the body and the preservation of life, and without which permanency of *nafs* is hindered.

Ḥuẓūẓ ("delights") signify whatever (of desire) is in excess (of rights).

The firm *'ulamā'* and the great ones of ṣūfism know that *nafs* is unworthy of kindness, or of the gift of delights, so long as it resteth not from stirring, striving in wickedness, stubbornness, and is not reproved against contentions with the heart.

When under the sway of orders, *nafs* becometh quiet and the veins of its attachment to the heart are torn out, there appear integrity and concordance between it and the heart, and it becometh worthy of delights and of kindness.

Then the "delights" of *nafs* become its "rights"; its pain becometh its remedy.

The "delights" of a *nafs* like this become its "rights," because the taking of delights becometh

1. "The rights" are that once every four nights, he should visit each wife.

not the cause of stubbornness. By every delight is its rank (in propinquity and devotion) greater.

When by taking delight, *nafs* gaineth delight,—there reacheth to the heart a great delight (the cause of increase of its rest).

Even so by his neighbour's joy becometh glad the kind neighbour. When the heart putteth on the rest-robe, it clotheth *nafs* with the ease-garment.

When the increase of the *ḥāl* of each (the heart and *nafs*) is the cause of increase of *ḥāl* of the other, then the delight of marriage for a *nafs* like this is excellent.

Sufyān b. 'Ainīyah saith: "(Better) than the whole world, is the increase (in number) of the woman (wives)."

For the Amīr-ul-Mū'minīn (the wisest, most pious, most austere of the Companions) had four wives and seventeen mistresses.

Such is the state of "the end ones," thereto the idea of the state of the man of "the beginning," or of the "middle," reacheth not.

Many are the pretenders and the deceived ones, who, by doubt of this stage, become proud; lay down in the plain of license their own *nafs* free from incumbrance; and travel in the desert of destruction.

The rule of the celibate traveller is:

So long as to this stage he arriveth not, in the heart, he advanceth no excess as to marriage, and no thought thereof, until, in the heart, the imaginary power showeth no sway. When a thought of it appeareth, he denieth it by penitence to God and by seeking His aid.

If it (*nafs*) be not repelled, he persevereth awhile in fasting.

If it gather strength, thereto he maketh no haste without the preferring of earnest prayer and of much knowledge.

Weeping and groaning he returneth to God; with submission and weeping, placeth his head in the dust; and uttereth this prayer:

"O God! this thought tormenteth me to commit this sin. Thy forgiveness for it I ask; before Thee I repent; me forgive and my repentance accept. Verily Thou art the Merciful and great Accepter of repentance."

If it depart not, he goeth to the *shaikhs* (living and dead) and to the brothers, and seeketh aid, and desireth them to refer these matters to God.

If after this, his heart is established, the brothers rely (according to excellent opinion) on God's will, and to them it becometh evident that they should aid him.

The rule of *ta'ahhul* is in choosing the wife, regard her faith, not the world.

As far as is lawful (*ma'rūf*) he should live with her; should observe her "rights," therein showing no negligence; and for the preservation of the *Shar'* should order her—as Ibn 'Abbās saith.

In marriage, he should preserve himself from three calamities.

(1) Inordinate lying with the spouse, which is the calamity of *nafs*. Therefrom appear three injuries:

(*a*) Decline in deeds and in readings (of the Qur'ān), wherefrom defects in *ḥāl* necessarily come.

(*b*) The inflaming the fires of praised nature, and the wolves of dead *nafs*. For, when with a *nafs*, *nafs* hath commerce, each (*nafs*), by kinship becometh the aider of the other. In each (*nafs*), a delight occurreth and the fire of nature kindleth.

(c) The superiority of *nafs* after being subdued. For through its own obedience and will, *nafs* never lowereth its head to the heart's devotion.

When, by the aid of divine attraction the heart gathereth power, and beneath its sway, *nafs* seeth itself like a powerless *amīr*—in the hand of a powerful *amīr* then, from itself, *nafs* effaceth the greed of wishing to be followed and by necessity and compulsion becometh submissive to the heart. The kindness, which in this state it gaineth from the heart, *nafs* seeth is the result of the heart's kindness and of its own submission and of its being subdued,—not the result of the heart's (vain) desiring to be followed.

When in passion, *nafs* exceedeth moderation, and from the heart hath no reproof, it thinketh that this negligence is through the heart's weakness and its own power; and in the heart's wishing to follow and in its own power (of being followed) reneweth vain desire.

(2) Solicitude as to daily victuals, which is the calamity of the heart.

This is the result of doubt; doubt is the calamity of *yaqīn* (certainty); *yaqin* is the light of vision; vision is the eye of the heart.

The sign of the light of *yaqīn* in the slave's heart and its not being veiled by the darkness of doubt is this—that, on God's surety and His pledge, the slave relieth; as to the acquisition of daily victuals (apportioned from the beginning of life to known death) wherein appeareth neither excess nor defect,—is void of doubt; and knoweth that the heart's sway (in solicitude for daily food) is the weakness of *yaqīn*, and the want of reliance on God's pledge.

Reliance on anyone by one's own deliberation is the result of want of reliance on God's power.

(3) Attachment of the heart to the beauty of the spouse, which is the calamity of the soul.

It is for him the prohibitor of sincerity of divine love, and, as regards the violence of *shauq* (desire) for God, and the torment of *dhauq* (delight), and the delight of love,—maketh him dull.

To the extent that he becometh attached to the net of beauty, verily changeable, affaceable and *ḥādith* (accidental),—he becometh deprived of viewing the beauty (of God), whole, eternal, permanent and lasting.

The repelling of these (and other) calamities becometh attainable if, at the time of lying with the spouse, two glances are his:

(1) One glance outwardly, in the way of desire, and of being engaged with the spouse.

(2) The other glance inwardly at God, from Him seeking aid for the repelling of calamity and in Him being engaged.

A crowd of deceived ones keep glancing at the visible (outward) beauty of the friend, and say: "In this spectacle-place, behold we the beauty of God!"

This claim is the essence of falsehood, and of slander.

When from the lawful glance resulteth the folly of the soul (*rūḥ*) and its opposition to the payment of the established portion of love to God—behold from the unlawful glance what (greater) calamities spring.

The source of error of this crowd is: When, in that (unlawful) glance, they rest from passion's assault, they think that the source of this is delight, not passion. This idea is false, for if it had not been the residue of *nafs*, the pleasure of the glance in a form (which is the stirrer of passion) would not have been special.

When in them this desire hath become slight, from its slightness, they gain not that passion.

When that (unlawful) glance is repeated, and, in it, the imagination gaineth sway—possibly it becometh gross and outwardly its effect appeareth.

Hence, for the quieting of love's assault, physicians order conjunction even with one, other than the beloved.

Who, in this way, claimeth the truth of *ḥāl*,—him, they should hear naught of, and regard as a mere pretender.

TAWAKKUL (TRUSTING TO GOD)

IX, 9

Tawakkul signifieth trusting one's affairs to the Absolute Agent (God), confiding it the suretyship of the surety of daily victuals.

After *rijā'* (hope) is this stage, because the matter (of trusting and of confiding) is that one's who first shall understand His mercy.

Tawakkul is the result of the truth of faith, by good deliberation and by fate.

This is faith in the rank of *yaqīn* (certainly), the possessor whereof knoweth that all affairs are predestined and distributed by fate (*taqdīr*), perfect of will, just of distribution, wherein, as to increase or decrease, is no change.

Its sign is that, to the grasp of fate (*taqdīr*), he entrusteth the rein of deliberation, and from his own power is up-plucked.

Even as have said Dhu'n-Nūn; Sarīy; Junaid; Ḥamadūn Qaṣṣār; Sahl 'Abdullah.

Every stage hath a beginning and a prosperity suitable to its face; and an end and a calamity suitable to the back of the head—except the stage of *tawakkul*, which is all beginning or prosperity, and which never terminateth in end and calamity, which signifieth the *tawakkul-i-'ināyatī* (the *tawakkul* of favour) trust to the beauty of the will of the Ancient One (God); not the *tawakkul i-kifāyat* (the *tawakkul* of sufficiency) which is an enterer that never returneth from *tawakkul-i-'ināyatī*.

The true *mutawakkil* (truster) is that one in whose sight is no existence save the existence of the Causer-of-causes. His *tawakkul* becometh not changed by the existence, or by the non-existence, of causes.

This is the *tawakkul* of that one who shall have reached the stage of *Tauḥīd* (the unity of God). Till he reacheth this stage the *mutawakkil*, in amending his own *maqām*, is in need of abandoning causes, because, in his *tawakkul*, the belief of the existence of causes is blameable.

Therefore, in repelling causes, he ever striveth.

In the amending of this *maqām* by abandoning causes, the state of Ibrāhīm Khwāṣṣ is well known.

In one place, he never sojourned more than forty days, and used to take great precaution to conceal his state from the people, so that their knowledge as to his *tawakkul* should not become a cause of the causes of his daily victuals. Generally, in deserts and solitudes, alone, void of food and of information,—he travelled.

That crowd, in whose *tawakkul* the existence of causes is blameable,—the existence of causes is the veil of their state, so that on them falleth not the glance of strangers, and beneath the towered dome of cause, they are concealed from the glance of others.

The people think that they are possessed of causes; with the Causer-of-causes they are, in *khilvat* of union, engaged in being benefited with the delight of holding talk at night, and with the *dhauq* of appearances and of presences (Divine).

As to the force of the *ḥāl* of the *mutawakkil*, the master of the *Sharī'at* (Muḥammad) hath decided.

In *tawakkul*, who is possessor of *yaqīn* (certainty) and of *tamkīn*, his head shivereth and trembleth not at any disaster.

An assembly asked Junaid: "If, in search of daily victuals, we make no effort, how will it be?" He said: "If ye know that the Provider of daily victuals hath forgotten you, strive in search of victuals." They said: "Then, will we sit in the house, and practise *tawakkul?*" He said: "By your own *tawakkul*, tempt not God; for, save disappointment, naught will ye have." They said: "What thought shall we take?" He said: "Abandon thought."

Thus it is in the gospel.[1]

1. The passage is : چه حیلت کنیم [what virtue (force, art) shall we practise?]

RIḌĀ' (CONTENTMENT)

IX, 10

Riḍā' signifieth:

the lifting up (and removing) of the abhorrence of *qaḍā'* and *qadr* (fate and destiny), and the sweetening of the bitterness of their orders.

After traversing the stages of *tawakkul* (trusting to God), is the stage of *riḍā'*.

For despite the *yaqīn* (certainty) of the past division (by fate) and the confidence in the Distributor, it followeth not that abhorrence should not exist, nor that the bitterness of orders should appear sweet.

Thus hath it appeared in some of the recorded prayers of Muḥammad.

With this difference, because he besought "the first certainty," whereby it becometh known that to none arriveth save what in eternity without beginning they (fate and destiny) have decreed.

To it (the first certainty), prayer, of *riḍā'* was added, so that it became known that over *qismat* (destiny) *riḍā'* is not appointed by *qismat*.

The *maqām* of *riḍā'* is the end of the *maqām* of holy travellers. The being joined to its exalted dignity and to its inaccessible pinnacle is not the power of every hastener. In this *maqām*, to whomsoever they gave a footing, him, in haste, they conveyed to Paradise.

For, in *riḍā'* and in *yaqīn*, they have established *rūḥ* (the soul) and joy, the requisites of men of Paradise.

At this, the naming of the guardian of Paradise with (the name of) *Riḍvān* hinteth. From *yaqīn* (certainty) is born *riḍā'*.

So long as, by the light of *yaqīn*, the heart is not diffused and dissolved, by it in the heart appeareth not the containing of events, of calamities, and of joy.

As have said Dhu'n-Nūn, Ravīm, Ḥārth Muḥāsibī.

The repelling of abhorrence (which is the source of the *maqām* of *riḍā'*) is the result of the repelling of one's own will.

Ibn 'Aṭā' observeth will, in whole, and in abandoning will in part, regardeth its excellence.

The source of *riḍā'* is *yaqīn* and the spreading of the breast is its necessary; the source of abhorrence is doubt, and the narrowing of the breast is its necessary.

Once in Junaid's society, Shiblī uttered *Lāḥaula* ... (there is no power nor virtue, but in God). Junaid said: "This is from the heart's narrowness, which is from the abandoning of *riḍā'*." Shiblī said: "Truly thou spakest."

Abhorrence is of two kinds:

(*a*) Abhorrence of the heart, which is the opposite to *riḍā'*.

(*b*) Abhorrence of the *nafs*, which is the opposite to the *ḥāl* and the *maqām* of *riḍā'*.

Possibly in some heart ariseth this doubt:

When its preface and source are *ḥāl*, how can the opposite to the *ḥāl* of *riḍā'* be collected with its *maqām*?

The reply is:

Only a gift is *ḥāl*, that, through exceeding fineness and

penetrating power, pervadeth all parts of existence; and thereby no suspicion of the desires of nature remaineth.

But *maqām* is mixed with *kasb* (acquisition); therefore is possible the suspicion of the temperament of the wish of nature.

Even as *riḍā'* is the result of *yaqīn*, which is the heart's special quality, so special to the heart is the quality of *riḍā'*.

In it, abhorrence of *nafs* is not blameable, save when the heart is the possessor of *yaqīn* like unto a wide sea, sometimes calm, sometimes rough. When, from the source of Divine favour, the winds of circumstances resolve to blow, the heart's sea cometh into tumult; and therefrom, the excess (foam) of a wave plungeth upon the shore of *nafs*; and, in the flowing of nature, goeth flowing By its means the effects of *riḍā'* and of rest appear in *nafs*; and become qualified with the heart's quality.

When these winds take rest, the heart's sea ceaseth from boisterousness; to its own boundary, the bounty of *'ilm-i-yaqīn* and of rest turneth its face; and perturbation and abhorrence of *nafs* return.

In that *ḥāl* of ignorance (the nature of *nafs*), *'ilm-i-yaqīn* becometh non-existent *nafs* putteth on by loan the garment of the heart's feelings, and to (*nafs*), the heart speaketh.

The *riḍā'* of *nafs* is the effect of *riḍā'* of the heart, which is the effect of the *riḍā'* of God.

When the glance of the Divine *Riḍvān* taketh attachment to the heart, in it appeareth *riḍā'*. Then the mark of union of the Divine *Riḍvān* with the slave's heart is the union of the slave's parts with

Him. Thus speaketh Sahl 'Abdullah.

Since the slave's *riḍā'* is the Divine *Riḍvān's* need,—union with the Divine *Riḍvān* appeareth not in the place void of *riḍā'* Thus speaketh Rābi'ah to Sufyān Thaurī.

The *maqām* of *riḍā'* is the *maqām* of those joined to God,—not the stage of holy travellers, as Bashar Ḥāfī in reply to Faḍīl hath said.

Besides that place where one cometh into the place of *riḍa'* of God,—is what *maqām*?

There, where is the glance of *riḍā* all sins appear good.

More pleasant than that where an abhorrent object reacheth none is what *ḥāl*?

Thus speak the Amīr-u'l-Mū'minīn and Yaḥyā Ma'ādh.

Necessary for the *maqām* of *riḍā'* is the *ḥāl* of love, because when all deeds fall into the place of *riḍā'*, where the Beloved is Agent, all deeds of the Beloved are beloved.

Neither in this, nor in the next, world separate from the slave *riḍā* and *maḥabbat* (love), contrary to fear and hope, which in the next world separate from him.

MAḤABBAT (LOVE)

X, 1

On *maḥabbat* is the foundation of all lofty *ḥāls*, even as on *taubah* (penitence) is the base of all noble *maqāms*.

Since *maḥabbat* is essentially gift all *ḥāls* that are founded thereon, they call *mawāhib* (gifts).

Maḥabbat is the heart's inclination to considering attentively beauty, and is of two kinds: (*i*) *maḥabbat-i-'āmm*. (*ii*) *maḥabbat-i-khāṣṣ*.

In the following table, the qualities of *maḥabbat* are given :

	Maḥabbat-i-'āmm	*Maḥabbat-i-khāṣṣ*
(*a*)	the heart's inclination to considering attentively the beauty of qualities.	the soul's inclination to viewing the beauty of *dhāt*.
(*b*)	a moon that from viewing the beauteous qualities appeareth.	a sun that, from the horizon of *dhāt*, ascendeth.
(*c*)	a light that giveth decoration to existence.	a fire that purifieth existence.
(*d*)	a token that saith—"Imitate what is pure; bid farewell to what is not pellucid."	a token that saith—"Live not and consume not."
(*e*)	the best wine, sealed, tempered (by age).	the absolutely pure fountain.
(*f*)	a wine (by reason of its temperament, possessed of desires) the porter of purity and of impurity; of fineness and of grossness; of lightness and of heaviness.	a wine (by reason of its being purified from defects) all purity in purity; fineness in fineness, lightness in lightness.

The fineness and the lightness of this wine affecteth the heaviness and the lightness of the cup; changeth its grossness to fineness, its heaviness to lightness, like the soul that giveth to the eye fineness and lightness.

In the cup of their souls, the lovers of *dhāt* drink this wine; and, on hearts and *nafs*, pour the dregs.

It giveth the lightness:

(*a*) of agitation to souls (*rūḥ*).

(*b*) of *shauq* to hearts.

(*c*) of devotion to *nafs*.

The relish of this wine affecteth all parts of existence. It giveth:

(*a*) to the soul, the delight of beholding.

(*b*) to hearts, the delight of remembering.

(*c*) to *nafs*, the delight of deeds,

to such a degree that, in *nafs*, the delight of devotion prevaileth over all natural delights.

From its exceeding pureness and fineness, the essence of the cup becometh in the colour of this wine so effaced that discrimination remaineth not and the form of unity appeareth.

Love effaceth all existence, on the condition that it be established in the *ḥāl* it giveth its own colour; and, like lightnings and flashings, becometh not quickly extinguished.

Junaid saith: "Love signifieth the entering into the qualities of the beloved in exchange for the qualities of the lover."

Maḥabbat is verily a link of the links of concord that bindeth the lover to the beloved; is an attraction of the attractions of the beloved, that draweth to himself the lover, and (to the degree that him to himself it draweth) effaceth something of his existence,—so that, first, from him it seizeth all his qualities; and then snatcheth, into the grasp of *qudrat* (God), his *dhāt*.

In exchange, the attraction of love giveth him a *dhāt* that is worthy of the description of its own qualities; and after that, his qualities (the enterer of that *dhāt*), become changed.

Junaid said: "In the exchange." He said not: "In the lover."

For as long as the lover existeth,—not fit to be described with the qualities of the beloved is his *dhāt*.

This *ḥāl* is the produce of *maḥabbat* and its end. Though its cause appeareth not, its marks are many. To the truth of his *maḥabbat*:

every hair on the lover's limbs is a witness.
every motion of the lover's limbs is a mark.
every resting of the lover's limbs is a sign.

Save by the eye of *maḥabbat*, one cannot behold this. For the sake of distinguishing the sincere ones from the pretenders, we sum up the ten marks of the lover of God:

(1) In the lover's heart is no love, either for this, or for the next, world, as God revealed to 'Īsā.

Possibly, in a heart Divine love together with compassion (for the people) may be collected, and to some that compassion may show (as) love.

Its mark that it is compassion is this, that, if they leave free to choice the possessor of these two qualities (Divine love and compassion),—he abandoneth the people's side.

(2) He should not incline to any beauty that they may present to him, nor turn his glance from the beauty of the Beloveḍ (God).

Once a man met a beautiful woman, and to her revealed his love. For trying him she said: "Beside me is one who is more beautiful of face than I and more perfect in beauty. She is my sister." Back, he looked. Against him, with rebuke, the woman extended her tongue: "O boaster! when I beheld thee afar, I thought thou wast a wise man; when thou camest near, I thought thou wast a lover. Now, thou art neither a wise man nor a lover."

(3) Means of union with the Beloved, he should hold dear, and be submissive. For that love and devotion are the essence of the love and the devotion of the Beloved.

(4) If of the number of hinderers of union with the Beloved should be his son, of him he should be full of caution.

(5) Filled and inflamed with love, he should be at the mention of the Beloved, and of it never be wearied. Every time that mention occurreth, greater should be his joy and exaltation.

The mention of the Beloved, he should hold dear to such a degree that, if, in the midst thereof, he hear his own reproach, therefrom he should gain delight.

(6) In respect of orders and of prohibitions, he should preserve devotion to the Beloved; and never oppose His order.

Thus have said Rābi'ah, Shal 'Abdullah, Ravīm.

(7) In whatever he chooseth, his glance, in desire of the Beloved's consent, should be,—not in

desire of another purpose.

Thus have said Abū Bakr Kattānī, Shiblī.

(8) Much he should regard a little regard of the Beloved; his own devotion (to the Beloved) little.

Thus saith God's word and the revelation that He sent to 'Uzair.

(9) In the ray of the light-splendours of beholding the Beloved, the vision of lovers becometh dulled and dimmed wherefrom spring jealousy, passion and sweat.

If he be in the *maqām* of *tamkīn*, and have the power of devouring (suffering) *ḥāl*, and if astonishment exceed not the soul's boundary, and prevent not the heart from arranging words and deeds,—his soul in beholding is the more astonished as his heart in appearing before another is the more sensible.

If he have not the power of such *tamkīn*, and, in the power of this *ḥāl*, the thread of discrimination becometh snatched from his hand, he crieth out: "In me, increase astonishment at Thee."

(10) The beholding of the Beloved and union with Him should not diminish his *shauq*.

In his nature should be evoked a new *shauq*, astonishment, and desire—every moment in beholding; and in every breath in union with the Beloved.

As the degree of propinquity to the Beloved becometh greater, to the degree of sublimity falleth his glance; and his *shauq*, agitation and desire for union increase.

Even so endless is the Beloved's beauty; and the lover's desire, endless.

Of many marks of love, these are a few; impossible in a book is love's limitation; according to the abundance of marks in love's praise is contrariety of words. According to another description and mark, each one, according to the *ḥāl*, dcscribeth love.

SHAUQ (DESIRE)

X, 2

Shauq signifieth:

the assault of the claim of delight on account of the Beloved in the lover's heart. Its existence is the requisite of love's truth.

Abū 'Uthman Ḥā'irī saith: "*Shauq* is the fruit of *maḥabbat* (love); who loveth God, with Him desireth union."

According to love's division, *shauq* is of two kinds:

(*a*) the *shauq* of lovers of qualities the understanding through the Beloved's grace, mercy and kindness.

(*b*) the *shauq* of the lovers of *dhāt* through union with, and propinquity to, the Beloved. This *shauq* from exceeding honour is like red sulphur rare of existence. Because generally people are seekers of God's mercy, not of God Himself.

Said a man of heart (a ṣūfī): Thou seest a thousand,

'Abd-u'r-Raḥmān, the slave of the most Merciful,

'Abd-u'r-Raḥīm, the slave of the Merciful,

'Abd-u'l-Karim, the slave of the Generous One, but scarcely one 'Abdullah, the slave of God.

The seekers of (God's) mercy are many; few, the seekers of God.

To the seekers of God, Paradise is the sight of

Him even if by Fate they be in Hell: Hell, separation from Him, even if they be in Paradise.

Thus saith Bāyazīd.

The *ḥāl* of *shauq* is an excellence such that, to their purpose, it conveyeth the messengers of the ka'baḥ of desire; joined to perpetuality of love, is their perpetuality; ever as long as love remaineth is *shauq* necessary.

Some of the ṣūfīs have denied *shauq* in the stage of being present with, and of beholding, the Beloved.

This denial would have been at the time when *shauq* was special in desire of beholding (the Beloved), which is not necessary because, beyond the beholding of the Beloved to special men are other desires, (desirous whereof they are) such as—union, propinquity, and increase of their perpetuality.

Not everyone who gained a sight of the Beloved, with the Beloved attained the fortune of union: not everyone who became a joiner gained the stage of propinquity: not everyone who became near attained the limit of the degrees of propinquity: not everyone who gained that degree lasting thereon remained.

The *shauq* of these desires, according to the exaltation of its degrees, is much more difficult than the *shauq* of beholding, as some of the great ones of *ṭarīqat* have said.

In the *Ḥadīth* of Dāwūd are words the meaning whereof is the strengthener of our spirit. Because in *ḥāl* when the glance is on the Beloved, *shauq* becometh (as is evident to those present and beholding) momently greater.

Then, in connection with what shall have been

gained, love is not desirous of beholding, or of being near to the Beloved; and is desirous in connection with what shall not have been gained.

The *shauq* of beholding is (in existence) the essence of certainty; its acquisition is in this world difficult.

In some places, *shauq* is the cause of death's delay, and in some (where the desired is an order from the Beloved, whose acqusition is as life) it becometh not its cause, but the negation thereof.

In this case, life may be beloved.

The cause of death's delay is not necessary, for *shauq* is the *ḥaqq u'l-yaqīn* and *maqām* of acquisition.

Possibly the cause of that *shauq* is the beholding of one whose acquisition is in this world difficult.

The word *liqā'* (beholding) signifieth *Mushāhidah* (manifestation), *wūṣul* (acquisition).

In this place, the second meaning is appropriate.

QABD (CONTRACTION) AND BAST (EXPANSION)

X, 7

When the holy traveller of the path of *ḥaqīqat* passeth beyond the *maqām* of *maḥabbat-i-'āmm* (common love), and reacheth to the beginning of *maḥabbat-i-khāṣṣ* (special love),—he entereth the crowd of the companions of heart and of the Lords of *ḥāl*, and upon his heart descendeth the *ḥāl* of *qabḍ* and of *basṭ*.

Ever between these two states, pursuant and expectant the Turner of hearts (God) keepeth his heart, so that out from it He graspeth sensual delights, and it, with His own light, expandeth.

Sometimes in the tight grasp of *qabḍ*, God twisteth his heart so that thereform becometh expressed the refuse of the existence of delight (*ḥaẓẓ*); and the effect thereof is shown in tears.

Sometimes in the broad plain of *bast* God lowereth His rein so that he (the traveller) may establish the marks of devotion and of sincerity.

Thus have said Wāsiṭī and Nūrī.

Qabḍ signifieth :

the extracting of delight (*ḥaẓẓ*) from the heart, for the sake of holding and capturing its state of joy (*surūr*).

Basṭ signifieth :

the flashing of the heart with the splendour of the light of the state of joy.

The cause :

(*a*) of *qabḍ* is the revelation of the qualities

of *nafs* and the veiling of the splendour of joy's state. The result is the contraction of the heart.

(*b*) of *basṭ* is the uplifting of the veil of *nafs* from before the heart. The result is the expansion of the heart.

Of the qualities of *nafs* (whereof many are the veil of *basṭ*) one is *ṭughyān* (exceeding iniquity).

In the state of the descending of joy, the heart listeneth to *nafs*; becometh admonished of its state; through joy cometh into exaltation; and through its motion becometh raised a great darkness like to a cloud, layer on layer, wherefrom springeth *qabḍ*.

To repel this calamity, the heart should at the time of the descending of joy, before listening to *nafs* take shelter in God; with truth and penitence, repent, so that He may lower between it and *nafs* the veil of purity, and preserve it from attachment to *nafs* and to *ṭughyān*.

Sometimes to "the first ones," appear in *nafs* resemblances to:

qabḍ (contraction)	grief.
basṭ (expansion)	joy.

On experiencing either grief or joy, they think that they experience either *qabḍ* or *basṭ*, and, thus, fall into error.

The end of *qabḍ* is *basṭ*; the end of *basṭ* is *fanā'*; in fanā', *qabḍ* and *basṭ* are impossible.

Since *qabḍ* and *basṭ* are of the crowd of *aḥwāl*:

(*a*) in them, "the first ones" share not.

(*b*) from them, "the last ones" having issued from the sway of occupations have turned.

(*c*) them, "the middle ones" have as their *ḥāl*.

In the place of *qabḍ* and of *basṭ*:

(*a*) "the first ones" have *khauf* (fear of God), and *rijā'* (hope in God).

(*b*) "the last ones" have *fanā'* (effacement) and *baqā'* (permanency).

Partners between "the first ones" and "the middle ones" are:

(*a*) fear and hope according to faith.

(*b*) grief and joy according to nature.

"The last ones" by putting off the garment of existence have neither *qabḍ* nor *basṭ*, neither fear nor hope, neither grief nor joy—except when to the heart's stage shall have reached their *nafs*; and to it (*nafs*) become revealed the qualities of the heart; and grief and joy become changed to *qabḍ* and *basṭ*, and thereby *qabḍ* and *basṭ* become left in their *nafs* and are never removed.

FANĀ' (EFFACEMENT) AND BAQĀ' (PERMANENCY)

X, 8

Fanā'[1] signifieth the end of travelling to God.

Baqā' signifieth the beginning of travelling in God.

Travelling to God (*fanā'*) endeth when, with the foot of sincerity, the holy traveller travelleth the desert of existence.

Travelling in God (*baqā'*) becometh verified when, after absolute *fanā'*, they give to the slave an existence purified from the pollution of impurities, so that, in the world of description (the material world), he advanceth in Divine qualities.

In the description of *fanā'* and *baqā'*, the contrarieties of the words of *shaikhs* agree with the contrarieties of *ḥāl* of the holy traveller.

According to his understanding and the amend-

1. *Fanā'* signifieth:

(*a*) The death of passion, of self-will, of self-consciousness, producing the spiritual resurrection to eternal life (*baqā'*).

(*b*) The thinking away of self; the emerging from self that veileth man's real essence (God) (Lahījī in *Gulshan-i-Rāz*).

(*c*) The prayer of rapture, wherein man is effaced from self, so that he is not conscious of his body, nor of things outward and inwatd. From these, he is rapt,—journeying first to his Lord and then in his Lord.

If it occur to him that he is effaced from self, it is a defect. The highest state is to be effaced from effacement (Imām Ghazālī in *Gulshan-i-Rāz*).

(*d*) The proximity to the light of lights wherein the flame of eternal love burneth, ere it transformeth; consuming self, ere it quickeneth the lover wlth the embrace of union (*Gulshan-i-Raz*, l. 120).

ing of his *ḥāl*, the *shaikhs* have answered each *murīd*, absolute *fanā'* and *baqā'*, they have less explained.

Some have said:

Fanā' signifieth:	*Baqā'* signifieth:	The sense is a requisite:
(*a*) the *fanā'* of contrarieties.	the *baqā'* of concordances.	of the *maqām* of penitence of *Nasūḥ*.
(*b*) the decline of worldly delights.	the permanency of pleasure in the next world.	of the *maqām* of *Zuhd* (austerity).
(*c*) the decline of delights of this and of the next world.	the permanency of delight in God.	of the sincerity of natural love.
(*d*) the decline of blameable qualities.	the permanency of laudable qualities.	of the purifying and of the glorifying of *nafs*.
(*e*) the concealment of things.	the presence of God.	of the intoxication of *ḥāl*.

Fanā' is of two kinds: outward and inward.

(*a*) *Outward* fanā'. This is the *fanā'* of deeds and is the glory of Divine deeds. The possessor of this *fanā'* becometh so immersed in Divine deeds that, neither on the part of himself nor on the part of others, seeth he deed, or desire, or will—save the deed, the desire and the will of God.

In himself, no will for any deed remaineth; he plungeth into no work; and, from the free manifestation of Divine deeds without the pollution of deeds of other than God, gaineth delight.

Some holy travellers have remained in this *maqām*, wherein they have neither eaten nor drunk, till God hath appointed over them one who (with eatables, potables, and other things) might support them.

(*b*) *Inward* fanā'. This is the *fanā'* of qualities and of *dhāt*. The possessor of this *ḥāl* in the revelation of the qualities of the Ancient One is immersed sometimes in the *fanā'* of his own qualities; and, sometimes, in the manifestation of the effects and of the grandeur of the Ancient One.

Immersed in the *fanā'* of the *dhāt* of the Ancient One, he is immersed in the *fanā'* of the *dhāt* of *Wujūd* (the Absolute Existence, God)—until that time when, over him prevaileth the existence of God when his heart becometh cleansed of all temptations and thoughts.

God knoweth that, in connection with that one who shall not yet have passed the stage of *fanā'*, his *baqā'* is *shirk* (infidelity); and not *shirk* in connection with that one who, after *fanā'*, shall have reached *baqā'*.

In this *maqām*, the being hidden from feeling (being unconscious) is not a requisite. To some, it may chance; to others, not. The cause of his not being hidden from feeling is his amplitude of prayer, and capaciousness of mind.

Therein is contained *fanā'*. The presence of his inward (the heart) is immersed in the abyss of *fanā'*: the presence of his outward (the body) is present in what goeth forth from words and deeds.

This may be at a time when he shall have found dwelling in the *maqām* of manifestation of *dhāt* and of qualities; and shall have come from the inebriety of the *ḥāl* of *fanā'* to sobriety. He who is in the beginning of this *ḥāl*, him, concealeth from feeling the intoxiçation (of *fanā'*).

Muslim b. Yasār was in prayer in the *masjid* of Biṣra, when suddenly one of its columns fell. Of the circumstance, all the people of the bāzār knew, yet he in the *masjid* felt it not.

The *baqā'* that is in support of outward *fanā'* is this:

After *fanā'* of desire and of will, God maketh the slave master of desire and of will and in absolute sway of the rein (of guidance). Whatever he desireth, he doeth with the will and the desire of God. Even so the giver up of absolute will is in the degree of the degrees of *fanā'*; the giver up of will wholly in affairs (until he is allowed) and partly in them (until he first returneth in heart to God) is in the degree of the *maqām* of *fanā'*.

The *baqā'* that is in support of inward *fanā'* is this:

The *dhāt* and the qualities of *fanā'* become evoked from the bond of violence in the assembly place of manifestation in the garb of remaining existence; and from before it, the veil wholly riseth (and departeth).

Becometh neither God the veil of creation; nor creation, the veil of God. To the possessor of *fanā'*, God is the veil of creation,—as to those who have not reached the stage of *fanā'*, creation is the veil of God.

After *fanā'*, the possessor of *baqā'* beholdeth each veil in its own *maqām*, without one (the veil of the Creator) being the veil of the other (the created).

In him are collected and included the possessor of *fanā'* and of *baqā'*. In *fanā'*, he is *bāqī* (lasting); in *baqā'*, *fānī* (effacing).

Outward *fanā'* is the portion of the Lords of heart and of the Companions of *ḥāl*.

Inward *fanā'* is special to the noble ones, who may have become free from the intoxication of the sway of *ḥāl* have issued from beneath the veil of the heart; and, from the society of the heart, have joined the society of the converter of hearts (God).

THE AURĀD (PRAYERS)

VII, 7

Before the crepuscule, the seeker should have completed his ablution, and should be sitting before the *qiblah* in expectation of the prayer of morn.

When he heareth the cry of prayer, he should answer the *mu'adhdhin*,—whatever he saith, he should repeat except in:

(*a*) ḥayyi alā'-ṣ-ṣalāt, rise to prayer,

(*b*) ḥayyi alā'-l-falāḥ, rise to goodness,

when he should say: "There is no power nor virtue but in God the Great, the Mighty!"

In every *adhān*, he should observe this rule; in the morning *adhān*, he should generally say:

O God! this is the face of Thy day, the back of Thy night, and the sound of Thy prayer.

O Merciful of the merciful! through Thy mercy, me forgive, and my parents, and all the faithful, male and female.

When the morning dawneth, he should utter the renewal of the *shahādat*:

Welcome to the two kind recording angels! God bless ye! in my record, write that I declare

that there is no god but God.
that Muḥammad is His Prophet.
that Paradise is true.
that the fire (of Hell) is true.
that *ṣirāṭ* (the bridge) is true.
that the question (in the grave) is true.
that the balance is true.
that the account is true.

that the punishment is true.

that the book (of record) is true.

that the intercession (of Muḥammad) is true.

I declare that, in the hour given, God will cause (the dead) to rise from the grave.

O God! to Thee, I entrust this declaration for the day of my need. O God! for its sake,—stop my sin; forgive my sin; make heavy my balance; make me deserving of safety; and forgive me my faults through Thy mercy, O Merciful of the merciful!

Then he should perform two rak'ats of the prayer of the *sunnat*[1] of the crupescule

with Sūrat-u'l-Kāfirūn, chapter 109.

with Sūrat-u'l-Ikhlāṣ, chapter 112.

Several times he should repeat:

the Kalimah-i-tasbīḥ,

the Kalimah-i-istighfār,

and should say: "I ask pardon of God for my sin; to God, be glory by the praise of my God."

For the *masjid*-prayer, he should resolve to go to the *masjid*. On going out from his house, he should say: "O God! by the true ingress, make me enter; by the true egress, make me pass out."

On the way to *masjid*, he should utter this prayer:

By the incliners to Thee, by the beggars towards Thee, by this my going and coming out to Thee,—I pray to Thee, O God!

With evil and hypocrisy, I have not issued. To avoid Thy curse and to meet Thy blessing, have I come out. To save me from hell-fire and to forgive me my sin,—I pray to Thee, for none save Thou forgivest sins.

1. There are three kinds of prayer:
   wājib, necessary prayer (five).
   sunnat, prescribed prayer.
   nafl, voluntary prayer.

On going into the *masjid* and planting his foot on the prayer-mat, he should advance his right foot and say:

In the name of God, to God be praise! peace and blessing on the Prophet of God! O God, me forgive and open me the door of mercy.

When he performeth the enjoined observances in the *masjid* and giveth the salutation,[2] he should say ten times:

There is no god but God, the One, with Whom is no partner. Dominion, His; praise, His; life, He giveth and taketh; and is ever living without death. In His hand, is good; over all kings, He is powerful.

Then he should say:

There is no god but God, the One. Sincerity is His promise; victory, His slave; popular, His army. There is no god but God, the master of grace. To Him, be praise. There is no god but God, save Him, we worship none. Who have faith in Him are saved.

Then he should utter the ninety-nine names[3] of God; and say:

O God! bless Muḥammad, Thy slave, news-bringer, prophet, the illiterate but truthful messenger; and this descendant of Muḥammad with blessing such as is Thy will. Give him the means and the blessed degree[4] that Thou promisedest.

Bless his brethern the prophets, the true ones, the martyrs, the pious ones.

O God! to the day of faith (the judgment-day) our chief

2. *Salām* signifies "Peace (be) on thee, O Prophet, and the mercy of God and His blessing; peace on us and the devout slaves of God; peace on you and the mercy of God and His blessing!" Every prayer must conclude with this salutation.

3. See Brown's *Darvishes*, p. 116.

4. The degree is the *maqām al-Maḥmūd*.

Muḥammad bless—

among the ancient ones,
among the last generations,
among those in lofty regions.

O God! bless the soul of Muḥammad among the souls; his body among the bodies; and bestow all the excellences of the blessings of Thy mercy.

His two hands, he uplifteth, and the above traditional prayer of the Prophet (in *dhikr* whereof, after this a single section[5] will pass) he uttereth as he wisheth.

The Lords of deeds and the companions of stages have cherished this time; on its preservation, established the base of the structure of times and of hours; and in this rule:

by negation of lusts,
by abandoning words,
by assiduity in *dhikr*,
by reading without defect,
by attendance before the *qiblah*,

have ordered seekers and ṣūfis.

When, by anticipation, he shall have perferred a prayer, best it is that in the *masjid*, he should sit; be assiduous in *dhikr* and in reading; and utter naught till he preferreth the prayer of sunrise.

On the condition that, sitting, in that place, there shall be no thought of calamity; and that he shall be void of causes of defect of deeds and of states.

Otherwise, he should return to his dwelling and be engaged in reading till the sun ascendeth.

Of Muḥammad, the story is

5. This is given in chapter vii, section 8 of the *Miṣbāḥ*.

He who, from morning-prayer till sunrise, sitteth in *dhikr* of God is dearer to me than one who saveth four necks (lives).

He should read the following passages of the Qur'ān:

	Chapter	Verses
The Sūrat-u'l-Fātiḥah . .	1	
The Sūrat-u'l-Baqarah . .	2	1-5, 164-165, 255-257, 284-286
The Sūrat-u'l-'Imrān[6] . .	3	190-200, 18-19, 26-27
The Sūrat-u'l-Kahf[7] . .	18	107-110
The Sūrat-u'l-Ḥadīd . .	57	1-6
The Sūrat-u'l-Ḥashr . .	59	21-24

Then he should utter:

Thirty-three times the Subḥān Allāh,	glory be to God!
Thirty-three times the al-Ḥamdu Li-llāh,	praise be to God!
Thirty-three times the Allāhu Akbar,	God is great!
Once Lā ilāha ill-Allah,	there is no god but God.

His is no partner;
He is God.
He is single.
He is one.
He is divine.
He is unity.

He is immortal.
He is imperishable.
He is eternal.
He is perpetual

His is order; His is Praises; He is powerful over all.

Till near sunrise he should be assiduous:
in reading.
in praying.
in *adhkār* (*dhikrs*).

6. After this are omitted four passages not identified (see below).
7. After this are omitted three passages not identified (see below).

Verses of the Qur'ān

From	*To*
"Verily your God."	"of the benefactor."
"Verily, to you the prophet come."	the end.
"Upon God, I call."	the end.
Verily those that have faith.	the end.
and Dhu'n-Nūn.	"the best of heirs."
Praise to God.	the end.
To thy God, praise.	the end.

Then he uttereth the seven prayers, whereof the tenfold utterance is obligatory,—that is, the ten adhkār (repetitions).

				Chapter
(i)	the Surat-u'l-Fātiḥah	...	...	1
(ii)	the Surat-u'l-Falak [8]	...	...	113
(iii)	the Surat-u'l-Nās [9]	...	...	114
(iv)	the Surat-u'l-Ikhlāṣ	...	...	112
(v)	the Surat-u'l-Kāfirūn	...	...	109
(vi)	the Āyat-u'l-Kursī	...	...	2 v.255

(vii) glory to God; praise to God; no god but God; God is great; there is no power nor virtue but in God, the great, the mighty.[10]

O God! upon Muḥammad and his offspring send Thy blessing:

O God! me, forgive and my parents and all the faithful, male and female:

O God! towards me and them, do so, soon or late, in this and in the next world, as befitteth Thee; towards us, do not as befitteth us,—for Thou art the gentle Pardoner, the generous Bestower, the merciful Merciful.

This ended, he should engage:

in the *tasbīḥ*, repeating *Subḥān Allah*, glory to God,

in the *istighfār* repeating *astaghfirullāh*, I ask God to forgive me,

in the *tilāwat*, reading the Qur'ān,

till the sun riseth a spear's length. Then, in the afore-mentioned way, he performeth the prayer of sunrise.

8, 9. Together, these two are called—*ma'ūẓatain*, the two *ma'ūẓ* "shelter in God."

10. The clauses are:

1st—the *tasbīḥ*.
2nd—the *taḥmīd*.
3rd—the *taḥlīl*.
4th—the *takbīr*.
5th—the *hawla*.

If he have an important worldly matter, in it (for himself, or for his family) he engageth.

If God shall have given him the bounty of leisure, he should regard as booty the being engaged in worship of God; should without defect be assiduous in deeds and in devotion, till the time of the prayer of ḍuḥā[11] cometh, when he performeth it.

If still he have power for deeds, and no languor enter his soul,—he should be assiduous in deeds. If not, he should rest himself for a while.

Deeds are of two kinds:

(*a*) outward:

ṣalāt, prayer.
tilāwat, reading.
dhikr, repeating God's name.

(*b*) inward:

muḥādirah, being present before God.
murāqibah, fearful contemplation.
muḥāsibah, calling one's self to account.

The arranging of deeds is in this wise. As long as possible, the seeker should unite outward deeds with inward deeds; and in order advance *ṣalāt*, *tilāwat*, and *dhikr*—on the condition of the heart being present with God, and of its being in fearful contemplation.

If, through languor union with an inward deed (*muḥādirah*, *murāqibah*) be impossible, he should be content with an outward deed.

Murāqibah is that contemplative state wherein he ever regardeth God, his preserver and watcher: and this is the essence of *dhikr*.

If, in respect of *murāqiqah*, he be languid; and

11. *Duḥā* (or *chāsht*) is the middle hour between sunrise and noon.

temptations and thoughts prevail,—he should awhile rest himself in sleep so that *nafs* may rest from languor and torment; and, again, with joy may turn to deeds. Otherwise, through sorrow, *nafs*, with confused tale, entereth the heart; complaineth; prevaileth over it; and therein causeth hardness.

Before the declining of the sun (from the meridian), he should be awake for an hour, to arrange for ablution, so that at the time of noon, he may have finished his ablution; and may, engaged in *dhikr* and *tilāwat*, be sitting before the *qiblah*.

When the sun declineth from the meridian, he performeth:

four rak'ats,
one salutation,

and, thereby, becometh prepared for the prayer of ẓuhr.

After that:

he performeth the *sunnat* of ẓuhr.
he sitteth expectant of the *jamā'at*.
he engageth in *tasbīḥ*, and in *istighfār*.

It is laudable if, between an enjoined observance and the *sunnat* of the morn, he utter a prayer.

The *ṣalāt-i-ẓuhr* being ended, he uttereth:

	Chapter	
the Sūrat-ul-Fātiḥah	1	
the Āyat-ul-Kursī	2	255

the *tasbīḥ*, Glory to God.
the *taḥmīd*, Praise to God.
the *takbīr*, God is great.
the *tahlīl*, There is no god but God.

It is an excellence if, here, he should utter the

āyāt (verses) and the prayers previously mentioned after the *ṣalāt* of the morn.

Alive with holy deeds in the afore-mentioned way, he should make the time between ẓuhr (noon) and 'aṣr (afternoon).

This is for that one who hath no other occupation, and who passeth his time in devotion.

When 'aṣr cometh, he preferreth four *rak'ats* of the *sunnat*; and readeth:

	Chapter
in the 1st *rak'at* the Sūrat-u'l-Zilzāl[12]	99
in the 2nd *rak'at* the Sūrat-u'l-'Ādiyāt	100
in the 3rd *rak'at* the Sūrat-u'l-Qāri'ah	101
in the 4th *rak'at* the Sūrat-u'l-Takāthur	102

When he performeth the ordinance of 'aṣr no time remaineth for the *ṣalāt* of *nawāfil* (works of supererogation); it is the time of *dhikr* and of *tilāwat*. At this time, naught is more excellent than the society of:

a learned *zāhid*, possessed of *zuhd*, for the blessing of whose breathings he may borrow the splendours of advantages; and—in respect to abandoning the world, to perpetuity of devotion and of desire—may increase his resolution.

When he wisheth to come out from the stage he saith:

"In the name of God: what God pleaseth; God is my sufficiency; there is no power nor virtue but in God the great, the mighty. O God, towards Thee, I go out; and me, Thou makest go out."

12. The significations are:

Zilzāl	the earthquake
'Adiyāt	the war-horses that swiftly run
Qāri'ah	the striking
Takāthur	the emulous desire of multiplying

He uttereth:

	Chapter
the Surat-u'l-Fātiḥah	1
the Surat-u'l-Falak	113
the Surat-u'l-Nās	114

Between 'aṣr (afternoon) and maghrib (evening prayer) he uttereth a hundred times each of the following prayers:

(*a*) There is no god but God, Who is single, Whose partner is none; His is the dominion; His the praise; powerful is He over all things.

(*b*) the *tasbīḥ*.
the *taḥmīd*.
the *taḥlīl*.
the *takbīr*.

(*c*) Glory to God, and to Him, praise; glory to God, the mighty, and to Him, praise; I ask forgiveness of God.

(*d*) There is no god but God the ruler, the Just, the Visible.

(*e*) O God! upon Muḥammad and his offspring, send benediction.

(*f*) I ask forgiveness of God, the mighty,—save who is no God,—the Eternal, the Ancient, penitence, I offer.

(*g*) Whatever pleaseth God: there is no power but in God, the great, the mighty—save who is no god—the Eternal, the Ancient, penitence, I offer.

(*h*) Whatever pleaseth God; there is no power but in God.

Daily, once, at the beginning, and at the ending, of day, he should say:

O God, me Thou createdest, guidedest, fedest, quenchedst, causedest to die, causedest to live: Thou art my God; save Thou, none is mine; save Thou is no God; single, Thou art; no partner is Thine.

Whatever pleaseth God; there is no power save in God:
Whatever pleaseth God; from God, are all favours:

Whatever pleaseth God ; in the hand of God is all good :
Whatever pleaseth God ; save God, none wardeth off sin.

Before sunset, he must perform ablution ; and seated before the *qiblah*, be ready for the approach of night.

Till the sun setteth, he should utter :

(*a*) the seven prayers whereof the ten-fold utterance is obligatory.

(*b*) the *tasbīḥ*.

(*c*) the *istighfār*.

At sunset, in answer to the *adhān*, he uttereth :

	Chapter
the Sūrat-u'l-Shams,	91
the Sūrat-u'l-Lail,	92
the Sūrat-u'l-Falak,	113
the Sūrat-u'l-Nās,	114

O God ! the face of Thy night this is, and the back of Thy day.

Between the *adhān* (of sunset) and the *iqāmat*, as his time is little, he quickly performeth two *rak'ats* of the *sunnat*; and uttereth :

	Chapter
in the 1st *rak'at*, the Sūrat-u'l-Kāfirūn,	109
in the 2nd *rak'at*, the Sūrat-u'l-Ikhlāṣ,	112

He reneweth "the *shahādat*," and saith : "Welcome to the angels of the night ; welcome to the two kind angels."

In the *masjid*, he joineth the two 'ishā' (evening prayers) until he joineth the blessing of being in the *masjid* (*i'tikāf*) and of the union of the two 'ishā'.

If therein he see increase of safety of faith, of perfection, of sincerity, and of tranquillity,—he may go to his own corner ; and (of all the prayers which he performeth between maghrib and 'ishā') may utter:

	Chapter	
(*a*) with two rak'ats		
the Sūrat-u'l-Burūj,	85	
the Sūrat-u'l-Ṭāriq,	86	
(*b*) with one *rak'at*		
the Sūrat-u'l-Baqarah[13]	2	v. 1-16
the Sūrat-ul-Ikhlāṣ[14]	112	
(*c*) the Āyat-u'l-Kursi[15]	2	v. 255
the Sūrat-u'l-Ikhlaṣ[16]	112	

Well it is if he unite (*b*) and (*c*) with (*a*).

After performing the enjoined duty of 'ishā' and the two *rak'ats* of the *sunnat* he goeth to his dwelling or to his *khilvat*-place.

Before sitting down, he performeth four *rak'ats* with:

	Chapter
the Sūrat-u'l-Luqmān	31
the Sūrat-u'l-Yāsīn	36
the Sūrat-u'l-Dukhān	44
the Sūrat-u'l-Mulk	67

If he wish to shorten the prayer, he uttereth:

	Chapter	
the Āyat-u'l-Kursī[17]	2	v. 255
the Sūrat-u'l-Ḥadīd[18]	57	
the Sūrat-u'l-Ḥashr[19]	59	

Then he performeth eleven *rak'ats*, and uttereth

13. After the Sūrat-u'l-Baqarah cometh a passage from "Your God is God the One" to "For this tribe that hath come to reason," which passage in the Qur'ān I have been unable to identify.

14. This is to be repeated fifteen times.

15. And "The Prophet believeth."

16. To be repeated fifteen times.

17. And "The Prophet believeth."

18. The beginning.

19. The end.

the Sūrat-u'l-Ṭāriq, 86, and delayeth not, save when he is engaged in devotion of vigilance of his own *nafs*, wherein delay is excellent.

When he wisheth to sleep, he should (as to purity and to *dhikr*) be as before stated; when he awaketh and wisheth to make the *tahajjud* he maketh it standing as before stated.

Some short-sighted ones (whose vision may not have found the collyrium for the observing of the beauty of perfection of rule) may regard the repairing of times according to rules,—the portion only of *'ābids*.

They see no great need of it for the Lords of stages and for the Companions of union.

Possibly this is the mark of him who, in search of, and in love for, God, is sincere that he regardeth not much the expenditure of his own times and the being immersed in deeds and in devotion; and becometh not vexed.

For when, in respect of its Beloved, true love gaineth the opportunity of happiness and of meeting and the possibilities of the good fortune of prayer, and, in His presence, hath the power

of weeping,
of flatering,
of paying homage (with the ground kiss),
of doing service,

it recogniseth its own exceeding hope and great prosperity.

RU'YAT (BEHOLDING GOD)

I, 6

Clearly beholding God is:

(*a*) in this world, difficult, because *bāqī* is not contained in *fānī*.

(*b*) in the next world, promised to the faithful (*Muslim*) and denied to the *kāfir*.

The faithful (*Muslim*) seeth God:

(*a*) in this world, with the eye of faith and with the glance of vision.

(*b*) in the next world, with the glance of sight and of vision (as in the *Ḥadīth*).

In the matter of seeing, the purport of this resemblance is the glance of the next world with the glance of vision in this world—not the (vain) resemblance of God (possessed of glory) to the moon (void of glory), because this spectacle resembleth no other spectacle.

The truth of true faith is this:

In his own belief, the faithful reacheth to the degree of *yaqīn*, and as to this, belief is diverse.

In this world, a crowd:

(*a*) know by *'ilm-i-yaqīn*; and the promise of their *'ain-u'l-yaqīn* is in the next world.

(*b*) see with *'ain-u'l-yaqīn* and the promise of their *ḥaqq-u'l-yaqīn* is in the next world.

Hence said he what he said: "In my heart, my God, I saw."

This is faith. For Mu'ādh used to pass by the

door of the house of the *Ṣaḥābah* and used to say: "That I may have faith for an hour,—come."

When *'ain-u'l-yaqīn* reacheth to perfection, it gaineth the degree of beauty of vision wherein he seeth no increase of form as Amīr-u'l-Mū'minīn 'Alī hath related of this *maqām*: "If rent were all the veils, not at all would increase my *yaqīn*."

The error of the crowd that denied the seeing (of God) in the next world, twofold it its error:

(*a*) obligation to God's word—"Him, the eye understood not."

(*b*) the idea of the next world (founded) on this world.

As to (*a*):

Seeing is one thing (possible), understanding another (difficult). The sun's form, one can see; it, one cannot comprehend.

As to (*b*):

With seeing of this world, the seeing of the next world hath no connection.
What connection hath *fānī* with *bāqī*?

The mistake is this, that the crowd thought that even as in this world so in the next world, for seeing the five following conditions are necessary:

a side.
a description.
a quality.
an air.
a splendour-light.
a surrounding of light.

Vain imaginings, are all these fancies; and great is this error that, in respect of his own *ḥāl* and *maqām*, a person conjectureth in a degree superior thereto.

Today, the affairs of the next world gaineth that one, who, from the world and from its delights, shall wholly have turned his inclination.

He is:

(*a*) in heart, in the next world, in the hidden world, dwelling in *qudrat*.

(*b*) in body, in this world, in the world of *shahādat* and of *ḥikmat*.

This crowd performeth deeds for cash and giveth not itself to credit.

What, from beholding the promise, others have tomorrow, is for them the essence of cash today.

Despite this, for them also is a promise, which is the cash of another crowd; and for it, cash reacheth the Absolute Banker (whose promise is not the cash of another; and that is, Muhammad, whose cash is the promise of other Prophets).

The promise of saints is the cash of Prophets; the promise of the faithful (Muslim) the cash of saints.

According to his own *ḥāl*, Muḥammad hath a promised *maqām*, the signification whereof is the *Maqām-i-Maḥmūd*, the praised *maqām*.

In it, with him none hath partnership. In this sense, the signifier is the word that occurreth in invitation to faith; and thereto the speaker is the word of the Kalām-i-Majīd (the Qur'ān).

THE WITNESSING OF PROPHECY AND ITS ENDING (WITH MUHAMMAD)

I, 8

Through the witnessing by God and the proving by endless miracles, people of faith have had faith in Muḥammad's mission, and in the demand of the traditions of the Kalām-i-Majīd, by the revelation of the faith, whereby all other religious rites and orders are abrogated.

The perfection of prophecy in Muḥammad's mission placed, on the door of other prophecy, the seal of decline. After him, closed became the path of prophecy ; and all invitations (to faith).

Who from the path of following him turneth his face ; and considereth not necessary to himself the rules of his *Sharī'at*, is the friend of Shaiṭān, the enemy of the Merciful, and of the crowd of infidels.—Them, God requite !

If from the miracles [1] other than by the Prophets, something becometh apparent, it, they should call deceit, not miracle [2] (of the Prophets).

At one time when Fir'aun used to go by the Nīl-bank—as he went, the Nīl went ; as he stood, the Nīl stood.

Not of the crowd of miracles (of the Prophets) was this, though doubtless to him and to his people

1. *Khwāriq 'Ādāt.*
2. *Karāmāt.*

it appeared as the essence of power. Nay, it was Divine deceit that daily, in his own *kufr*, he might become more firm ; and, from the acceptance of faith, more astray.

Possibly, by the blessing of following Muḥammad, some of the miracles other than by the Prophets may be revealed to the *auliyā'* (saints) ; and to them they may be a blessing, whereby greater may become their *yaqīn*.

Not necessary is it that the truth of the *ḥāl* of a *walī*, or of a sincere one, should be manifested by miracles (of the Prophets). Because it is possible that the rank and the *ḥāl* of the master of miracle may be lower than the rank and the *ḥāl* of him who is not master of miracle.

By reason of the manifestation of miracle is commonly the strengthening of manifestation and the aiding of the faith of the master of miracle.

To the crowd (whose power of *yaqīn* is in perfection) is no need of the effects of *qudrat* free from *ḥikmat*.

For this reason, hath come the tale of :

karāmat, miracle (of the Prophets).

khwāriq-i-'ādat, miracle (of other than the Prophets).

On the part of the *Ṣaḥābah*, seldom ; on the part of modern *shaikhs*, often,—despite the fact that superior to their *ḥāl*, is the *ḥāl* of the *Ṣaḥābah*.

The cause is that mention whereof hath passed. Nay, in their opinion, through beholding the lights of absolute *qudrat* through *ḥikmat*, the glance of their vision is neither strange nor rare ; and, in the strengthening of their *yaqīn*, is no excess of effect.

When something became disclosed to those, for whom was no continuance of manifestation,—by it, they become impressed; and the power of their *yaqīn*, greater.

As the Prophets are special by *waḥī* (revelation), the *auliyā'* (saints) are from others of the faithful distinguished, by *ilhām-i-rabbānī* (Divine inspiration).

To them, either in *khwāb* or in wakefulness, God bestowed good inspiration; a part of the parts of prophecy is true *khwāb* (sleep, dream).

MA'RIFAT-I-DIL (DEEP KNOWLEDGE OF THE HEART)

III, 6

The *ma'rifat* (knowledge) of the qualities of the heart are difficult, and its signification abstruse by reason of the continuance of its power in the forms of *ḥāl*, and its advancement in the degrees of perfection.

Hence they call it.

qalb (the heart).

qullab (a cheat).

Since *ḥāl* is the gift of God and His gifts are boundless, endless are the power and the advance of the heart in degrees of perfection and in ascents of the beauty and of the grandeur of eternity without beginning.

Contained, in the limits of number and in the number of limit, are not its qualities and its *ḥāls*.

In limiting and numbering it, whoever spake knoweth of very truth, that the establishing of the limit of understanding and the making it dear becometh not the portion of his own capacity.

In the ocean of *ma'rifat-i-dil* thousands of divers of the seas of *ma'ārifat* have dived;—its abyss, none hath reached, or renounced its rarities and wonders.

Not everyone, who found a trace thereof, thereof news gave back to the heart. From it, to whom fell the precious jewel—it, he placed on the platter of desire.

The meaning of *dil* (the heart) is that point

wherefrom the circle of existence came, into motion and wherewith it found perfection. With it is joined the mystery of eternity without beginning; and in it, the source of sight reached the limit of vision, and therewith glorified became.

The beauty and the grandeur of the aspect of *bāqī*; the throne of the Merciful; the stage of the Qur'ān and of the *Furqān*; *Barzakh*,[1] between the being absent and the being present; *rūḥ* (the soul) and *nafs*; the seas of the country and of dominion; the observer and the observed of the king; the lover and the beloved of God; the bearer of the load and the load of the mystery of the deposit of God's grace —all are its (the heart's) qualities.

The purport of the marriage of *rūḥ* and of *nafs* (is) the result of its (the heart's) existence; and the object of the links of the country and the dominion of God (is) the reverberation-place of vision and the pasturage of beholding (Him).

Its form (is) pictured with the essence of love; and its vision, illumined with the light of beholding.

When, free from the soul, became *nafs*, on both sides love and contention appeared. From the marriage of the two loves (*rūḥ* and *nafs*), was born the heart's form; like to *Barzakh*, it intervened between the sea of *rūḥ* and the sea of *nafs*; to both inclined; and between them became the hinderer of contention.

That the heart's form appeared from love's source is proved thus:

Wherever it seeth a beauty, with it it allieth itself: wher-

1. See the Qur'ān, iii. 24; ix. 114.

ever it findeth an associate, with it, it intertwineth.

Not without a chosen one, nor a beloved, nor a heart-adorner,—ever is it. Firm is its base on love, and love's existence on it.

In their existence, the heart is like unto the throne of the Merciful. The throne is the heart of the greatest in the great world; the heart is the throne of the least in the least world (Ādam).

Included, beneath the sway of the throne's surrounding, are all hearts,—even as in the sway of the greatest *rūḥ* (God), are the parts of *rūḥ*; and, in the sway of universal *nafs*, the parts of *nafs*.

A form and a truth hath the heart ever as hath the throne. Its form is that piece of cone that, in the left side of the body, is a deposit: its truth is that Divine grace mention whereof hath been made.

Between this truth and its form, rational *nafs* and the animal *rūḥ* intervene, because the heart's truth is purely grace, and its form the essence of grossness. Between absolute grossness and grace, resemblance is in no way.

The rational *nafs* and the animal *rūḥ* (which have, each, a face to the world of grace; and a face to the world of grossness) intervene between the heart's form and its truth,—so that every trace (that may issue from the heart's truth) may first reach *nafs*; may by affinity take its aspect of grace; and may, to the animal *rūh*, convey its aspect of grossness.

Even so, by affinity, the animal *rūḥ* taketh its form of grace; intrusteth to the heart's form the aspect of grossness; and, therefrom, becometh diffused in the quarters of the body.

Even so the grace of mercy first is from God; becometh spread upon the truth of the throne; reacheth from it to all thrones; joineth by their means to the throne's form; and, hence, reacheth the quarters of the material world.

The affinity of the throne's form is to its truth. Because every bounty (whereby truth reacheth the material world) first reacheth its form, and thence penetrateth to other bodies.

So is the affinity of the heart's form to its truth.

All hearts find bounty from the throne:

(*a*) its truth from the throne's truth.

(*b*) its form from the throne's form.

At a time when, by means of prosperity, opposition as to God between the heart and the throne appeareth, nothing of creation is greater than the throne. Of its greatness God's word speaketh.

Muḥammad hath said the hearts are four:

(*i*) the heart, pure, luminous, wherein the lamp is kindled. This is the heart of the faithful *Muslim*.

(*ii*) the heart, dark, head-lowered. This is the heart of the *kāfir*.

(*iii*) the heart addicted to hesitation between *kufr* and faith. This is the heart of the hypocrite.

(*iv*) the heart, inclined, possessed of sides, whereof one side is the place of faith; and the other, of hypocrisy.

In it are the aid of faith from the holy world, and the purification like to freshness that increaseth from pure water; and in it are the aid of hypocrisy from the world of pollution, and a stain like a wound that increaseth from purulence and ichorous pus.

Whichever of these two is superior, ordereth the heart.

The source of contrariety of these four kinds of heart is the result of contention between *rūḥ* and *nafs*.

To its own world, *rūh* wisheth to draw *nafs*; and *nafs*, *rūḥ*. Ever in this contention they are. Sometimes *rūḥ* prevaileth and draweth *nafs* from the low centre to the lofty *maqām*, sometimes *nafs* prevaileth, and draweth *rūḥ* from the summit of perfection to the abyss of loss.

Ever obedient to that side that prevaileth is the heart until when dominion becometh established wholly on one. In following it, the heart accepteth contentment.

On these two attractions are established happiness and misery.

If the happiness of eternity without end and the favour of eternity without beginning arrive and give to *rūḥ* (the soul) the aid of grace, whereby it gathereth strength; conquereth *nafs*; escapeth from contention; advanceth from the descending-place of creation to the rising-place of *qidam*; and, turned wholly away from *nafs* and *qalb* (the heart), approacheth to the viewing of God—then *dil* (the heart) in its following from the *maqām* of *qalb* (the conversion whereof is necessary) ascendeth to the *maqām* of *rūḥ* and in *rūḥ's* dwelling resteth.

Then following *dil* (the heart), *nafs* issueth from its dwelling (which is the world of nature) and reacheth the *maqām* of *dil* (whose child it is).

Such is the heart of the faithful wherein is no atom of *shirk* (partnership with God) and *kufr* (infidelity).

If, otherwise, be the state and the effect of

misery and the hardness of eternity without beginning arrive and make *rūḥ* captive to *dil* and *nafs* victorious, so that it gathereth strength, and, to its own world, draweth *qalb* and *rūḥ*—*rūḥ* descendeth from its own *maqām* to the place of *qalb*; *qalb* entereth from its own *maqām* to the place of *nafs*; and, in nature's soil, firm becometh *nafs*.

Such is the heart of the *kāfir*, who is lowered of heart, black with *kufr*,— altogether seized.

If, on either side, be not total victory, the inclination of *dil* is generally :

(*a*) to *nafs*, if *nafs* be powerful and *dil* hesitating in the middle. Such is the heart of the *munāfiq* (hypocrite).

(*b*) to *rūḥ* (or to both sides), if *rūḥ* be powerful. Such a heart is inclined and hath two faces—one towards faith, the other towards hypocrisy.

MA'RIFAT-I-MURĪD VA MURĀD VA SĀLIK VA MAJDHŪB

Deep knowledge of the Murīd (*the Follower, the Lover, the Disciple*), *of the* Murād (*the Followed, the Beloved, the* Shaikh) *of the Holy Traveller, and of the Attracted One*

III, 9

Ṣūfīs assign two meanings:

to *murīd*, the follower, the lover (the disciple).
to *murād*, the followed, the beloved (the *murshid*.

The *murīd* (disciple) is called *muqtadī* (the follower) because:

the eye of his vision becometh, with the light of guidance, the seer; and gazeth at his own defect. The fire of desire of perfection kindleth in his nature; and never resteth except by the acquisition of the *murād* (the followed) and of propinquity to God.

Impressed with the travelling of the man of desire, whoever was; and, in the two worlds, hath a desire other than God, or resteth a moment from desire for the *murād*,——for him, illusory is the name of desire.

Thus say Shaikh 'Abdullah Ḥāfiẓ, Abū 'Uthmān Ḥā'irī.

The *murād* is called *muqtadā* (the followed) because:

The power of his sway (over *murids*) hath reached to the degree of perfecting imperfect ones to the diversity of ways of capacity; to the ways of directing and of instructing with the glance of the eye.

Like this is the person, or the holy traveller, (who is) the attracted one, who, with the foot of travelling, hath traversed all the deserts and the dangerous places of sensual qualities; and then, with the aid of Divine attraction, passed from the degrees of the *qalb* (heart) to the ascents of *rūḥ* (the soul); reached to the world of *kashf* (revelation) and of *yaqīn* (certainty); and is ever in beholding (God).

Or like this is the (God) attracted one (who is) the holy traveller, who first, with the power of attractions, hath traversed the plain of the *maqāms*, reached to the world of revelation and of beholding; and then, with the foot of travelling, beheld the stages and the halting-places; and found, in the form of *'ilm*, the truth of *ḥāl*.

To these two is preserved the rank of being a *shaikh*, or of being a *muqtadā'* (a followed).

Neither of the two following hath the right of the dignity of being a *shaikh*.

(*a*) The imperfect holy traveller, who from the strait place of effort to the plain of manifestation, hath not reached.

(*b*) The imperfect attracted one, who, in respect to the subtleties of holy travelling and to the truths of *maqāms*, of stages, and of dreadful places,—hath not gained knowledge.

To them becometh not committed the ruling over the capacity of the *murīd* and the instructing him in the rules of *ṭarīqat*.

For this reason, more than its good is the evil of every control that they exercise.

The exercise of the *murīd* and his capacity of perfection is like unto an egg, wherein is existent the capacity of being a bird.

If it be worthy of the power and of the impressing of the blessing and of the protection of a matured bird (wherein the vehemence of the power of begetting is overpowering),—while in the egg, the power of the spiritual life and the specialities of its perfection of flying penetrate. At last, off from itself the egg pulleth the egg-garment; putteth on the honour-robe of being a bird; and conveyeth itself to the perfection of capacity.

On the contrary, if he place the egg beneath a (young, immature) bird, that hath not the power of flying—a time lapseth, and in the egg the capacity of the existence of flying becometh corrupted. Then the egg is not worth restoring.

Even so, if—beneath the sway of a perfect *shaikh* (who shall have attained to the degree of perfecting imperfect ones; and in whom, are joined together the travelling on, and the flying on, the Path, and attraction) the sincere *murīd* make obedient his own existence—the bird of truth, "God created Ādam in His own form," issueth from the egg of his existence; flieth in the liquid air of Divine Essence; and reacheth the degree of producing.

If beneath the sway of the imperfect holy traveller, of the imperfect attracted one, the *murīd* come, corrupt in him becometh the capacity of the perfecting of humanity; and he reacheth neither to the perfection of man, nor to the stage of perfection.

Even so in the material world, the demand of

God's mature *ḥikmat* and current *sunnat* is this

that, despite the capacity for producing, appeareth not the permanency of species, except after union of the two producers with the bond of lust, by the means of the deed, active and passive; and by the impressing and the impression.

So, in the spiritual world, the mystery of the *ḥaqīqat* of man (which is purely service) cometh not into existence

except after the union of the *murīd* and of the *murād* with the bond of love; and the *murīd's* acceptance of the *murād's* sway. This is "the second birth".

Though in the *qudrat* of God, possible is the existence of the son without the father,—yet, in *ḥikmat*, it is prohibited just as is prohibited the spiritual birth without the union of the *murīd* and of the *murād*.

In *qudrat* it is possible (as is shown by the existence of some attracted ones); in *ḥikmat*, difficult.

Further, in birth without the father, calamity may be expected as in the birth of 'Īsā, who (in divinity and in humanity) became the source of error of the Christians—him they called—"the Son of God"

If an attracted one become master of revelation, not through the directing of a consummately perfect *shaikh*,—not secure are others from calamity.

In the sense of lover, *murīd* is the traveller, who is (God-)attracted. In the sense of beloved, *murād* is the (God-)attracted one, who is the traveller. Among them, restricted is the sense of *shaikh*.

Whose labour (as to revelation and manifestation) is preceding is lover; whose revelation (as to the form of effort) is preceding is beloved. In this way, the sense of *murīd* and *murād* is the essence of *murād.*

The Qur'ānic verse comprehendeth the explanation of the *ḥāl* of the lover and of the beloved.

Divine Will, not the slave's acquisition, is the cause of choice; the condition (of acceptance) of guidance is the forerunner of repentance (which is the slave's deed).

In this form, the choice is the *ḥāl* of the beloved. Only by arrangement and by degrees are the guidance of the *ḥāl* of the lover, and the travelling of lovers in the regions of *maqāms.*

Until he fulfilleth the lowest *maqām*, he reacheth not to the lofty *maqām.*

They ascend:

from the 1st to the 2nd degree.
from the 2nd to the 3rd degree.
from the 3rd to the 4th degree.

Thus, by arrangement, they travel all the *maqāms.* Then, changeth, travelling to attracting; endeth, travelling in flight; joineth, labour with manifestations; and reacheth, the being absent to beholding (God) face to face.

In this *maqām,* do they write for the lovers the mandate of *khilāfat*; give the honour of being a *shaikh*; and order power over the *murīd.*

For this degree is the middle *maqām*:

(*a*) between the hidden and the manifest.
(*b*) between God and man.

In this *maqām,* like to the throne of the merciful

is the slave's existence that hath one side towards the hidden world; and the other towards the material world.

With the former, he taketh the bounty of God's mercy from the hidden world; with the latter, he conveyeth it to the material world and to the people.

When at the beginning of *ḥāl*, beloved ones take the path by the aid of attraction they traverse the regions of *maqām* with a single attraction, and, therein, are comprehended the acquisition of all deeds of beloved ones.

Included in the purity of their *ḥāl* is the purifier of the crowd of *maqāms.*

The binding by *maqāms* is for common lovers, who have not yet reached the world of *kashf*; whose travelling is in the removing of the darkness of the qualities of *nafs*; and from whom, in every *maqām*, becometh effaced the darkness of a certain quality till that time when, by this effacing, their *nafs* gaineth, with Divine light, full refulgence.

As in *nafs* the inclination of nature is a darkness (which, in the *maqām* of sincere penitence, becometh effaced); and delight in the world is a darkness (which, in the *maqām* of austerity, becometh effaced); and poverty of trust on the surety of provision of God is a darkness (which, in the *maqām* of *riḍā'*, ariseth and departeth)—accordingly, in every *maqām*, a darkness becometh effaced till all the darknesses of *nafs* (by the travelling of the crowd of *maqāms*) arise and depart; and from the veil of darkness becometh revealed the beauty of the face of *yaqīn*.

By reason of the preceding of revelation on the

path, when all the quarters of existence and of the interior (before the travelling of the stages of *maqāms*, of travelling, of effort) are, with the light of *yaqīn*, illumined; and cut off from them are the darknesses of the qualities of *nafs*.

In them is existing the abstract of all *maqāms*; separate from all *zāhids* they are, despite delight (in the world); reliant on God, despite attention to the chattels of the world; and contented with God, despite abhorred sins of nature. Because on God is their existence, not on themselves.

The absolute *murād* (the followed, the beloved, the *murshid*) and the absolute *maḥbūb* (beloved) is Muḥammad, the Sayyid of created beings: the purpose of creation was his existence; created beings are all his offspring.

To none save to him did they give the honour robe of being "a beloved". Even to the *tābi'īn* advance from the *maqām* of being a lover to being a beloved is only by implicitly following Muḥammad.

Then from Muḥammad came the address in respect of Mūsā, who had the degree of being "a lover (of God)" and who wished to be "a beloved (of God)".

When 'Īsā desired this degree, at a time when He was desirous of Muhammad God kept him detained some years in the sky, till after the mission of Muḥammad, so that—

by God's order He might descend (to earth), and (by reviving the faith of Muḥammad and by following the *sunnat* of prophecy) reach the *maqām* of being "a beloved (of God)"

God, none reacheth by being a lover,—only by

being a beloved: God, none reacheth save by God.

Abū Ali Daqqāq hath said:

"As Mūsā was a murid (lover), he said: 'O God! open me my heart.'

"As Muhammad was a *murād* (beloved), to him, God said: 'Thy heart, opened We not?'"

Mūsā said: "Let me see." Came the answer—"Me, thou shalt never see." To Muhammad, God said: "At thy God, shalt thou not look? (Yea, thou shalt)."

In the attraction of truth, the similitude of the love of the Ancient One (God) is Muhammad—even as, in the attraction of iron is the quality of the magnet.

As the magnet giveth its own quality (the attraction of iron) to its own attracted and beloved one, so that it can attract another (piece of) iron—so, in its own attracted one, the speciality of every attracter permeateth.

From the magnet of love for the Ancient One (God), the *rūḥ* (soul) of Muhammad (which is the first attracted and beloved one) acquired the speciality of the attraction of the souls of the faithful (Muslims).

From the quarters and regions of the world, to himself Muhammad drew thousands of souls of the *Ṣaḥābah*, each one of whom found a portion of that speciality suitable to his capacity.

To himself, he drew the souls of the *tābi'īn*.

So, œon after œon, womb after womb, from the souls of the *tābi'īn* to the souls of the *shaikhs* and of the firm *'ulamā'*,—that speciality became transported; of the *murīd* to the *murād*, the chain (of attachment) became arranged; and every *murīd*, a *murād* became.

Such is the effect of following Muḥammad.

By perfection of following and by the link of union with the souls of *shaikhs*, whoever gained union with the soul of Muḥammad—in him appeared love for God, and the degree of being a beloved (of God) and of being a *murād*.

For, according to arrangement, the souls of *shaikhs* are united with the soul of Muḥammad; thereby, in all permeate—love, following (the followed), and love for God.

The *murīd*, whose soul with the soul of the consummately perfect *shaikh* (who shall have slipped out from his own desire, and gained from another *shaikh*, the heritage of love for God) uniteth not,—never reacheth the degree of being a beloved (of God), nor gaineth the *maqām* of sway over another (the *murīd*).

I'TIQĀD (BELIEF), THE PLACE WHENCE IT IS TAKEN, AND THE BINDING OF ONE'S SELF TO THE TRUE FAITH

I, 1

The words *i'tiqād* and *ittiḥād* signify the binding of a form of *'ilm* in the heart of the existence of mysteries. Its place of origin, in the beginning of *ḥāl*, is the repetition of the hearing of news; and the continuance of the following of impressions as in children's pure *nafs*, which, by the passing of time, becometh the cause of iniquities of ideas and fancies; of the following of the people's faith.

In their mind, the form of those beliefs becometh, like the (imperishable) sculpture on stone,—firm to such a degree that, in it, the power of another form appeareth impossible.

Whom, they see declining from the *sunnat* of their own faith, and the good of the religious order, they charge with perversion and error.

Of them is a crowd that hath, according to its own idea, held to the arguments of its own religion, and of itself imagined the verifying of, and the expelling (of deniers) from, its own circle of following.

If verily they look, they see themselves even so in the degree of following their own *Imāms* and *'Ulamā'*, from whom by reason of good opinion (and by the fancy of goodness of that opinion), they may have accepted arguments; from whom fancies and understandings may have issued; and with whom the thought of *yaqīn* and by the abundance of verification, they may have become pleased.

By reason of diversity of opinion is the contrariety of desires, wherein human *nafs* is innate, and the existence of disputing and of forbidding worldly positions and demands (by the disease of seeking which, hearts are commonly distressed).

From the ancient to modern ones hath arrived this contrariety in the happy state.

Gradually, in the midst, the parties became diffused and dispersed; drew to enmity and hate; and it, by way of heritage from ancestors, descendants have taken.

Œon after œon become pressed together its darkness (of hate), till it reached the limit of enmity, and ended in execration and *kufr*.

Then wherever the past favour of eternity without beginning joineth, and wisheth to bestow faith upon the slave

it releaseth him first from effects; customs and manners; conveyeth him to the purity of the first creation; teareth up from his heart the root of obstinacy and of desire; till he becometh worthy of the form of true faith; and clear to him becometh the manifestation of the pure God.

In the time of the society of Muḥammad, by the blessing of the effects of descent of *vaḥī* (revelation), and of the ray of light of prophecy the *nafs* of the people had become eradicated from the darkness of customs; and hearts, purified from the pollution of nature and from the impurity of desire, turned away from this world, turned to the next world; seekers of God, with the light of faith,—had beheld through the veil the form of the hidden.

Therefore free was their belief from the reproach of contrariety, and their heart, from the ills of desire.

One of heart, of opinion, of tongue were all.

When the sun of prophecy became veiled in the veil of the hidden; and the light of purity, concealed in the veil of grandeur,—the darkness of the land of *nafs* of the people (who, by the light of prophecy, had gained effulgence) became effaced in its light.

By the sun's being veiled and hidden, it again cast its shadow; and, little by little, forth from the concealed ambush, came the darkness of its desire.

Hearts turned their face from the moderation of steadfastness to turning aside; contrariety, to the degree of turning wholly away, appeared; and open to shaiṭān, became the path of sway.

According to the distance from the time of prophecy and of being veiled, the light of innocence daily became greater through the darkness of the descendings of *nafs* in the world; and contrariety commonly appeared.

Who is the seeker of the true faith should follow the first crowd of the "Companions"; should turn his heart from love for the world, so that, by the light of *yaqīn*, the eye of his vision may be opened; and to him may be discovered the pure God.

This appeareth only—

- by true purity.
- by excellent refuge in the giver.
- by the complaining of the evil of *nafs*.
- by keeping one's self pure of sin by God's grace.

For, the associate of answer, God maketh every

question that is through sincerity and perturbation.

To whom God gave the favour of change of desire away from the world, the root of contention He plucked up from his heart and made it the glancing place of His mercy.

Its mark is this:

By the glance of mercy, he becometh not joined with the veiled ones; nor with them treadeth the path of contention.

This is of the specialities of the ṣūfīs, whose hearts have wholly turned to the ecstasy of the sweetness of love (for God) away from the love for the world; whose veins of contention have become extirpated; and who, with the glance of mercy, have gazed at the commonality of the people, gained safety from enmity, and who are entitled—firqah-i-nājiyah.[1]

1. This is the name of an Arab tribe.

‘ILM-I-FARĪḌAH (THE KNOWLEDGE OF GOD’S ORDINANCE)

II, 3

That *‘ilm* the desire whereof is for all Muslims an ordinance of God, is, in the opinion of the *‘ulamā’*, contradictory.

Some have said it is :

(*a*) the *‘ilm-i-ikhlāṣ* (sincerity), because even as devotion to God is God’s ordinance, so sincerity in devotion is also God’s ordinance; as for *‘ilm* practice is necessary, so practice is necessary for the *‘ilm-i-ikhlāṣ*.

(*b*) the *‘ilm-i-āfāt-i-ikhlāṣ* (the calamities of sincerity); or the quality of *nafs*, the revelation whereof is the power of *ikhlāṣ*. Then the *‘ilm-i-ikhlāṣ* is dependent on the *‘ilm* of the qualities of *nafs*. Dependent on it whatever may be a necessity is on it also necessary.

(*c*) the *‘ilm-i-waqt* (period), or the knowing in what thing (deeds or words) it is best to be daily engaged.

(*d*) the *‘ilm-i-ḥāl* (mystic state), or the knowing the *ḥāl* (that may be between the slave and the Lord God), and the rule which is special to that *ḥāl*, and the learning its excess (or defect) at any period.

(*e*) the *‘ilm-i-khawāṭir* (thoughts); attached thereto is the distinguishing between the sources of the acts of thoughts and the goodness and evilness of acts.

All this is *faḍīlat* (excellence), not *farīḍah* (God’s ordinance).

Not lawful is the abandoning of *farīḍah*. If *‘ilm-i-farīḍah* be one of those *‘ilms*, not lawful to Muslims is its abandoning.

What Muḥammad hath said is enjoined to all Muslims; the knowing of it is to all Muslims impossible.

Not every nature can be prepared for these *'ilms*; not lawful is unbearable trouble.

Most true is the *qaul* (word) of those of former times.

The *qaul* of Shaikh Abū Ṭālib Makkī is:

> It is the *'ilm* of the source of Islam, or the five columns:
> (*i*) the *kalimah-i-shahādatain*, the two creeds.
> (*ii*) the *ṣalāt*, prayer.
> (*iii*) the *zakāt*, alms.
> (*iv*) the *ṣaum*, fasting.
> (*v*) the *ḥajj*, pilgrimage.
> It is the *'ilm-i-bay'* (purchase).
> It is the *sharā* (sale).
> It is the *ṭalāq* (divorce).
> It is the *nikāḥ* (marriage).
> Enjoined on high and low is the knowing of these; for the understanding of them is, for all reasonable men, possible.

The (totality of all *qauls* is the) *qaul* of Shaikh Shahāb-u'd-Dīn 'Umar Sahrawardī: "It is the *'ilm-i-mutafarraḍ* (the enjoined *'ilm*); or the *'ilm* of orders and of prohibitions (of God)."

Because though the slave is ordered as to doing, and prohibited against abandoning, them,—incumbent on him is their *'ilm*, so that the practice of them may be established.

The rules of the *Shar'*, as regards orders and prohibitions, are of two kinds:

> (*a*) the comprehender of the chosen common people,
> the *'ilm-i-mubānī-Islām*
> the *'ilm-i-bay'*

the *'ilm-i- sharā*
the *'ilm-i-nikāḥ*
the *'ilm-i ṭalāqat*

which are incumbent on all Muslims by reason of :

requisites,
necessity,
need.

(*b*) the *'ulūm-i-faḍā'il* (excellences) :
the *'ilm-i-ikhlāṣ* (sincerity)
the *'ilm-i-khwāṭir* (thoughts)
the *'ilm-i-ḥāl* (state)

and other *'ilms* already mentioned.

These are enjoined on some special folk, who have the capacity and the power of knowing them; and not enjoined on common folk who have not the power.

For some special ones, whose capacity is fit, these *'ilms* are of the number of God's ordinances By them, they are ordered and prohibited.

Some of the *Ṣaḥābah* have grieved and said :

"We have the power not to bring into action impure thoughts; impure thoughts, we have not the power to prevent. If as regards them, go a reckoning and a requital, difficult is the work."

Came this *āyat* : "Save to its limit, *nafs*, God troubleth not."

Whoever cannot perform the ordinance is by it not ordered; and for the abandoning of it not reproved.

Whoever can restrain impure thoughts,—on him, is enjoined the ordinance.

The *shaikhs*, who have made *yaqīn* of something and reckoned it God's ordinance, have spoken according to their own state.

This limit is the comprehender. Those *'ilms,* which others have mentioned; and according to their own *ḥāl,* reckoned God's ordinance, they have called:

the *''ilm-i-dirāsat* (teaching).

the *'ilm-i-wirāthat* (heritage).

THE ḤAL OF MAN

III, 10

According to diversity of degrees, the ranks of men are of three kinds:

(*i*) The *wāṣil* (those joined to God) and the *kāmil* (the perfect. The *wāṣil* are the *muqarrab* (those near to God) and the *sābiq* (those gone before others in faith) (The Qur'ān, lvi. 10-11).

(*ii*) The *sālik* holy travellers of *ṭarīq* (the path) of perfection. These are the pious; the *aṣḥāb-i-yamīn* (companions of the right hand) (The Qur'ān, lvi. 8).

(*iii*) The *muqīm* dwellers of the essence of defect. These are the wicked; the *aṣḥāb-i-shumāl* (the companions of the left hand) (The Qur'ān. lvi. 9).

The men of *wuṣūl* (union with God) are of three crowds:

(*a*) The *anbiyā'*, prophets, whom, after union and perfection, God sent to the people for the sake of perfecting the imperfect ones; and whose existence He made the link of the hidden and the material world to invite people to Him, and to keep prosperous the realms of God and of the angels.

(*b*) The *mutaṣawwifah, shaikhs*, who, by perfection of following Muḥammad, have gained union (with God); and who were, after that, ordered to invite the people by the *ṭarīq* of following Muḥammad.

Consummately perfect are these two crowds, to whom, after their being immersed in the essence of *jam'* (collected), and in the abyss of *tauḥīd* (unity of God), the grace of eternity without beginning bestowed freedom and salvation from the belly of the fish of *fanā'* (effacement) to the shore of *tafraqah* (dispersed) and to the plain of *baqā'* (permanency), —so that, to salvation and to degrees, they might guide the people.

(c) The *jamā'at* (crowd), to whom, after arrival at the degree of perfection, the trust of perfecting (the imperfect ones) in reference to inviting the people (to Islam) passed not; who became immersed in the sea of *jam'* (collected) and in the belly of the fish of *fanā'* (effacement), who became naught so that neither news nor trace of them reached to the shore of *tafraqah* or to the region of *baqā'*; who became threaded on the thread of the dwellers of the towers of *ghairat* (jealousy), and of the inhabitants of the land of *ḥairat* (astonishment); and to whom after perfection of union the power of perfecting the imperfect ones was not entrusted.

The men of *sulūk* (the path of travelling) are of two kinds: (*a*) the seekers of lofty purpose, and the *murīds* of the face of God; (*b*) the seekers of Paradise, and the *murīds* of the next world.

The seekers of God are:

(*a*) *The* Mutaṣawwifah. These are that crowd that have gained freedom from some of the qualities of *nafs*; become qualified with some of the *ḥāls* and some of the qualities of the ṣūfis; and become the beholder of the excess of their *ḥāl*.

Yet with the proud trailing residue of the qualities of *nafs* are they left distressed, and therefore deprived of the acquisition of the end of the man of propinquity to God and of *ṣūfiyā'* (ṣūfism).

(*b*) *The* Malāmatiyah, *the reproached*. These are that crowd who, in the observance of the meaning of *ikhlāṣ* (sincerity) and in the preservation of the rule of *ṣidq* (truth), have expended much effort; who in the concealing of their devotion and in the veiling of their almsgiving from the people's glance regard necessary great effort; who neglect not the minutest matter of holy deeds; who regard an enjoined duty all the excellences and the *nawāfil*; whose religious order is at all times the verifier of the sense of *ikhlāṣ*; and whose taste is for the singularity of God's glance upon their deeds and *ḥāls*.

As the sinner is full of caution, as to revealing his sins, so (lest there be suspicion of hypocrisy) as to revealing their devotion, do they practise hypocrisy that the order of *ikhlāṣ* may suffer no injury.

Although they are precious of *wujūd* and exalted of *ḥāl*, yet from their glance not wholly rent is the veil of creation. Therefore are they left veiled from beholding the beauty of *tauḥīd* (the unity of God) and the essence of *tafrīd* (inward solitude), because the concealing of deeds and of their *ḥāl* from the people's glance is known and allowed in the sight of the people and of themselves, who are the forbidders of the sense of *tauḥīd*.

Nafs is of the crowd of strangers. As long as on their own *ḥāl*, they keep their glance, not wholly have they expelled strangers, from the viewing of their own deeds and *ḥāls*.

The difference between the Mutaṣawwifah or *Ṣūfiyā'* and the Malāmatiyah is this :

From the Malāmatiyah, the attraction of the grace of the Ancient One hath wholly uptorn the existence of *Ṣūfiyā'*; and from the glance of their witnessing uplifted the veil of creation and of egotism.

In making their devotion, in issuing their alms, the Malāmatiyah see not in the midst themselves and the people. They are secure from the knowledge of the people's glance; and bound to the concealing neither of their deeds nor of their *ḥāl*.

If good they see in revealing their devotion, they reveal it; otherwise, they conceal it.

The Mutaṣawwifah or *ṣūfiyā'* are *mukhlas* saved. The Malāmatiyah are *mukhliṣ*, sincere.

The description of their *ḥāl* is : "Them, by sincerity, We (God) saved."

The seekers of the next world are four crowds:

zuhhād (sing. *zāhid*), *zāhids*, dry austere men.
fuqarā' (sing. *faqīr*), *faqīrs*.
khuddām (sing. *khādim*), servants of God.

'ubbād (sing. *'ābid*), those dedicated to God.

The *zuhhād* are those who with the light of faith and of certainty behold the beauty of the next world; clearly see this world in the form of ugliness; turn their desire from inclining to the worthless decoration of the *fānī* (perishable); and incline to the true beauty of the *bāqī* (imperishable).

Against the *ṣūfiyā'*, the opposing of this crowd is

because the *zāhid* is, by the delight of his own *nafs*, veiled from God; and because Paradise is the *maqām* of delight of *nafs*.

By beholding the beauty of eternity without beginning and the love of eternal *dhāt*, the ṣūfī is veiled from both worlds.

As in respect to this world, he may have expended delight, so in respect to the next world, is his delight.

The *Ḥadīth* saith:

"Unlawful for the people (of the next world) is this world; unlawful for the people (of this world) is the next world; unlawful for the people (of God) ars both worlds."

In the degree of *zuhd* (austerity) is the ṣūfī above the degree of the *zāhid* far wherefrom is the delight of *nafs*.

The *fuqarā'* are those who possess naught of the chattels of the world; who, in desire of excellence and of the Divine *Riḍvān* (God), have separated from their native land; and who have abandoned accustomed objects.

The cause is one of the following three things:

(*i*) The hope of lessening the fearful reckoning of punishment (on the Day of Judgment). For necessary is the reckoning as regards lawful deeds; and, punishment as regards unlawful deeds.

(*ii*) The hope of excellence of reward and of excelling on entering Paradise. Glad tidings, brought Jibrā'īl one day to Muḥammad: "By half a day (equal to five hundred years) will the *faqīrs* of thy *ummat* (tribe) enter Paradise before the rich of thy tribe."

(*iii*) The desire of tranquillity of heart, and of freedom of mind—for the sake of much devotion; and therein the presence of the heart.

Against the Malāmatiyah and the Mutaṣawwifah, the opposing of the *faqīr* is:

because the *faqīr* is the seeker of Paradise and is desirous of his own delight. They (the Malāmatiyah and the Mutaṣawwifah) are the seekers of God and desirous of propinquity to Him.

Above this degree in *faqr* is a *maqām* superior to the *maqām* of the Malāmatiyah and of the Mutaṣawwifah.

'Tis the special description of the ṣūfī. Though the degree is above the degree of the *faqīr*, yet the abstract of the *maqām* of *faqr* is included in his *maqām*. The cause is that, for the ṣūfī, the traversing of the *maqām* of *faqr* is of the crowd of enjoined conditions; every *maqām*, wherefrom he advanceth, its purity he rendeth and thereto giveth the colour of his own *maqām*.

In the *maqām* of the ṣūfī is another description for the *faqīr*:

On his part, the denial and the absence of possession, of all deeds, *ḥāls*, and *maqāms*.

On his part, he beholdeth no deed, no *ḥāl*, no *maqām*; and regardeth them not special to himself. Nay, himself of himself he seeth not.

Then his, is

no *wujūd* (existence).
no *dhāt* (essence).
no quality.

He is *mahv* in *mahv* (obliteration in obliteration);

fanā' in *fanā'* (effacement in effacement).

Such is the truth of *faqr*, in excellence whereof the *shaikhs* have spoken. What, in the sense of *faqr*, before this has been mentioned,—is the impression and form of *faqr*.

The superiority of the *maqām* of the ṣūfī above the *maqām* of the *faqīr* is because

the *faqīr* is ruled by the desire of *faqr* and of the delight of *nafs*. The ṣūfī hath no special desire; in *faqr* or in wealth, effaced is his desire in the desire of God—his desire is the essence of the desire of God.

If he choose the form of *faqr* and its way, it becometh not veiled by his own desire and choice; his desire is the desire of God.

Some have said: "Who is void of impression and of quality is the ṣūfī: who is void of things material is the *faqīr*."

Abu'al-'Abbās Nihāvandī saith: "The end of *faqr* is the beginning of *taṣawwuf*."

Some of the *shaikhs* have said:

As cautions of wealth, should be the *faqīr* as the wealthy one of *faqr*.

By the entrance of wealth, the *faqīr* feareth that *faqr* may become abhorrent to him; by the entrance of *faqr*, the wealthy one, that wealth may become abhorrent to him.

Once a wealthy one brought ten thousand dirhams to Ibrāhīm Adham and asked him to accept them. Ibrāhīm refused, saying: "With ten thousand dirhams, thou wishest to efface, from the record-book of *fuqarā'*, our name."

Between *faqr* (poverty) and *zuhd* (austerity), the difference is this:

Possible without *zuhd* is *faqr*. Thus, with firm

resolution a person abandoneth the world through the desire of *yaqīn*; yet in him is left the heart's delight.

Possible without *faqr* is *zuhd*. Thus is a person possessed of chattels, wherefrom his delight is turned.

Faqr hath a custom,—the want of property. Its truth is the expelling of qualities from orders; and the denying to one's self the choice of a thing.

Faqr is the form of *zuhd* and its sign. The meaning of *zuhd* is the expending of desire (for God) away from the world.

When, beneath the towers of pomp, God wisheth to veil, from the glance of strangers, some of His saints, He outwardly clotheth them with the garment of the wealthy one (which is the form of desire), so that them, the outward people may regard as of the crowd of desirous ones of this world; and thus, from the glance of the unprivileged, the beauty of their *ḥāl* may be concealed.

The kernel of the *ḥaqīqat* of *faqr* and of *zuhd* is the special description and requisite of the *ḥāl* of the ṣūfī. The custom of *faqr* is the choice of some of the *shaikhs* of the ṣūfīs; and in it, their purpose is—the following of the Prophets, the abandoning of the world, the inciting and the inviting of seekers with the form of *faqr* and with the tongue of *ḥāl*.

In this sense, their choice is proved by the choice of God, not by the desire of the delight of the next world.

The *khuddām* are those who choose the service of *fuqarā'* and of the seekers of God; who, after the performance of the ordinances of God, have expended their time in ceasing to labour, and in making tranquil the heart as to solicitude for matters of livelihood and for capacity for the next world; who prefer this service to *nawāfil,* and who in their need enter on every way not forbidden by the *Shar'*—in acquisition, in beggary and in receiving gratuitous income.

In taking and giving money, their glance is on God.

In taking money, they regard the people the link of God's giving to them, and, in giving money, they regard them as the means of their acceptance (with God).

On account of the honour of this *maqām* appeared similitude in respect to the crowd of the *ḥāl* of the *khādim* and of the *shaikh.* In respect to the *khādim,* they have established no difference from the *shaikh.*

The difference is this :

The *khādim* is in the *maqām* of the *abrār* (the pious).

The *shaikh* is in the *maqām* of the *muqarrab* (those near to God).

In the choice of service, the purpose of the *khādim* is the reward of the next world; otherwise not bound by service is the *khādim.*

Standing in the purpose of God, not in his own purpose, is the *shaikh.*

The *'ubbād* are those who, ever on the portions of devotion and on the rules of *nawāfil,* display assiduity for the sake of the reward of the Nil of the next world.

Existent in the ṣūfī is this description but free from the impurities of desire. For they worship God for God, not for the reward of the next world.

Between the *'ubbād* and the *zuhhād*, the difference is this: with the existence of (despite) desire for the world the form of *'ibādat* (devotion) is possible.

Between the *'ubdād* and the *fuqarā'*, the difference is this: with the existence of (despite) wealth, a person may possibly be *'ābid* (dedicated to the service of God).

Then, it became manifest: (*a*) that the *wāṣil* (those joined to God) are three crowds; (*b*) that the *sālik* (the holy travellers) are six crowds.

Each one of these nine crowds hath two similitudes: (*a*) *Muḥiqq*, the verifier, (*b*) *Mubṭil*, the abolisher.

To the Prophets of both crowds, the similitude of the verifier is:

> the *shaikh* of *ṭarīqat* (the Path) and the *'ulamā'* of *ṣūfiyā'*, —who, by following Muḥammad, invite the people through the desire of vision.

The similitude of the abolisher is this:

> In calumny, he layeth claim to prophecy; and falsely and slanderously attributeth to himself *waḥy* (revelation).

Him, they call. *Mutanabbī*, "one who calleth himself a prophet".

After the expiration of the time of mission, in the brain of a *jamā'at* (assembly), the bird of this desire wished to lay an egg. In the end, to the wind of destruction, they gave their head, and rolling fell into Hell.

To the ṣūfīs, the similitude of the verifier is:

> *mutaṣawwifah*, who are exceedingly informed and desirous of the *ḥāl* of ṣūfīs; and by the residue of their attachments to the qualities of *nafs* are detained from the maturity of purpose and forbidden it.

To the ṣūfīs, the similitude of the abolisher is :

a *jamā'at* (assembly) who in life reveal themselves ṣūfīs ; who are void of the power of their belief, deeds and *ḥāl* ; and who, having taken off from their neck the halter of devotion, graze free from encumbrance in the meadow of revelation.

They say :

The binding to the orders of the *Sharī'at* is the portion of the common folk, whose glance is restricted to outward things. Loftier than that is the *ḥāl* of the special folk and of the man of *ḥāqīqat*. For they (the common folk) give attention to outward customs, while their solicitude for viewing the inward presence is not great.

This crowd they call Bāṭiniyah,[1] Mubāḥiyah.

To the *majdhūbān-i-wāṣil* (the joined attracted ones), the similitude of the verifier is :

a crowd of the men of *sulūk*, whose travelling is yet in the traversing of the stages of the qualities of *nafs* : and whose existence, from the burning of desire's ardour, is in agitation and perturbation.

In the *maqām*, of *fanā'*, before the revelation of the tidings of the morn of the manifestation of *dhāt*, of resting and of dwelling,—sometimes a flash of the flashings of that manifestation glittereth on the glance of their witnessing ; and from the breeze-place of *fanā'*, a breath of the breathings of union joineth the perfume-place of their heart.

So, in the flashing of the lights of lightning, the darkness of the qualities of their *nafs* becometh folded ; and to their heart, from the heat, the bubbles of that breath give fire of search, agitation, *shauq* of the soul, and restfulness.

1. The Bāṭiniyah (Ismā'īliyah, the Assassins) were founded in the eleventh century by Ḥasan Ṣabbāḥ Shaikh-u'l-Jabal.

When that lightning expireth and that breath ceaseth, the manifestation of the qualities of *nafs*, the heat of desire, the agitation, and the *shauq* return; and the holy traveller wisheth to be wholly drawn out from the clothing of his own qualities, and to be immersed in the sea of *fanā'*, so that he may rest from the ruining of his existence.

When that *ḥāl* hath not become his *maqām*, and sometimes it descendeth on him, his interior becometh wholly informed and desirous of this *maqām*.

His name was the similitude of the verifier to the joined attracted ones.

To the joined attracted ones, the similitude of the abolisher is:

a crowd, who lay claim to being immersed in the sea of *fanā'*, and to being annihilated in the essence of *tauḥīd*: who, to themselves, assign not any moving or any resting.

They say—our moving is like unto the moving of doors, which without a mover is impossible. Though this sense is true, it is not the *ḥāl* of that *jamā'at* (assembly).

From this matter, their purpose is:

(*a*) the framing of excuse for sins.

(*b*) the assigning of it to desire for God.

(*c*) the repelling from themselves reproach.

This crowd they call Zanādiqah, *zanādīq* (sing. *zandīq*)—infidels.

To Sahl 'Abdullah, they said: A certain one saith: "The connection of my deed with the desire for God is as the connection of the motion of the door with its mover." He said:

"If the speaker be one who preserveth the sources of the *Sharī'at* and the limits of orders of worship,—he is of the crowd of the *sādiq* (sincere).

If he be one who, in opposition of the rules of the *Shar'*, hath no fear of falling into destruction, he speaketh so that he may make apparent the way of assigning his deeds to God, and of causing to fall from himself reproach—together with the being uptorn from faith and religion,—he is of the crowd of Zanādiqah.

To the Malāmatiyah, the similitude of the verifier is a crowd, who, for the repairing and the destroying of the people's glance, show not much consideration. Much of their effort is in ruining customs and habits, and in loosening the bonds of rules of association; the source of their *ḥāl* is naught save freedom of heart and disposition of heart; and on their part, appeareth neither the gazing at the usages of the *zuhhād* and the *'ubbād*, nor the issuing of acts of *nawāfil* and of devotion.

No bond do they make for the resolution of deeds; they persevere only for the performance of the enjoined ordinances; not ascribed to them is the amassing of the chattels of the world; contented with goodness of heart, they desire no increase of substance.

Them, they call Qalandariyah, *qalandars*.

Through the absence of hypocrisy, this crowd resembleth the Malāmatiyah.

Between the Malāmatiyah and the Qalandariyah the difference is:

The Malāmatiyah seek union with all *faḍā'il* (excellences) and *nawāfil* (works of supererogation), but keep them concealed from the people's gaze.

The Qalandariyah pass not beyond the *farā'iḍ* (enjoined ordinances), and, as regards the revealing, or the concealing, of their deeds from the people's gaze, are unfettered.

The crowd, at this time called Qalandariyah, have taken from off their neck the halter of Islam; and are void of these mentioned qualities.

For them, the name of Qalandariyah is illusory; fit is the name Ḥashwiyah, the padded ones.

To the Malāmatiyah, the similitude of the abolisher is a crowd (also of the Zanādiqah) who claim sincerity, and greatly strive in revealing iniquity.

They say : From this, our purpose is the reproach of the people, and the taking away of the glance (of approval) of man ; no need of the people's devotion, hath God. By their sin, uninjured they consider the sin restricted to the people's injury, and devotion among laudable actions.

To the *zuhhād*, the similitude of the verifier is:

a crowd whose delight hath not wholly been expended away from the world; and who from it desire at once to turn.

These, they call (Mutazahhid), self-denying.

To the *zuhhād*, the similitude of the abolisher is

a *jamā'at* (assembly), who (for the acceptance of the people) abandon the world's decoration; from off all the world's chattels, take up their heart; and thereby desire the acquisition of rank among men.

It is possible that their *ḥāl* may be obsecure :

(*a*) to some. They think that they have wholly turned away from the world; and that they themselves, by abandoning wealth, have purchased rank.

(*b*) to themselves. They think that (since outwardly they are not engaged in desire for the world's chattels) they have wholly turned from the world.

This crowd, they call Marā'iyah), acting hypocritically.

To the *fuqarā'*, the similitude of the verifier is :

he whose exterior is painted with the custom of *faqr*, and whose interior is desirous of the *ḥaqīqat* of *faqr*. Yet hath he inclination to *fanā'* and, with difficulty, endureth *faqr*; regardeth the true *faqr* of the *fuqarā'* a special favour from God; and therefore ever preferreth portions of thanks.

To the *fuqarā'* the similitude of the abolisher is: he whose exterior is painted according to the custom of *faqr*; and whose interior is, as to its *ḥaqīqat* (truth), void of information.

His purpose is purely the revealing of claim, of mandate, and of the people's acceptance (of him).

Him, they call Marā'iyah, acting hypocritically.

To the *khuddām*, the similitude of the verifier is: he, who ever remaineth standing in the service of the slaves of God; who, in his heart, wisheth to do them service unmixed with the suspicion of worldly design or rank; and ever to free his resolution from doubts of inclination and of desire.

Yet to the *ḥaqīqat* (truth) of *zuhd*, he shall not have reached.

At one time by reason of the superiority of the light of faith and by the concealing of *nafs*, some of his powers fall into the place of merit.

At another time, by reason of the superiority of *nafs*, his service is mixed with desire and hypocrisy. The crowd who are not in the place of merit, he preferreth, with the expectation of laudation, to full service; and some, who are worthy of service, he excludeth.

Him, they call Mutakhādim.

To the *khuddām*, the similitude of the abolisher is he who in service hath no resolution for the next world. Nay, the people's service, he hath made the snare of worldly advantages, so that thereby he may attract bequests and chattels. If, in the acquisition of his design, he see not effected his purpose, he abandoneth it.

Then is his service restricted to desire for rank, for wealth for numerous followers and approvers, so that thereby, in assemblies and companies, he may seek precedence and glorification.

In every service, his glance is on his own delight.

Him, they call Mustakhdim, an employer of many

servants.

To the *'ubbād*, the similitude of the verifier is:

(*a*) He, who desireth his own times immersed in devotion; but by reason of the residue of the pretensions of nature, and of the want of purification of *nafs*, languor momently falleth on deeds, or prayers and on devotion.

(*b*) Or he who hath not yet found the delights of devotion and who, in them, standeth with difficulty.

Him, they call Muta'abbid, devout.

To that one of the crowd of Marā'iyah, the similitude of the abolisher is:

He, whose glance in devotion is on the people's acceptance (of him); and, in whose heart is no faith as to the reward of the next world.

So long as he seeth no stranger attentive to his own devotion, in it he remaineth not.

THE ĀDĀB OF MUḤAMMAD'S MISSION (OF PROPHECY)

VI, 3

Known it is that, in the opinion of men of investigation and of sincere lovers, the beloved of the beloved is the beloved.

Who loveth not the beloved of the beloved, its sign is that, with design, his love is distempered.

Verily, such a one is the lover of himself, not the lover of the Beloved; he loveth the Beloved for the reason that he regardeth Him the source of pleasure and the place of delights to himself,—not, really and truly.

Sincere lovers, who have become free from the sickness of *hawā'* (desire) and the design of *nafs* (lust), and pure of the impurities of existence,—desire themselves for the sake of the Beloved, not the Beloved for the sake of themselves; desire for His sake the sacrifice of their own existence,—not, for themselves, His existence; and prefer to their own purpose His purpose,—nay, no purpose is theirs save the Beloved's purpose.

As the beloved of the beloved may be beloved, so the means of union with the Beloved is the beloved.

Munifest it is to the man of faith and of *yaqīn* that Muḥammad is the beloved of God and the agent of the King, great and holy. Then demandeth love for God sincerity of love for Muḥammad.

When it became known that wherever love may be, necessary is the observance of *ādāb* to the beloved (Muḥammad), to men of faith (especially to the Lords of revelation and of beholding), were requisite the observance of *ādāb* to him, and the preservation of the magnificence of his mission.

Though in form and body, Muḥammad is hidden and concealed from the glance of outward beholders, —in quality and spirituality, he is clear and revealed to the Lords of vision. The form of his *Sharī'at* is the mould of his spirituality.

Then as long as is left his *Sharī'at* in the body, —in truth, his form is present; and continuous and perpetual is the aid of his life for souls and for *nafs*. The verifier of this is the ancient word.

Though the *Sharī'at* is in this way the link of the bounty of life, in another way it is the means of the acceptance of life. Muḥammad calls the causing of his *sunnat* to live (in men's hearts) the causing himself to live.

Thus, for the nations, his *Sharī'at* and *sunnat* are life-giving and life-accepting.

The source of doors (of opening) and the column of *ādāb*,—after the strengthening of love's links, and the perfecting of love's conditions,—is ever viewing the person of the beloved, and the contemplating of hearts.

As, in all his *ḥāls*, outwardly and inwardly, the slave seeth God known and informed,—so informed and present, he should regard Muḥammad in respect to his own exterior and interior.

Towards Muḥammad, the beholding of his form

of grandeur and of dignity may ever be the guide to the preservation of *ādāb*; towards him, he may be ashamed of opposition, secretly or openly; and of the subtleties of the *ādāb* of his society, he may let go no subtlety whatever.

The greatest part of *ādāb* is this:

In his heart, he should not conceive that to any created being should be possible that perfection, rank, and loftiness of degree that are Muḥammad's; that to God, any travellers can find the path except by his guidance; that to any *Walī*, should be the power of perfecting and directing another save by borrowing from the light of his power; that to a *maqām*, should reach an arriver, who may be independent of his aid, although in his stage of propinquity, he may have attained to perfection.

The distributed bounty of all existing things is the purified soul of the Prophet (Muḥammad) and his holy *nafs*. Without his means, no aid floweth from God.

Who by Shaiṭān's deceit becometh haughty and proud, and in whose mind the idea of power and of wealth gathereth—becometh doubtless the rejected of *ulūhīyat* (God), and the banished of the court of *rubūbiyat* (God); and, wrapped with groans, returneth from the *maqām* of propinquity (to God) to farness (from Him).

Let us flee to God for shelter.

Another *ādāb* is:

After establishing the rule of belief, and after perfect following of his *sunnat* and *ṭarīqat*, it is necessary that, learned in following his *sunnat*, he should make every effort; in it should regard negligence unlawful; and should verily know that the degree of being a beloved he cannot gain save by observing the *sunnat* and the *nawāfil* (works of supererogation).

He should not imagine that fulness of *nawāfil* is the degree of lovers and of *murīds*; independent of it, is the beloved or the *murād*, for whom the performance of the enjoined ordinances is sufficient.

The sign of being a beloved is service in the following of the *sunnat* and of the *nawāfil.* At the inn of the narrow path, they keep every *sunnat* of Muḥammad's *sunnats*, distributed from the sea of the existence of prophecy,—by whose aid, bounty and currency flourish, in the soil of *nafs* and of the heart, the bubbles of love, the tulips of truths and the odoriferous plants of *yaqīn*.

With Muḥammad, whoever hath connection, apparently or really, as:

the *sādāt* (plural of *sayyid*),
the *'ulamā'*,
the *mashā'ikh* (plural of *shaikh*),

who are, outwardly and inwardly, the offspring and the heirs of *'ilm* (knowledge) and of prophecy,—all, for the sake of love for Muḥammad, he should love; and their honouring, regard necessary.

In all *hāls* of *i'tiqād* belief, of *qaul*, of *fi'l* deed, he should associate the reverencing of Muhammad with the reverencing of God; and devotion to him, the requisite of devotion to God.

Not true, nor acceptable, is faith in God and in His Unity,—without association with faith in Muḥammad, and with confession as to his (prophetic) mission.

Not the *ṭarīq* of union with God is the performance of the enjoined ordinances without the *sunnat* of tradition.

In nearness to God, to liken his similitude to two bows' length is fit.[1]

1. From God, Muḥammad is not farther than two bows' length.

They call the honouring of him, the essence of the honouring of God; devotion to him the essence of devotion to God.

"Who submitted to Muḥammad submitted to God; with thee who made *bai'at*, *bai'at* made with God" (see the Qur'ān).

As in speaking and in books, they mention the name of God with magnifying and reverencing, so should they mention the name of Muḥammad—

with *ṣalawāt*, benedictions.
with *taslīmāt*, salutations.
ta'ẓīm, reverence.
tamkīn, honour.

ĀDĀB (DUTIES, OBSERVANCES) TOWARDS GOD

VI, 2

The preservation of *ādāb* is both love's fruit and also its seed. As love is more perfect, greater is its solicitude for the preservation of *ādāb* towards the beloved; as the form of *ādāb* is more evident to the lover, for him greater is the glance of the beloved's love.

Then every slave, in whose heart love for God shall be firmer, his solicitude is greater for the preservation of *ādāb* towards Him; and more powerful for the purifying of the exterior and of the interior in a way, that to himself may represent to his sight in the form of the sick for God (not in the garment of the sinner).

Although his propinquity to God is greater, stronger are the desires in his nature for the subtleties of (additions to) *ādāb*.

For doubtless, than the work of servants and of followers (who, in the thread of the remote and of the stranger, are disobedient), the work of others (*wazīrs*, courtiers, others) near to the majesty of kings —is more difficult and dangerous, and more are their desires for accessions of *ādāb*.

There are seven *ādāb* of God.

(1) By viewing another, they should not keep back the glance from beholding the beauty of God.

In the **Ḥadīth** it is said:

When, for prayer, the slave arose, verily present with God he was. Then if at another he look, the Provider of the world saith: "O slave! at whom lookest thou? Than I, who is better? O son of Ādam! to me turn thy face; for to thee better than that whereat thou lookest, am I."

(2) Though propinquity to the King (God) and his honouring; and through gaining the power of conversing with, and travelling in, God, the slave should not forget his own (low) degree, nor transgress beyond the limit of service and of the revealing of his *faqr* and misery—that to rebellion he become not addicted.

Once Maḥmūd (of Ghaznī) desired (to prove) the trust of (his favourite slave) Ayāz. When he was present, he saw that, on a nail, before him, Ayāz had suspended a rent *postīn* (sheepskin coat) and an old blanket. He asked, saying: "What is this?" Ayāz replied: "When the hand of power threaded me on the thread of service, it drew from off my head this garment of poverty, and clothed me with the honour-robe of liberality. Them, for repelling forgetfulness and forbidding disobedience (the requisites of the *nafs* of man), I arranged before my face, so that at them, momently, I might look; (by repeating and calling to mind) recollect past events; my own (former) degree (of poverty) forget not; and of the cap (of sovereignty), of the bejewelled girdle, and of the gold-woven cloth (which, through the graciousness of the king, I have obtained) become not proud."

In respect to the Sayyid of both worlds (Muḥammad), the Kalām-i-Majīd giveth news. Of his observing these two *ādāb* in the presence of God.

Although in inclining to God, Mūsā was not accused of dimness of sight, yet by reason

(*a*) of abundance of descent of *ḥāl*,
(*b*) of the delight of the *samā‘* of God's word,
(*c*) of the *dhauq* (delight) at the sources of propinquity,
(*d*) of intoxication of the heart from drinking cups of *tauḥīd*,

forth from his hand, he gave the thread of discrimination; transgressed the limit of worship; and, through joy, entered upon asking (God).

Opposed to his desire, the back of its hand dashed the word of God: "Me, thou shalt never see." Immediately came this voice: Between the dust (of man) and the Lord of Lords,—what?

(3) The ear's listening to the word of God, and truly hearing orders and prohibitions against the abandoning of listening to the *ḥadīth* of *nafs*. The hearing of the word of God worketh in that way that whenever on his own tongue, or on another's tongue, in prayer or out of prayer, a phrase or a verse of the Qur'ān-i-Majīd goeth,—it, he heareth from a true speaker; and knoweth his own tongue or another's tongue (to be) the means whereby God conveyeth to his ear His own word—as, by the (burning) olive bush, He conveyed to Mūsā His own ancient address.

The purifying of the stations of *‘ilm*, and the congratulating of the subtleties of the understanding of words of the Qur'ān by the moderating of *nafs*, and the abandoning of listening to the *ḥadīth* of *nafs* is attainable; and its purport is this *āyat*: "When the Qur'ān is being read, to it listen and refer if thou wishest to be pitied (by God)."

(4) The *ādāb* of asking and of address. As, from the form of order and of prohibitions, the sense of the question is farther, nearer it is to *ādāb*.

In asking the Pardoner (God) and (seeking) mercy from his tribe, Ibrāhīm preferred, out of the form of order, the words of prayer, saying: "Me, those have sinned against; but, the most merciful pardoner, Thou art." He said not: "Them, pardon and forgive."

In the desire of repelling torments from nations, and of asking pardon from God he kept out from the form of order his address, saying: "Them, if Thou torment—they are Thy slaves; them, if Thou forgive, the precious Wise One, Thou art." He said not: "Them, torment not; but forgive them."

Out from the voice of order, Ayūb kept his desire of recovery: "Me, ailment hath afflicted; the most Merciful of the merciful, Thou art." He said not: "On me, have mercy!"

In answer to God's address: "Art Thou He who told the people—'As gods besides Allah, accept Me and My mother?'" 'Īsā said: "Verily, Thou toldest the people; to the people, Thou madest known."

(5) Concealing *nafs* in the fold of diminution, and depreciating one's own existence in the manifestation of the effects of God's power, when he mentioneth a favour of God's favours to himself.

Muḥammad said: "At the earth, I glanced—east and west." He said not: "I saw."

By not mentioning the deed, to himself he concealed his own existence; and thus was nearer to *ādāb*.

(6) The preserving the mysteries of God. When the slave gaineth knowledge of a mystery of the mysteries of God; and becometh the place of deposit and one with whom is deposited aught,—its revealing he should hold unlawful.

Otherwise, far from the degree of propinquity, he goeth and becometh the place of punishment.

In the *Ḥadīth*: "The betraying of secrets is *kufr*."

(7) The observing the times of asking, of praying, of resting, of keeping quiet.

This sense is dependent upon the *ma'rifat* of the times:

of grace (of God).
of mercy (of God).
of *basṭ* (expansion of heart).

In the times of grace, is the plunder of leisure:

for praying.
for asking.

In the times of wrath, of severity, and of *qabḍ* (contraction of heart), is the season:

of being silent.
of abstaining from asking.

Who preserveth not this *ādāb*; who, at the time of prayer, is silent; who, at the time of being silent, is vociferous,—his time is the time of hate.

At the time of prayer, the slave should ask (of God) according to his *ḥāl* and *maqām*.

If he be in the first of the *maqāms* of propinquity and, notwithstanding that, in respect of joy, he be not permitted,—not possible is it that on the carpet of joy, he should place the foot of inquiry.

Against asking for trifling matters, cometh the forbidder,—the majesty of God's grandeur.

One day, Shiblī sent to one of the sons of the world; and, from him, desired something of the world. That one replied: "From God, desire this world also, since, from Him, thou desirest the next world." Reply, Shiblī sent back: "Thou art ignoble; ignoble is this world: God is noble; noble is the next world. The ignoble from the ignoble, I seek; the noble from the noble."

If he be at the end of propinquity, and in respect to joy permitted by God, it is lawful to travel the path of joy—in praying and asking.

In the beginning of *ḥāl*, on account of the world's contempt and reproach, Mūsā used not to seek from God worldly needs; otherwise, the need of the next world and of asking trifling matters in the veil of grandeur would have been until that time when God conveyed him to another degree in propinquity (to Himself), superior to that (previous) degree; and, in the asking of mean matters, permitted him saying: "O Mūsā! ask of Me, even if it be the salt of thy (worthless) ferment (the dust elements of the body)."

When he became necessitous for food, Mūsā said: "O God! on me whatever thou causeth to descend is the best for the *faqīr*."

Known it became that there is an *ādāb* for every:

Waqt (period).
ḥāl.
maqām.

Hence, is the *qaul* of Abū Ḥafṣ Ḥaddād:

"All *ādāb* is *taṣawwuf*; for *ādāb* is the *waqt*, *ḥāl*, and *maqām*. Who performed the *ādāb* of *waqt* reached the pinnacle of manliness; who wasted the *ādāb* was far from propinquity (to God) and rejected of His acceptance.

Whoever guardeth as to keeping these seven *ādāb*, the hope is that, from observing the subtleties of the other *ādāb* he will not be portionless.

In short, from off the slave, the *ādāb* of God should fall in no *ḥāl* except in the *ḥāl* of *fanā'* and in the immersion in the essence of *jam'*. For the observance of *ādāb* demandeth change of *wujūd* and acquireth duality.

In the *ḥāl* of *fanā'*, the slave's existence (the demander of change) becometh up-plucked. Hence the qaul :

Saith God the great, the praised : Necessary is *ādāb* for him who observeth *qiyām* in My name and with love for Me ; necessary is destruction for him to whom is revealed the truth of My *dhāt*. *Ādāb* or *'aṭāb* (destruction),—either of the two,—he can choose.

The explanation is : "The glory of God's *dhāt* demandeth *fanā'* ; in fanā', *ādāb* weakeneth ; the glory of names and of qualities demandeth existence ; in existence, the protection of *ādāb* is necessary.

Junaid saith : "When love becometh true, dropped are love's conditions."

Because the end of love's demand is this :

When the love becometh *fānī* in the beloved, and the twofold custom ariseth (to depart) ; the way of *ādāb* becometh the change of existence. Nay, in a *ḥāl* such as this, the observing of *ādāb* is the abandoning of *ādāb*.

Once Abu'l-'Abbās b. 'Aṭṭār, while in the midst of some of his *ṣaḥābah* extended his foot, denying : "In the midst of people of *ādāb*, the abandoning of *ādāb* is *ādāb*."

Once when Muḥammad was sitting with Abū Bakr and 'Umar, a part of his auspicious thigh became exposed. Suddenly 'Uthmān approached. Muḥammad covered his thigh saying : "Him, whom the angels regard I must regard."

Though this *ḥāl* pointeth to 'Uthmān's esteem in Muḥammad's opinion, yet compared with that *ḥāl* (which was between Muḥammad, Abū Bakr, and 'Umar) it was lower—for nearer to concord was that *ḥāl*.

ĀDĀB-I-MA'ĪSHAT (THE RULE OF LIVELIHOOD)

VI, 7

Diverse, according to contrariety of degrees, are the *ḥāls* of the (*mutaṣawwifah*) in causation and in reliance (on God).

(*a*) Some, through weakness of *ḥāl*, for the amending of time, in search of daily food rely on chattles. These are called *mutasabbib*.

(*b*) Some, through power of *ḥāl* and denial of will, suffice themselves with the surety of God ; on Him, rely ; and in no way seek reliance on daily distributed food (through man's effort). These are called *mutawakkil*.

(*c*) Some strive in *kasb* (acquisition) ; some in beggary ; some (for the amending of their time) now in *kasb*, now in beggary.

Ibrāhīm Adham, sometimes for the maintenance of the *ṣaḥābah*, used to obtain a morsel of lawful food by watching over sown fields, or by reaping ; and sometimes when alone, at the time of need and to its extent, used to travel the path of beggary. Awhile, he was a dweller in the *jām'* (*masjid*) at Biṣra and used to break his fast every three nights ; on the night of breaking the fast, he used to come forth, and to take morsels from the doors of houses ; to the eating of these morsels, he restricted himself.

Abū Ja'far-Ḥaddād (Junaid's *murshid*) used to go forth, every two or three nights, in the first two watches (of the night) ; and to the extent of his need, at doors, used to beg.

In the beginning of *ḥāl*, Abū Sa'īd Kharrāz used,

when he was very necessitous to hold forth the hand (of beggary); and to say: "The prophet of God!"

So long as the necessity for concord was not complete, they have not seen this crowd in beggary whereof they are full of caution. Because of it the *Sharī'at* hath cautioned them in the way of inciting and of terrifying.

(*a*) *Inciting* In the history of Thaubān, it is related that one day Muḥammad said to the *āṣḥab*: "Who in one thing will join me,—him, in Paradise, I will meet." I said: "O prophet of God! I will." He said: "Of the people, ask naught."

(*b*) *Terrifying*. In the *Ḥadīth* it is said:

"Urge not thy prayer (of beggary) till God permitteth; till only a piece of flesh remaineth on thy cheek."

The *ādāb* of the beggar is:

So long as no necessity ariseth, he should not enter upon beggary. As long as he hath power, he maketh *nafs* desirous of patience of its handfuls till from the hidden, the door openeth.

When, in places of need, by giving patience, *nafs* displayeth levity, true wealth from all exterior to God is acquired.

The second crowd *mutawakkil* on account of perfection of being engaged with Him,—viewing the grandeur of *tauḥīd* and the light of *yaqīn*,—seek the causing in no cause of the causes of daily food; and from no created being, seek aid,—so that the Causer of causes (God) may as He desireth convey to them daily food.

One day, they inquired of Bāyazīd, saying: "Thee, we see engaged with none: whence is thy livelihood?" He replied: "The (unclean) dog and the (filthy) pig, my Master feedeth, wherefore should he not feed Abū Yazīd?"

Some are those who, whatever they ask, ask of God, so that He giveth them one of these things:

(*i*) the giving of the desired object.
(*ii*) the power of patience.
(*iii*) the erasing of desire from the heart.

Some ask naught, either from the people, or from God; because in His *'ilm*, they have effaced their own *'ilm* and desire; they know that in their affairs, more comprehending is the *'ilm* of the Eternal than their own *'ilm*; attachment to their affairs, on the part of Universal Desire (God) is greater and more complete than partial desire on their part; therefore on account of His *'ilm*, they are independent of begging.

They call the *mutawakkil* "the companions of gratuitous income," because their taking is from the income received gratuitously from the hidden. Although he seeth that, from the hidden is gratuitous income without their *nafs* being desirous, they accept it, even if in need of it they be not.

Some are slow in taking and in giving, because, in both *ḥāls*, they have suspected the residence of desire in their own *nafs*.

Some are slow in taking, not in giving, because in giving they less regard the pleasure of *nafs*.

Some are slow in giving, not in taking, because in taking they regard only the will and the act of God,—in giving, their own will and act.

Some are slow neither in taking nor in giving, because their existence is annihilated in the light of *tauḥīd*, their giving in Divine causes, is their safety from the calamity of desire. In the world, the existence of this crowd is more precious and less often found than (rare) red sulphur.

The *ādāb* of the *mutasabbib* (or *ṭāriq*), the *mutawakkil*, is this, that before arrival at the degree of the glory of *dhāt*, of qualities, and of deeds (which are the source of glories), they haste to taking gratuitous income and to giving it without the connection of a new permission, or of a ready knowledge.

Before the rules of the *maqām* of freedom, they plant not the foot, in the foot-place of the free.

In respect to the *Aṣḥāb* of *tamkīn* and to the Lords of *yaqīn*, they regard not their own *ḥāl* without a true proof.

By the residence of the veil of seduction, the truth of the *shaikh's* *ḥāl* may appear to him obscure; but at the time of examination (the fact) that the cash of his *ḥāl* is counterfeit is not concealed to the assayer of vision.

As long as he is bound by the residence of the residence of his own habits, for him is not reserved the *maqām* of freedom.

Shaikh Ḥammād used to eat no food unless, in dream or in sleep, he saw the order: (*a*) certain food of such a quantity from such a one,—take; (*b*) certain food of such a quantity to Ḥammād take. Then he used to take it.

To one of the crowd of his own *murīds*, Shaikh 'Abd-u'l-Qādir Ḥiblī sent, despite that the depositor was absent, saying: "In thy presence, a certain one hath a desposit; thence, some gold and some food thou shouldest send me." That *murīd* came before the *shaikh* and said: "Rule over the deposit, how is it lawful for me to exercise? If they ask thee, thou wilt give a decision that it is not fit (to do so)." With compulsion, the *shaikh* ordered him (to take from the deposit). Immediately after that, from the master of the deposit arrived a letter saying so much gold and so much food, take up from the deposit; and take to 'Abd u'l-Qādir.

Its quantity was exactly as the *shaikh* had stated.

Then in respect to his delaying in (the matter of) submission (to his order) the *shaikh* reproved that *murīd* and said: "Void of the truth of *'ilm*, thou thoughtest was the commanding of the *fuqarā'*".

The truth of gratuitous income is this:

From God, they should take it, not from the people—whether its cause be the hand of man, or not; whether it be known or not—on the condition that in its preface there be no wishfulness.

The *Shaikh-u'l-Islām* relateth that once to Shaikh Abu'l-Sa'īd a man came, and said: "I wish to make a fixed quantity of a daily allowance that they should bring for thy use; but I think that the ṣūfīs have said: 'Sinister, is what is known.'" The *Shaikh* said: "This, we say not: because the known that God willeth for us,—in it, His deed we see; and it auspicious, not sinister, we regard."

ṢALĀT (PRAYER)

VII, 5

When a person wisheth to begin the *ṣalāt* (*namāz*, prayer), its *sunnat* is that, in its preface, if it be an enjoined ordinance, he should prefer the *iqāmat*.[1]

Generally in the *ṣalawāt*—except in the *nawāfil* of *safar* in respect to the *rāḥilah*—the condition is:

In body, he should look towards the *qiblah* and in heart, towards the Master of the *qiblah*, from the wickedness of the temptations of Shaiṭān and from the thoughts of *nafs* should take shelter in God; and to himself should utter: the Sūrat-u'n-Nās, chapter 114, the Qur'ān.

Both hands, he should uplift in such a way that the two palms are level with (and parallel to) the two shoulders, the two thumbs near to the two lobes of the ear, and the finger-tips level with the ears.

According to the appointing, he should in his heart perform the established *ṣalāt*; if he urge it also orally it should be continuous as in the *namāz* (prayer)

1. The *adhān*		the *iqāmat*
(*a*) 4 *takbir*		the *iqāmat*
(*b*) 4 *Shahādat*	2 of God	the *iqāmat*
	2 of Muḥammad	the *iqāmat*
(*c*) 4 *Ḥayy-i-'alā*	2 for *salāt*	the *iqāmat*
	2 for *falāḥ*	
(*d*)		2 *iqāmat*
(*e*) 2 *takbir*		2 *iqāmat*
(*f*) 2 *taḥlil*		1 *taḥlil*

After the four *ḥayy-i-'alā* the Sunnī Muslims add twice *Aṣ-ṣalātu khairun min-an-naum* (prayer is better than sleep).

The Shī'ah Muslims say:

(*a*) *Ḥayy-i-'alā khair-il-'amal* (rise for the best deed, prayer).

(*b*) Either one (or two) *shahādat* of the *vilāyat* (*walīship*) of 'Alī after the two *shahādats* of Muḥammad.

of morn. He should say : "I utter the enjoined prayer of this morn."

In confirming resolution in his heart, he lowereth his hands and saith : "*Allāhu Akbar*, God is greatest," so that the first portion of the *takbīr* may agree with the falling of the two hands. With the *takbīr* should be associated—the end of the *takbīr*, the end of the falling of the hands, and the *niyyat*.

In Allah, he observeth the *maddā* (the lengthening of *alif*) ; in the *dhamma* (ُ) of the ه he exaggerateth not.

In *Akbar* he addeth not an ا (*alif*) between the ب (*bā*) and the ر (*rā*), but maketh it *majzūm*.

In letting fall the hands, he avoideth swinging so that he may be with deliberation, dignity and *khushū'* (humility).

At the time of *takbīr*, he should be the beholder of God's majesty.

In his glance, the people should appear contemptible and feeble ; he should not turn his attention as to their being informed about his *ḥāl*. Thus, may he come into the crowd, of the *ṣādiq* (the sincere ones) and draw not on himself the line of falsehood.

The most excellent of the *takbīrs* is the first *takbīr* (the *iḥrām*) as Junaid saith : "Of everything is a chosen part ; the chosen part of the prayer is the first *takbīr*.

The first *takbīr* is the place of resolution ; resolution is the life of practice. Whenever resolution is for God, and free from the impurities of causes,—its order is applicable to (other) parts of deeds.

If through the beholding of shaiṭān, through

error or neglect, practice becometh defective,—resolution hath no great effect.

From Ibn Salīm, Abū Naṣr Sarrāj quoteth :

"Resolution is to God, for God, from God ; otherwise is destroyed whatever is added to the slave's prayer after the resolution, even if it be to God and for God."

After the *takbīr*, and the falling of the hands, he should advance his hands midway between his breast and his navel ; should place the right hand on the left hand, the forefinger and the middle-finger on the left wrist ; should seize with the three other fingers both sides of the end of the wrist ; should lower his head ; should keep his glance on the place of prostration ; should stand so that his stature may be firm and erect ; should not bend his knees ; should keep his feet apart to the extent of four fingers ; should make effort to keep his feet parallel to each other ; should not lift a foot ; should not place one foot on the other.

In the *sharī at*, *dhaghn* (the lifting of the feet) and *ṣafd* (the joining of the feet) are prohibited.

Thus, he standeth, and saith :

"To Him, who created the heaven and the earth, obedient and faithful, my face, I turn : not of the crowd of *mushrik* (believers in partnership with God) are we ; verily, from God, the Provider of the world, are—my prayer, my devotion, my life, my death. His is no partner ; to this belief, we are commanded : of the crowd of *mushirs*, are we."

In the preface to the *talāwat* (reading) to this extent (if he have not the power of prolonging it) he should not abridge the enjoined ordinances.

If he have the power of prolonging the reading, he should, after reading the *āyat* of *tawajjuh*, utter the prayer *istiftāḥ* (asking aid):

"To Thee, O God—glory! to Thee, praise! Auspicious is Thy name, lofty Thy rank; save Thou, is no God. O God! Thou art king; there is no God but Thou, my Lord; Thy slave, I am; I have oppressed my *nafs*; I confess my sins; my sins, forgive. Verily none forgiveth sins save Thou; lead me to goodness of heart; to goodness of heart, verily none leadeth save Thou; pass over my sins; over sins, verily none passeth save Thou; I stand in service of Thee; by Thee, I stand; in Thy hands, is all good and evil none.

"To Thee, I cry; to Thee, I approach; Thee I extol; of Thee, I ask forgiveness; to Thee, I repent; from the accused shaiṭān, I flee to God. In the name of God, the merciful, the compassionate."

After this, he will utter the *Fātiḥah* and that Sūrah that he desireth; between them if there be an *Imām*, he should delay awhile and slowly utter:

"O God! between me and my sins, place distance—as distance, Thou hast placed between the east and the west; cleanse me from my sins as, out of the filthy garment, Thou hast made the white garment. O God! with water, with snow, with hail,—wash out my sins."

This prayer, he should (if alone) utter before the *Fātiḥah*. In uttering, in praying,—he should be fully present (conscious). The words of the Qur'ān that he urgeth on his tongue,—their meanings with the desire of being present (conscious), he should comprehend.

Thus, the speech of the tongue (which is the interpreter of the heart) may be the author of the speech of the heart. For the credit of the heart's speech is not the tongue's. If the tongue's speech be not the author and the interpreter of the heart's speech, the prayer-utterer is neither the speaker in the way of needs to God, nor the hearer in the way of understanding Him.

In respect to the hearing together the word of God, the men full of presence (consciousness) and the Lords of propinquity, are comprehenders of three *ḥāls*, only found among them.

(*i*) *Regarding the outward signification of the world of dominion.* This is the special power of *nafs*, so that it may stand in the place of its *ḥadīth.*

(*ii*) *Regarding the inward signification of the world of angels.* This is the special power of the heart, so that it may forbid the heart from turning to the world of dominion.

(*iii*) *Regarding the pomp of the Speaker* (*God*) *from the world of* jabarūt. This is the special power of the *rūḥ* (the soul), so that it may protect men from turning to other than God; and may reach a place where the soul is so immersed in the sea of *shuhūd* that the prayer-utterer is hidden from feeling (consciousness).

One day, Muslim b. Yasār was offering prayer in the *masjid* of Biṣra. Suddenly a column fell, and of the fall thereof all the people of Biṣra knew; but he, in the *masjid,* knew of it naught.

Awhile, he should rest; and then proceed to the *rukū'* (bowing the body from the hips).

In the *rukū'*, he should keep his stature well-bowed, the neck and the back straight; should place the palms of the two hands, with extension of the fingers, on the two knees; should not bend the knees; should keep in the state of standing, the lower half of the body (hips downwards), and his glance on the feet.

When he establisheth himself in the *rukū'*, he should, three times, say: "To my God, the greatest, —glory; to Him, praise." If he say it ten times it is full. Then, he saith:

"O God! to Thee, I bow; to Thee, I make humble my limbs; to Thee, I incline; to Thee applied are my ear, my eye, my flesh, my limbs, and tendons."

Restricted to it he should keep all his spirit; for these significations become the qualities of his *dhāt*.

When from *rukū'*, he uplifteth his head, he saith: "Him, who praiseth Him, God heareth."

When he standeth erect, he saith: "O God! the praise of the heaven and of the earth—to Thee!"

After that, if it be in the second *rak'at* of the enjoined ordinances of the morning, or of the *witr* of the latter half of the month Ramaḍān, he should utter the prayer of *qunūt*.[2]

"O God! guide us whereto Thou wishest to guide; protect us whereto Thou wishest to protect; cause us to love what Thou wishest us to love; make auspicious to us what Thou hast bestowed. Save me from the evil of what I have neglected; give benediction to Muḥammad, the noblest of the prophets; forgive and pity, for Thou art the Most Merciful.

Before standing in *qiyām*, he should go to *sujūd* (prostration). The *Ḥadīth* saith: "Him, who raiseth not erect his spine between *rukū'* and *sujūd*, God looketh not at."

Then into *sujūd* he goeth; and, as he goeth, uttereth a *takbīr*. He placeth on the prayer-mat first the lower limbs, then the upper limbs. That is, he placeth on the ground first the knee, then the hand, the forehead, and the nose; keepeth open the eyes, and his glance on the tip of his nose; placeth on the prayer-mat his two bare palms, keepeth the head right between the two hands; placeth on the

2. The uplifting of both hands and joining them before the face, at a distance of a foot, palm upwards, parallel to the prayer-mat.

prayer-mat his hands parallel to the shoulder and the tip of the elbow against his side; holdeth joined together the fingers opposite the *qiblah*; extendeth on the prayer-mat the wrist; and saith three times: "To my God, the loftiest,—glory; and praise to Him." If he say it ten times, it is full. Then he saith: "To Thee, I prostrate myself: in Thee, faith I have; to Thee, I bow. Auspicious is God the best of makers."

In the presence of God, a crowd in *sujūd* seeth its own *nafs* fallen on the dust of *fanā'*.

By reașon of the residue of existence, this crowd is affected by the majesty of pomp, and humility is the custom of its *ḥāl*.

A crowd of the men of revelation and of beholding in the state of *sujūd* becometh described with the truth of *fanā'*; in the light of the *shuhūd* of the *dhāt* of *Wāḥid* (God the One), seeth the existence of created beings, high and low, obliterated,—like to the obliterating of the shadow in the sun's light; and seeth itself entered in *sujūd* into the spaciousness of *fanā'* on the border of the sheet of the grandeur of God.

By reason of *fanā'*, this crowd is not impressed with the form of the grandeur of *dhāt*; in the essence of affection it is plucked forth from the garment of submission.

Besides these two crowds of the manifestations of the mysteries of *sujūd* is a crowd (in which, for the sake of prolonging prayer, and of the loftiness of being described with *baqā'* after *fanā'*,—are collected affection and fear).

This crowd is:

(*a*) in heart and in *nafs* submissive through the manifestation of the fire of grandeur (of God).

(*b*) in soul and with head uplifted and exalted, through the viewing of the light of affection of the beauty (of God).

Then, he uplifteth his head from *sujūd* and uttereth the *takbīr*; sitteth erect on the left foot; uplifteth the right foot so that its toes are opposite the *qiblah*; placeth his hands on the knees without an effort of joining, or of separating, them; and saith: "O God! me, forgive; on me, have mercy; me save; pass over my sins."

Again into *sujūd*, he goeth; and when from it he raiseth his head. If again he wisheth to rise, for the sake of sitting at ease, he sitteth and lightly riseth. In the last *tashahhud* he sitteth on the prayer-mat on the left foot; placeth his hands near the tip of the knee on the thigh; draweth to the palm the fingers of the right hand, except the forefinger; keepeth expanded from the palm the fingers of the left hand; and saith:

"O Prophet! auspicious blessings, holy benedictions from God; to thee, salutation and the mercy of God and His peace; on us and the pious slaves of God, salutation.

"I declare that there is no god but God; I declare that Muḥammad is His slave and His prophet. O God! on Muḥammad and his offspring, bestow Thy benediction; on Muḥammad and his offspring, have mercy; Muḥammad and his offspring, congratulate as Thou hast bestowed benedictions, congratulations, and mercy on Ibrāhīm and his offspring.

"Verily, Thou art glorious and honourable. O God! me forgive what is past, last, secret, and open and what Thou knoweth more than I. Verily! Thou art the first and the last. There is no God save Thou."

When, in *shahādat*, he reacheth to——(*ill Allāh*),

he uplifteth the forefinger, and inclineth it to the right side.

At the end of *tashahhud*, for loosening the knot of the *iḥrām*, he again giveth the salutation; turneth his face to the right side, so that the people on the right may clearly see over his cheek.

In that state of resolution of issuing from—

ṣalāt,

salām,

he bringeth into his heart those present of the angels, of the faithful jinn and men; and a moment delayeth.

Again, he turneth his face slowly to the left side, and giveth another salutation.

Of this form, motion, resting, words and deeds (which in the form of *ṣalāt* are mentioned) are some enjoined ordinances and some *sunnats*.[3]

3. These are described in the *Miṣbāḥ-u'l-Hidāyat*, chapter 7, section 6.

THE (MYSTIC) ROSE OF THE QĀDIRĪS [1]

[Brown's *Darvishes*, pp. 89-93]

Every *tarīq* (path) hath its sign; the sign of the Qādirīs is a rose which is green, because the word *Ḥayy* (the Living one) was manifested in green colour to one of the *shaikhs*. It hath:

	WHITE RINGS[2]		SERIES OF LEAVES		COLOURS		PETALS	
	Number	Signification	Number	Signification	Number	Signification	Number	Signification
outside	(1) *sharī'at* (Muslim law)	is my word	(1) five leaves	five virtues of Muslims	(1) yellow	*sharī'ut*	seven	the seven beauteous names of God
	(2) *ṭarīqat* (the path)	is my practice	(2) six leaves	six characteristics of faith	(2) white	*ṭarīqat*		
inside	(3) *ma'rifat* (Divine knowledge)	is the chief of all things	(3) seven leaves	seven verses of the Qur'ān	(3) red	*ma'rifat*		
	(4) *ḥaqīqat* (truth)	is my condition	The whole series (18 leaves)	Muḥammad brought mercy to eighteen worlds	(4) black	*ḥaqīqat*		

1. This order was founded by Shaikh 'Abd-u'l-Qādir Jīlānī (*b.* 1078, *d.* 1166). His titles were:
(a) *Pir-i-dasigir*, the hand-seizing *Pir*.
(b) *Muhy-u'd-Din*, collected in faith.
(c) *Ghauth-u'l-A'zam*, the greatest *Ghauth*.

2. The white colour signifieth submission to the *shaikh*. The first three circles signify the acquisition of *ḥāl*, that is, of *ḥaqīqat*. The green cord surrounding the rose signifieth "the living one".

Shaikh Ismā'īl-ū'r-Rūmī, successor to 'Abd-u'l-Qādir, adopted this rose as emblematic of the seven names[3] of God uttered during the *dhikr*.

Name of God	*Signification*	*Colour of its light*	*Number of times the name must be repeated*
Lā ilāha ill Allāh	no god but God	blue	100,000
Allah	Allah, (the beauteous) name	yellow	78,586
Hū	He	red	44,630
5 *Ḥayy*	the Living One	white	20,092
6 *Wāḥid*	the One	green	93,420
'Azīz	the Dear One	black	74,644
Wadūd	the Loving One	none	30,202

The seven colours are emblematic of the lights (splendours) of the seven names; its eighteen gores (*tark*), of the numerical value of the two letters in: *Ḥayy* (the Living One).[4]

In the centre of the rose is the seal of Sulaimān, the signification whereof is:

س freedom from defect
ل gentleness of disposition
ى power of spiritual vision
م familiarity with his companions
ن prayers and salutations belong to God (the Qur'ān, i. 4)

— The rose is embroidered on felt of camel's hair, emblematic of the felt *khirqah* that Muḥammad gave to Uvais Qarnī, Sulṭān of faithful lovers.

3. The ninety-nine beautiful names of God are given in Brown's *Darvishes* (p. 116).

4.

ح	=	8
ى	=	10
Total		18

In the word *gul*, the rose, the letters گ and ل are the first letters of the two lines of the Qur'ān, xxxix. 37.

The origin of the rose of the Qādirīs is as follows:

Shaikh 'Abd-u'l-Qādir Jīlānī, under the direction of Khaḍir (Elias), proceeded to Baghdad.

When he arrived, *Shaikh* 'Alī-u'l-Vāḥidī al-Qādirī sent him a cup full of water, which meant the Baghdad being full of holy men, there was no room for him.

Whereupon 'Abd-u'l-Qādir put a rose into the cup, which meant that Baghdad would find a place for him.

Then all present exclaimed: "The *shaikh* is our rose!"

THE BAI'AT (THE PLEDGE) OF THE MURĪD

[Brown's *Darvishes*, pp. 94, 95; 97-101; 103, 215, 216]

As appointed by its *Pīr* (founder), the *mubāyi'at* (the pledging) of a *murīd* of the Qādirīs is as follows:

The *murīd* sitteth with his right hand[1] in the right hand of the *shaikh* (the *murshid*); expresseth his repentance, and his readiness to take the *'ahd* (the pledge).

The *shaikh* addresseth him thus:

"The *Faqīr* must be of an active mind, brilliant in thought, of good repute, near in approach to God, of a good heart, of a meek demeanour, of serious deportment, of a mind easy to acquire knowledge, prepared to teach others who are ignorant, disposed to trouble no one, though they trouble him.

"It is incumbent on him to speak only of those things which belong to his faith; to be generous of his means; to avoid what is forbidden and wrong; to be careful in refraining from what is doubtful; to aid those who are strangers; to be a parent to the fatherless; to be of a pleasant countenance; to be gentle of heart and joyful of spirit; to be agreeable and happy.

"Even in poverty, not to expose his secrets to others, nor to divulge them; to be gentle in conduct and in intercourse; to be bountiful of his benefits, kind in language, few in words; to be patient with the ignorant, and to refrain from doing them

1. The two thumbs must be raised against each other. This is the *bai'at*, the pledge.

The *bai'at* (the giving of the hand) of the *murid* taketh place several years after his admission to the Order of Dervishes. The period dependeth on the *shaikh* (*murshid*) and on the degree of knowledge (*ma'rifat*) and acquisition (*kasb*) of the *murid*.

The *shaikh*, or the *murid*, is held to see in a vision either the Prophet, 'Alī or the *Pir* (founder of the Order).

This ceremonial is a secret which the *murid* takes an oath never to divulge.

any wrong; to show respect to great and small; to be faithful to those who confide in him, and to keep aloof from all duplicity; to be strict in his religious duties; to refrain from sloth and slumber; to speak ill of no one; to be sedate, easily satisfied, and thankful for benefits bestowed; to be much in prayer and fasting, truthful of tongue, permanent in abode; to curse no one; to be without calumny, hatred, of a grave heart, and careful of the perfect performance of the religious duties of the Order; and to be as correct in thought as in deed."

Having uttered this counsel, the *shaikh*, holding the *murīd's* hand in his own, reciteth from the Qur'ān:

i. Sūrat-u'l-Fātiḥah.
x. Sūrat-u'l-Yūnus.
xlviii. Sūrat-u'l-Fatḥ (first 10 verses).
xxxiv. Sūrat-u'l-Aḥzāb (the 56th verse).
xxxvii. Sūrat-u'l-Ṣāffāt (the 180th-182nd verses).

Then the *shaikh* offereth the *istighfār* (prayer for pardon):

"O great God, I beseech Thee to pardon me,—Thou, like to whom is none other.

"To Him, I repent of my sins; Him, I ask to pardon me, to accept my repentance, to lead me in the true path, and to have mercy on all those who repent of their sins. Accept my oath of fealty, the oath which Muḥammad administered to the *aṣḥāb* (companions)."

Then the *shaikh* addresseth the *murīd*:

"All Muslims are bound to offer up their devotions to give alms and religious advice, to disbelieve any association with God (Father, Son and Holy Ghost), to abjure wine, not to waste their means, not to commit adultery, not to kill forbidden food, not to calumniate anyone.

"These I command you to observe as implicitly as the dead body is submissive in the hands of the preparers for interment.

"Rebel not against what you know hath been commanded thee of God; commit not what is forbidden; make no innovations in your prayers; commit no sins, distinguish between the wrong and the true path.

"Bear your *shaikh* ever in mind in this world and in the next.

"The Prophet is our prophet, and the Shaikh 'Abd-u'l-Qādir Jīlānī is our *Pīr* (founder); the oath of fealty is the oath of God; this hand is the hand of Shaikh 'Abd-u'l-Qādir Jīlānī, and the hand of the Director of the True Path is in yours;

"I am the *Khalīfah* of 'Abd-u'l-Qādir; he accepted this hand; with it, I accept you (as his disciple)."

The *murīd* replieth: "I also accept you (as my *murshid*)." The *shaikh* respondeth: "I therefore do now admit you."

Then the *shaikh* pronounceth the *dhikr*, which the *murīd* repeateth three times after him; and directeth him to recite with him the *Fātiḥah* (Qur'ān, i.); and, the *salāt va ṣalām* (the prayer of peace for the Prophet).

The *murīd* kisseth the hand of the *shaikh*, and of all the dervishes present.

This act is called *muṣāfaḥat* (taking by the hand).

The *shaikh* offereth up the *istighfār* (the prayer for pardon of the sins of the *murīd*) and addresseth the assembly:

"The acceptance of this initiation by the *murīd* is a source of future advantage to him. The prayer which we have offered for him is for the submission of his body to his spiritual will, just as when the angels, before addressing the Creator, prostrate themselves humbly before Him,—so hath the *murīd* by his acceptance of this *bai'at* (giving of the hand) submitted to my rule."

Our *shaikh* ('Abd-u'l-Qādir) hath said: It is not proper for the *shaikh* to sit in the post of pillage, nor to gird on the sword of benevolence until he becometh qualified by the following twelve qualities :

Name of person	*Quality*
Allah (God)	to cover up and to forgive
Muhammad	to intercede and to accompany
Abū Bakr	truthfulness and benevolence
'Umar	to command and to forbid
'Uthmān	to feed the poor and to pray when others sleep
'Alī	to be knowing and brave

If these qualities be not possessed by the *shaikh*, he is unworthy of the submission of the *murīd*.

When he doth possess them, follow under his banner. When he doth not, Shaiṭān hath made him his friend ; and he will participate neither in the benefits of this life nor of the next.

The Prophet hath said : When to one of his *murīds* a *shaikh* giveth spiritual advice, and by it he refuseth to abide—God abandoneth him.

Shaikh 'Abd-u'l-Qādir hath said : When any one of my *murīds* is oppressed with affliction, let him walk three paces to the eastward and say :

"O Thou, much desired : Thou, the aid of all in the hour of trouble, in the deepest of darkness, as in the dangers of the desert, Thou seest all things.

"In the hour of shame and confusion, me only Thou canst protect.

"When I am overcome with affliction, in the hour of danger, me Thy supreme intelligence will support.

"O Thou, ever present, Thee I implore to free me from grief."

The ceremony may be varied as follows : When a *murīd* wisheth to enter an Order he is received in an assembly thereof. The *shaikh* toucheth his hand, and breatheth three times into his ear : "*Lā ilāha ill Allāh* (there is no god but God)," which he commandeth him to repeat daily 101, 151, or 301 times (*talqīn*).

The *murīd* voweth to spend his time in *khilvat*; and to repeat to the *shaikh* his *mushāhidah* (manifestations).

According to these *mushāhidah*, the *shaikh* knoweth the time when he may breathe into his ear successively

Yā Allah	O God
Yā Hū	O He
Yā Ḥaqq	O Just One
Yā Ḥayy	O Living One
Yā Qayyūm	O Existing One
Yā Qāhhār	O Avenging One

This exercise (*chillah*) requireth six to ten months according to the *murīd's* capacity.

When he reacheth the last *maqām* he hath acquired *takmīl-i-sulūk* (the perfection of travelling in the Path), and is fit for admission. During this novitiate, they call the *murīd*—*kūchak*.

The *murīd* liveth in the world and gaineth his livelihood. The *shaikh* attendeth only to his *takyah* convent and trusteth to God for his support.

The *shaikh* instructeth the *murīd* that there are :

	Number		Number
مقام station ...	40	اقليم clime ...	7
درجه degree ...	360	كره globe ...	4
منزل stage ...	28	عالم world ...	18,000
دائره circle ...	12	آيت Qur'ānic verse ...	7
ساعت hour ...	24	حرف letter ...	
فصل section ...	4	فاتحه Qur'ānic openings	7

The dervish reacheth *quwwat-i-rūḥ-i-bāṭinī* (the power of the inward soul) through :

tawajjuh, turning the face devoutly in prayer to God
murāqibah, fearful contemplation of God
taṣarruf, self-abandonment to pious reflection
taṣawwuf, mystic spiritualism.

The exercise of this power is called *quwwat-i-irādī* (the power of the will) which is traced to Divine power, man's soul being connected with the Supreme Soul (God).

There are three *dhikrs* :

dhikr-i-khafī (the silent *dhikr*) when in solitude
dhikr-i-jahrī (the audible *dhikr*) when in society
dhikr-i-Allah, the *dhikr* of God (Qur'ān, xxiv. 37)

Ṭarīqat is composed of columns, of precepts and of principles as below :

Ṭarīqat

Columns	*Precepts*	*Principles*	*Result*
1 توبہ repentance ...	علم knowledge ...	احسان benevolence ...	معرفت Divine knowledge
2 تسلیم resignation ...	سخاوت generosity ...	ذکر repetition (of God's name)	حلم meekness ...
3 دیانت fidelity to the Order	قرب nearness to God	ترک معاصی abandoning sin ...	صبر patience ...
4 خشوع و خضوع humility (of limbs and of the heart)	دین faith ...	ترک دنیا abandoning the world[2] ...	طاعت submission ...
5 رضاء contentment ...	تفکر meditation ...	خوف خدا fear of God	ادب manners ...
6 خلوت retirement ...	توکل reliance on God	عشق خدا love for God	صرق sincerity ...

2. Muḥammad said : "This world is forbidden to those of life in the next world ; life in the next world is forbidden to those of this world ; both are forbidden to the slaves of God."

DHIKR, MURĀQIBAH, TAUḤĪD, DAUR AND ḤĀLAT

[Brown's *Darvishes*, pp. 215, 227]

The statutes of nearly all the dervishes require them to repeat daily :

Lā ilāha ill Allah, no god but God

Yā Allah	O God
Yā Hū	O He
Yā Ḥaqq	O Just One
Yā Ḥayy	O Living One
Yā Qayyūm	O Existing One
Yā Qahhār	O Avenging One

These names (*asmā'-i-ilāhī*) refer to :

(*a*) *sab' samā'* (the seven heavens)

(*b*) *anvār-i-ilāhī* (the Divine splendours)

The exercises of *murāqibah* (fearful contemplation), and of *tauḥīd* (the unity of God) are as follows :

(*a*) on their heels, elbows touching, the dervishes sit in a circle; and simultaneously make slight movements of the head and of the body.

(*b*) or they balance themselves slowly right to left, left to right; and incline the body forwards and rearwards.

(*c*) or, seated, they begin these motions in measured cadence with a staid countenance, eyes closed, or fixed upon the ground; and contiune them on foot.

The convent-hall (wherein these exercises are carried out) is of wood; and is called **the *tauḥīd-khānah*** (the house of unity).

The Daur (*Rotatory Dance*). The dervishes holding each other by the hand put forward the right foot, increasing at every step the strength of the movement of the body.

They uncover their hands, take off their turbans; form a second circle within the first; intertwine their arms; lean their shoulders against each other; raise the voice; and unceasingly utter—*Yā Allah* ! *Yā Hū* ! They do not stop till strength is exhausted. Each one leaves when he pleases.

To the *shaikh* seated before the *qiblah*, the dervishes offer praise.

The four senior dervishes approach the *shaikh*; embrace each other; and place themselves, two on his right, two on his left.

The other dervishes, arms crossed, heads inclined, advance. Each one boweth to the tablet whereon the founder's name is inscribed; putteth his hands over his face and beard; kneeling before the *shaikh*, kisseth his hand; and taketh his place on the *pūstīn* (sheepskin) spread in a half circle in the hall.

The circle being formed, they all chant together

the *Takbīr*	*Allāhu Akbar*
the *Fātiḥah*	The Qur'ān, i.

The *shaikh* repeatedly pronounceth the words: "*Lā ilāha ill Allah* ! No god but God !".

Balancing themselves from side to side and placing their hands on their face, breast, abdomen and knee—the dervishesexclaim : Allah !

One of the dervishes on the *shaikh's* right chanteth the *Ḥamd-i-Muḥammad*, while the other dervishes, moving their body to and fro, continue to exclaim *Allah* !

After a few minutes, they rise, approach each

other, press their elbows against each other, balance from right to left and then from left to right—the right foot being firm; the left foot in periodical movement, the reverse of that of the body.

All observe great precision of measure and of cadence. In the midst, they cry: *Yā Allah* ! *Yā Hū*.

Pale of face, languishing of eye,—some sigh, some sob; some weep, some perspire great drops.

In the middle of a hymn, chanted alternately by the two dervishes on the *shaikh's* right, they accelerate their movements. One putteth himself in the centre to incite them by example.

During this hymn, the dervishes take off their turbans; bear their shoulders against each other; and compass the hall at a measured pace, striking their feet against the floor, and all at once springing up and exclaiming: *Yā Allah* ! *Yā Hū* !

When they would stop from sheer exhaustion, the *shaikh*, making violent motions, inciteth them anew.

The two senior dervishes take his place, double the quickness of the step and the motion of body, and all dance till entirely exhausted.

Ḥālat (*Ecstasy*). Two dervishes take down from niches cutlasses; heat them red-hot; and present them to the *shaikh*.

After breathing over them prayers and invoking the aid of the *Pīr* of the Order, the *shaikh* raiseth them to his mouth, and then giveth them to the dervishes, who eagerly ask for them.

Transported by frenzy, the dervishes seize upon the glowing irons, gloat upon them, lick them, bite them, hold them between the teeth, and cool them in their mouth!

Others stick cutlasses into their sides, arms and legs.

If they fall under their sufferings they cast themselves, without a complaint, or a murmur or a sign of pain, into the arms of their Brothers.

Some minutes after this, the *shaikh* visiteth each; breatheth upon his wounds, rubbeth them with saliva, reciteth prayers, and promiseth speedy cure.

It is said that twenty-four hours afterwards, nothing is to be seen of their wounds.

They call the red-hot irons *gul* (the red rose), because the use of them is as agreeable to the soul of the dervish as the perfume of the rose is to the voluptuary.

THE DANCE OF THE SAMĀ'

The dervishes (nine to thirteen) sit on sheepskins on the floor at equal distances from each other. Thus for half an hour,—arms folded, eyes closed, heads bowed,—they remain in profound meditation.

The *shaikh* on a seat, on a small carpet, breaketh silence by a hymn in honour of God. Then he inviteth the assembly (*majlis*) to chant with him the *Fātiḥah.*[1]

"Let us chant the *Fātiḥah*, in glorifying the holy name of God; in honour of the blessed religion of the Prophets, especially of Muḥammad Muṣṭafā, the greatest, most august, magnificent of all heavenly envoys; in memory of the first four *Khulafā'*; of the sainted Fāṭimah; of chaste Khadījah; of the Imāms Ḥasan and Ḥusain; of all the martyrs of the memorable day (battle of Karbalā, 680 C.E.); of the ten evangelical disciples, the virtuous sponsors of our Prophet; of all his zealous and faithful disciples; of all the *imāms*, *mujtahids*, of all the *'ulamā'*, of all the *auliyā'*, of all the holy women of Islam.

"Let us chant in honour of Hadrat Maulānā, the founder of our Order, of Hadrat Sulṭān-u'l-'Ulamā' (his father), of Sayyid Burhān-u'd-Dīn (his teacher), of Shaikh Shams-u'd-Dīn (his consecrator), of Vālidah Sulṭān (his mother), of Muḥammad 'Alī-u'd-Dīn (his son and vicar), of all the successors, of all the *shaikhs*, of all the dervishes, and all the protectors of our Order, to whom the Omnipotent deigneth to give peace and mercy.

"Let us pray for the constant prosperity of our society; for the preservation of the very learned and venerable General of our Order, for the preservation of the reigning Sulṭān, the very majestic and clement sovereign of the Islam Faith, for the prosperity of the Grand *Vazīr* and of the *Shaikh-u'l-Islām*, and of all the Muḥammadan soldiery and of all the *Ḥujjāj* to Mecca.

1. The *shaikh* reciteth first the Fātiḥah, then uttereth the following prayer.

"Let us pray for the repose of the soul of all the *pīrs*, of all the *shaikhs*, and of all the dervishes of all other Orders; for all good people.

"Let us pray for all Muslims of one and of the other sex, of the east and of the west, for the maintenance of all prosperity, for preventing all adversity, for the accomplishment of vows, and for the success of praiseworthy enterprise.

"Finally, let us ask God to deign to preserve in us the gift of His grace, and the fire of His love."

After this, all chant together; the *shaikh* reciteth the *Fātiḥah* and the *salawāt*.

This being ended, the dervishes, standing in line to the *shaikh's* left, arms folded, head bowed, slowly approach. The first dervish having arrived nearly opposite to the *shaikh* profoundly saluteth the tablet, wherein is inscribed the founder's name; advancing by two leaps to the *shaikh's* right side he turneth to him, saluteth him, and beginneth to dance.

The dance consisteth in turning on the left heel, in advancing slowly, and in making the turn of the hall with closed eyes and opened arms.

This, in succession, all the dervishes do.

Interrupted by two short pauses, during which the *shaikh* reciteth prayers, the dance lasteth for two hours.

Towards the close, the *shaikh* joineth in the dance; then returning to his seat, he reciteth Persian verses for the prosperity of religion and of the state; and saith:

"Let us pray for the Sovereign of the Muslims and most august of Monarchs of the house of 'Uthmān, Sulṭān, son of a Sulṭān, grandson of a Sulṭān . . . and for the dervishes, present and absent; for all friends of our Order; for all the faithful, dead and quick, in the east and in the west."

The Fātiḥah is chanted; the *samā'*, concluded.

THE END